Image credit, Vince Ray

FOREWORD

Foreword – In case you didn't know . . .

A foreword is generally a short piece of writing sometimes placed at the beginning of a book. Often written by someone other than the primary author of the work, it usually tells of some interaction between the writer of the foreword and the book's primary author.

Doktor Haze a Showman or a Shaman?
Believe everything he says believe nothing he says.

Paul Peculiar

Cover Image by Seventhwave Imagery

Well everyone seems to have a foreword and I wouldn't want to disappoint, the only difference is I'm writing mine myself. Of course it's not clear which Doktor Haze has actually written it, with that in mind it seems perfectly appropriate to write it myself.

I consider I have lived a charmed life, from being born and bred in a Circus, being deserted by my Dad twice, the first time while only six months old.

Brought up in Preston before being reunited with my Dad when I was 11 and learning to fire eat in a day. Leaving school at 12, spending most of my youth in a Circus, then running away from the Circus.

Inspired by Marc Bolan I then pursued a career in Rock 'n' Roll. Eventually forming Britain's longest running alternative Circus and then taking the extreme to the mainstream on prime time Television. That's about it in a nutshell but if you think you needn't read the book well think again, its packed with an abundance of anecdotal stories and amazing characters that I have had the pleasure of knowing.

The strange thing about writing a book is you seem to upset everyone. I have been featured in a few books and I think its perfectly normal to quickly head to the chapter that contains you and see what the author says about you, but maybe it's a ego thing. To assist with this I did think about adding an index at the back so people could find which page they were featured on, I decided against that option in preference to the dipping their hand into their extremely long pockets, buying it and spending many an hour digesting and hopefully enjoying a book covered in Mud, Blood and Glitter.

To test the water I wrote a condensed version of my life in my last album 'An Evil Anthology' and found it really divided people. Some pleased with what I had written, some pissed of when I didn't say anything about them, others breathing a sigh of relief because I hadn' said anything about them. Most neutrals though loved it and urged me to put pen to pape and compose the whole damned thing.

Most of what you read in this book is true, some is unbelievable, some exaggerated, bu generally it is a true story about growing up in a Circus, running away from the Circus on to return in a blaze of glory (excuse the pun). Most of the characters are genuine althoug some have had their names changed to protect and preserve their anonymity. In some case protecting people privacy whilst maintaining the integrity of the book.

Enjoy . . .

FIFTHWORD

Well where do I begin, I kinda hoped that I would have been given the opportunity of writing the foreword. I know they are normally written by someone famous who knows the author and although not famous I have certainly known Haze longer than most.

I suppose it was inevitable, after all I asked him to be my Best Man and then changed my mind, then asked him to be the Godfather to my son but changed my mind again, it was obvious then that I would be relegated to the 'fifthword'.

Anyway, here goes. Haze alias Doktor Haze is a truly wonderful human being, it's been my pleasure to know this Saint of a man for over 30 years and I can tell you he is the "Salt of the Earth". He is the greatest motivator of men I have ever known, Brian Clough had nothing on him. He has done so many wonderful things for humanity. Not many know of his extensive work for charity particularly un-wed mothers.

Right, now the truth, the slimy toad Haze only reads the first paragraph of anything, that's how I know I can get away with writing this, he simply won't get this far down the page, he's such a lazy git and now I'll tell you how it really is. He's a rat faced selfish mean swine, who has everyone working for him for nothing. For instance he threatened Captain Dan to be stretched (and thereby lose his livelihood) if he didn't go on the last tour. Not to mention forcing the poor guy to superglue his penis to a Hoover!

He knows no shame.

Then there's Hannibal – who was a respectable tax inspector in Munich before he made him get his entire body tattooed and swallow all kinds of nasty things. There are worse, much worse things he's done but I can't tell you for legal reasons. Many of the files are held by MI5 for another 50 years, but I can say they involve several high court judges a member of the Royal Family, the cast of Billy Elliot and Madam X of Lytham St Annes, allegedly. Mind you I bet they're all here in this damned book.

He'd sell his own Mother for a good story as you can read about in chapter seven.

Is the book truthful? Can he be trusted? Well as with everything with Haze, as I always tell anyone sad enough to ask, he's always serious, he's never serious if you get my drift, believe everything he says, believe nothing he says.

So enjoy the book, it's very well written – it's rumoured that Garry Stretch actually wrote it in Haze's basement in Wimbledon. Locked down there for months and fed on scraps of food, I wouldn't be surprised.

Also I have a much bigger Willie. Well if Keith Richards can get away with that in his book.

Paul Peculiar alias Paul "3 balls" Roberts MA. LSO. CDP. OBE. DIK ED.

PROLOGUE

I arrived at the Circus big top which had been erected on The Meadows, Edinburgh ready to appear at our 4th Edinburgh Festival. My friend Emilia Arata greeted me, she was screaming hysterically, half laughing and half crying. 'What's wrong' I asked, 'It's Dan' she replied, He's superglued his Dick to a Hoover, 'What?' I replied, I couldn't believe it and quickly went to the portacabin changing room where he was sitting. I found him with a corrugated plastic tube coming out of his trouser flies and attached to his Henry Hoover.

I can understand that this seems a little strange but there was some logic to it. During Dan's performance in The Circus of Horrors he places his Penis in the Hoover hose and pulls the Henry Hoover round the stage. Unfortunately, Denis Remnev had stood on the hose the night before and the crack in the tube caused it to lose it's suction.

To try and repair this Danny had come in early and had superglued the crack but did not read the instructions on the tube properly. They stated 'leave for 20 minutes', he did not have his glasses on and thought it said 'leave for 20 seconds'. When he tried out his repair it got well and truly stuck. I didn't know whether to take him to A and E or Specsavers but decided on A and E.

I quickly loaded him, Henry the Hoover and another girl called Carima into the back seat of the car (Carima had twisted her knee - so I thought I might as well do my bit to save the planet and take both victims together). With myself and Emilia in the front we rushed to Edinburgh General Hospital. We parked in the car park and Emilia and I went to A and E I spoke quietly and embarrassingly to the receptionist and tried to whisper an explanation 'I have a personal problem'.

The receptionist didn't seem to share my embarrassment and after my explanation shouted at the top of her voice in a pure Scottish accent. 'OK bring him in then'. I said 'are you sure you have a waiting room full of people and I have a guy in my car with a Hoover stuck to his Dick'. She suddenly realized, shot out of her seat, finally understanding the problem and went and got two nurses.

I walked with them to my car again explaining what had happened but at this point I did not tell them that Dan was a Dwarf, we opened the door and although trying to be professional you could see the smirk on their faces.

They went off and returned with two wheel chairs and one blanket, Carima was dispatched on one followed by Dan and Henry covered very appropriately by a tartan blanket. We waited patiently, Dan returned carrying Henry the Hoover, his wee man was throbbing but free and Henry emerged unscathed too. We had to wait a little longer for Carima who when about to get examined told the male nurse that she was embarrassed to take off her jeans because she had no knickers on, he said 'if you could see what the guy in the next booth had done then you wouldn't be embarrassed', little did he know.

Business at the Edinburgh Festival had been quiet until now but suddenly we hit the front pages. It was amazing, not only did we dine out with this story for years to come but it also ran and ran in the media.

Dan's story became my first piece of front-page news, this was followed by features everyday in The Sun. We re-enacted the stunt for The BBC programme 'Bizarre ER' and then again on 'Scott Mills Radio 1 show'.

A Tory MP even brought up the story in The House of Commons, 'How could the BBC waste the British public's license fee by making a film about a Dwarf getting his penis stuck in a Hoover'? The House of Commons erupted.

We consequently survived a potential ban in the next city we performed in, Derry, Ireland, again hitting the front pages of the Irish media condemning the Millennium Theatre for booking such an outrageous show. A Cambridge Professor even tried to ban Dan from performing in one of the cities Universities Freshens Ball, not this in case because of the 'Hoover Incident' but in case it offended other Dwarfs!

Again we hit the front pages. From there on, virtually every show in the UK was sold out. Thank God for Superglue. Life certainly is Strange.

Image credit to Sarah Photogirl

"We lived in a van, not a caravan but a converted Austin "Three-way" van. It was considered revolutionary when built in 1948 but this was the late 1950's and it had definitely seen better days. To cover the rust he pasted Circus posters all over it. It must have been cramped with the three of us and our pet dog Sheba all living in a tin box measuring 12' x 5'." By Haze.

CHAPTER ONE
THE NIGHTMARE BEGINS

R omantic notations declaring you were born in a Circus caravan with lions roaring outside in the middle of a thunderstorm are certainly stories of legend.

That wasn't quite the case with me, there was no caravan, instead a hospital in Manchester. There were no raging storms and no roaring lions. Just a cold, wet, winters morning.

But born into a Circus though I certainly was.

I'm not quite sure why we were in Manchester at this time, unless it was one of my Dad's soirees into club land.

My Mum claimed she could hear my Dad doing his Max Miller impersonations in the club across the road while she was in labour.

My father was the ultimate jack-of-all-trades, master of none. Former bear and lion trainer, clown, fire-eater, publicist, taxi driver, milkman, comedian, thief, fraudster and down right rotter. He had been married, divorced and had three children before he met my Mum while he was working as an ambulance driver in London.

As a youngster he won a grand piano after entering a competition searching for promising musicians in the Daily Express. His Mother refused to allow the piano in the house and this began a lifetime of hatred between them. This was further fuelled after he stole money from her and she went to the police, prosecuted him and in turn he was sentenced to his first of numerous stints behind bars.

His father was a Jewish insurance salesman, consequently, they had a nice large house in Folkestone and were fairly well off.

Between his prison stints and as a result of his Mother's imposed ban from his family home he ran away and joined a Circus, or more to the point it was various Circuses. Doing many different jobs, such as, beast man, publicist, clown, briefly a lion trainer as well as a bit part as a fire eater in The Curse of Frankenstein.

His fate however could have taken a very different course when he bought a troupe of performing cats, yes that's right cats, not lions or tigers but domestic cats.

Cats unlike dogs are notoriously hard to train and consequently you rarely see them in Circuses. He did manage to buy a troupe though and quickly got a booking touring Music Halls in Ireland. As the norm with my Dad he didn't stick at anything very long and at the end of his contract in Ireland decided to give all the cats away as domestic pets to the good folk of Dublin.

He returned home to the UK only to receive a letter, offering himself and his cats a lucrative contract promoting Whiskers Cat Food, including a TV ad. The money he could have received from the ads and the subsequent live shows he could have secured from being the 'Whiskers TV Cats' would have set him up for a long time.

My Mum was completely opposite, she came from a relatively poor family. She was an illegitimate daughter of a mental hospital nurse at a time when it was totally unacceptable to have a child out of wedlock. For a time it was planned that she would be sent to a children's orphanage or workhouse to protect my Grandma's embarrassment.

Thankfully that idea was dropped.

Of course my Grandma was not alone in her outer matrimonial affairs but it tended to be hidden in those days and consequently Mum was brought up by my Grandma, her two sisters, Aunty Nell and Aunty Rachel who, herself had four more children, Dennis, Charles, Will, Elsie who, with my Mum, were brought up as brothers and sisters.

My Mum was not in the best of health as a youngster, she was blind in one eye after it had somehow exploded and at the age of 12 contracted Meningitis. At this time it was a killer and she was in a coma for a month. Eventually she was given a pill that would kill or cure.

To everyone's relief it did cure her although the doctors told her it was only a temporary respite and predicted she would die before she reached her 21st birthday.

She was born and brought up in Portmadoc, a beautiful little town in North Wales where everyone knew everyone and everyone knew everyone else's business.

The Second World War had finished a few year's earlier although rationing was still prevalent.

Work also, was hard to come by and my Grandma, her sister, my Mum and various other family members moved to New Brighton to seek employment.

Their time there was short lived as my Grandma was offered work as a staff nurse in a psychiatric ward in a mental institution in Preston.

The family moved into a terraced house in Avenham Road in the Town Centre. It was very basic with an outside toilet and a tin bathtub that would be used once a week by each of the house's inhabitants. There were three small bedrooms, somehow squeezing in my Grandma, her sister, Aunty Nell and five adolescent Welsh kids.

Preston has a proud history, the name derived from Old English words meaning "Priest settlement" and in the Doomsday Book appears as "Prestune".

It's citizens know it as 'Proud Preston', however, it's once thriving textile industry was beginning to fall into a terminal decline and Preston subsequently faced similar challenges to other post-industrial northern towns, including economic deprivation and housing issues.

What it did have in the late 40's and early 50's was a thriving football team, Preston North End.

They were a founder member of the English Football League in 1888, they were the first English football champions and won the FA cup in the same year. Winning the league without losing a game and winning the cup without conceding a goal.

In the mid 20th century they weren't quite as consistent as their 'Invincible' ancestors but formidable opponents nevertheless. Led by the legendary flying winger Tom Finney, Preston was buzzing and proud to proclaim it had probably the greatest footballer of all time.

My Mum finished her schooling in Preston and for the next few years did various jobs, mainly as a hospital orderly. I believe she liked her time in Preston but longed for the bright lights of London and after a raging row with my Grandma decided to pack her bags and head south in search of the golden paved streets.

It was there, again as a hospital worker that she met, got engaged to and, within a few weeks, married my Dad. He worked in the same hospital as an ambulance driver until he got the sack for using the Ambulance for immoral purposes, picking up Prostitutes and their clients and allowing them to use the Ambulance as a sort of mobile brothel.

His severance pay, little as it was, enabled him to set up his own business and he started a taxi company where my Mum did the switch.

He had big ideas, bought a fleet of clapped out old bangers that consistently broke down usually after being sent down the wrong streets by my Mum.

Before long and with most of their money gone he persuaded her to do a flit, leaving the taxi firm behind and joining a travelling fun fair. In those days fairs did not only have rides but also travelled with attractions such as Wall of Death, Freak Shows, Boxing Booths etc.

My Dad hired a couple of Himalayan bears from a Circus owner Wally Lucken and presented them on a chain in pit, my Mum worked in an illusion cum freak show owned by Nippy

Appleton where she was a Spider woman - The head and torso of a woman and the legs of a spider.

My Mum always told me that my father was frightened of the bears and one day while the fair was in Grantham one of the bears escaped and ran down the High Street with my Dad and Mum dressed in her Spider Woman outfit in pursuit. It was caught just as it entered a pub. The incident was front-page news but was also the end of my Dad's bear training career.

They then moved to Lord George Sangers Circus, I'm not sure what my Dad's role in this fantastic and famous show was but I certainly hope that this was where I was conceived.

That winter they moved back to the North of England, firstly to Manchester and after my birth and after reconciliation with my Grandma back to Preston.

A few of my cousins had now moved out of Avenham Road so my Mum, Dad and me moved in temporally. Dad took a job as a milkman but it was not long before he was tempted by the smell of the greasepaint again.

In the late 50's Britain's towns and cities had numerous Theatres playing host to the Variety Shows of their time. Often headlined by one of the big name comedians of the time plus singers dancers and speciality acts.

One of these Variety Shows contained Rosaries Beauty and the Beast act where two topless models stood in a cage of performing lions. My Dad visited the show and found out they needed a new presenter for the lions. He quickly volunteered himself and amazingly got the job.

His new occupation failed to last the week though after my Mum told him to give it up as she didn't want to be young widow, although my Dad believed my Mum's real concern was the claws of the topless models.

Circuses in the years after the war though were thriving and by the late 50's there were 50 Circuses touring the UK including the big three – Bertram Mills, Billy Smarts and Chipperfields.

My Dad was offered a job in much more modest show than the big three, entitled, Winships Circus. It was a small show with no wild animals, only horses and dogs and smaller Circus acts. His first job as a white-faced clown and then as the advance manager.

o maybe not back into the lions den but a return to the Circus for my Mum, Dad and a three month old me.

We lived in a van, not a caravan but a converted Austin "Three-way" van. It was considered evolutionary when built in 1948 but this was the late 1950's and it had definitely seen better days. To cover the rust he pasted Circus posters all over it. It must have been cramped with th three of us and our pet dog Sheba all living in a tin box measuring 12' x 5'.

I can't imagine what the sanitary and washing arrangements must have been like and lucki I was too young to remember.

My Dad's job as an advance manager involved him booking the grounds for the Circus to c on, placing an ad in the local paper and then putting up the posters to publicize it.

Nowadays poster publicity is still vitally important in the promotion of Circuses but it combined with new media, viral campaigns, web sites, e shots, face book, twitter etc etc, plu of course newspaper, radio and TV adverts, stories and features. All part of the multi-med world in which we now live. In the late 50's you relied pretty well on the power of the poste

Publicizing Circuses in those days was relatively easy because everyone wanted to go, the ve vision of a big top turning up in a local park or farmers field was in it self a great advert, puttir up posters without permission was also commonplace, no town and country planners suir you for fly posting.

My first foray into the Circus world was about to be cut short however. Dad was as alwa restless and once Winships had reached it's furthest point Wick in Scotland, he decided to jum on his motorbike and do a runner.

He left my Mum, a now six month old baby and our dog Sheba with no money and living in knackered old Van that my Mum couldn't drive.

The Winships were diamonds as were the Bailey family who were also on the show and looke after us all. Giving my Mum small jobs and money. We stayed until the end of the season whe they then drove us to Preston.

We moved back in with my Grandma, leaving Sheba with the Bailey family so at least he carrie on our Circus connections.

My Grandma, was previously very mentally cruel to my Mum, destroying her confidence ar telling her she would never find a man to marry her, I think in many ways marrying my Da was a type of rebellion that backfired.

Returning back to Preston to live with my Grandma was very much 'I told you so'. The fami quite rightly, never liked my Dad and was sure it could never last.

It was this confidence battering that had caused the rift between them in the first place ar forcing my Mum to leave home, telling my Grandma that she would see her at her funeral.

Thankfully, they had made up and I'm sure my Grandma was pleased to see my Mum and her new Grandchild back home as opposed to trekking around the country in the back of a battered old banger. My Mum never really forgave her though and on my Mum's deathbed she threatened to punch my Grandma in the face if they met in the afterlife.

Another situation that must have grated on my Mum is the fact that she could never call my Grandma 'Mum' - still protecting her unacceptable illegitimate motherhood, my Mum had to call my Grandma , Auntie Bessie and I was brought up thinking she was my Auntie.

We shared the house with Bessie's sister, Aunty Nell (who was actually my Great Auntie) and Uncle Charles (who was actually my cousin). We first lived in Avenham Rd. until we were told the road would be knocked down as it was classed as a slum and was part of the town's redevelopment. In fact the road is still there, only our house was knocked down - The Devils Child lived here! Where are they going to put the blue plaque now?

While we were in Avenham Road I went to nursery and briefly to infant school in the centre of the town before we moved a mile or two out of town to 5 Barry Avenue, Ingol.

Ingol was a modern housing estate and as Preston was expanding, more and more of these estates were springing up around the town.

Can you spot the Doktor and Basher Briggs? Answer on page 18   *Photo credits, from Haze's personal collection*

We were the first family in the house, it was a three bedroom, with me and my Mum in one room, Bessie and Nell in another and Uncle Charles in the other. We even had an inside toilet and a bathroom.

I enjoyed my childhood and everyone was really good to me, we never had much money but I always somehow got lots of birthday and Christmas presents.

We regularly went on holiday, mainly to Portmadoc, and a great recollection was seeing Sanger Circus arrive in Port' while we were there. I was very small but the memories of this show were profound. It was certainly the first Circus I can remember seeing.

Me and my Uncle Charles in Avenham
Photo credits, from Haze's personal collection

The show featured a local boy 'Gwen Owen' making his debut on the trapeze, a troupe of bears, a clown called Fiery Jack and this amazing act called The Moreliys. It was tiny car with a guy sat in it that was on a track above all of our heads. It would flydown, do a loop de loop on the track until the track ran out above the ring. It would then go into free fall and project itself over the ring and into a net on the other side of the tent. Amazing.

Returning from my holiday to Preston, I moved school and went to Savick Junior School. I had lots of friends, one of which, Graham 'Basher' Briggs is still a friend to this day.

I found Savick a really pleasant school, and after school I loved going to the Cinema, usually twice a week. I'd go with my Mum to see the main features such as the Bond films, Dr. No, From Russia with Love, Goldfinger etc as well as the Disney classics of the time and the Carry On films. Uncle Charles would take me to the westerns and the military films, The Magnificent Seven and Zulu.

My favourite films though were Whistle Down the Wind and Jason and the Argonauts, which we saw, in a tiny cinema while on holiday in Portmadoc. Every Saturday morning I would go with my friends to the matinees, they were a mixture of cartoons and kids films. I remember one week the Odeon tried to get everyone to go in fancy dress with a cash prize to the winner. I went as a bandit and when it was time to go onto the stage to get judged I noticed I was the only one dressed up. Nevertheless I still went onto the stage and as the only person who had bothered to dress up was sure to win, only to be told that due to the poor turn out the competition would be rolled over to the next week.

My Mum shopping in Preston
Photo credits, from Haze's personal collection

I returned the following week, again in my bandit attire, this time there were other competitors. We all took our place on the stage but the result was declared a draw and we were given 1/2 a crown each (that's a 2d/6p coin - worth about 12p today). I felt a little conned but 1/2 a crown richer never the less. I would hardly call my dressing up as a bandit performing but I was about to make my debut treading the boards alongside Basher as a shepherd in Savick's Christmas nativity.

My Mum of course was over the moon watching her little solider and I think I was quite pleased too. The next year though I was hoping for a better role, maybe a King. Alas, I was cast as a shepherd again! I complained to our Headmaster Mr. English who pointed out that the girls have it much tougher with the only choices for them the Virgin Mary or an Angel.

My complaint prompted a discussion within the class though when Mr. English asked us to come up with some more female biblical characters that in a different time scale we could portray if we were girls. Basher chose Mary Magdalene not realizing she was a prostitute, I had no such modesty and opted for the Whore of Babylon.

Mr. English was none too happy with me or the rest of the class of eight year olds when they started asking him what a whore was. The rest of the class were not best pleased either as my nomination and their subsequent questions ended with the whole class given detention during our dinner hour come play time.

Of course we visited every Circus that came to Town. An amazing sight as a child was watching Billy Smarts mighty herd of 20 elephants being paraded through the streets from Preston Station to Moor Park, the Circus site. The big three in those day's, Bertrum Mills, Chipperfields and Billy Smarts were massive affairs with 4,000 seater big tops and lavish shows. They would alternate their visits to town bringing huge amounts of fantastic exotic animals with them.

During the mid sixties I was taken to my first football match with a group of friends by one of their Dads. I was in complete awe from the minute I walked into the floodlit Deepdale.

It was an evening game, a friendly I believe, against Leeds who had Jackie Charlton playing for them. Leeds were a dirty team even in those days and won 3-2, I didn't care, I had met my messiah, I had smelled the liniment.

I had tasted true excitement and as soon as I entered this historic stadium and heard the roar of the crowd the hairs stood up on the back of my neck and I knew, it was Preston till I die.

My heros were coming thick and fast but not always in the blue and white of Preston. I hadn't quite got into music but was aware of it, who wouldn't be in the sixties with the likes of the clean cut Beatles battling it out with the bad boys The Rolling Stones.

At this time I preferred the Beatles but it didn't take me long to change my allegiance. Other heros though tended to come at me from my TV screen, Steve Zodiac, expert pilot of Fireball XL5, Troy Tempest, heart throb captain of Stingray and the puppet boy band of their time Thunderbirds.

Other greats were Illya Nickovetch Kuryakin from The Man from Uncle. plus of course a great

boyhood hero (although I only saw him on Match of the Day), Georgie Best.

Surprisingly though there was a lack of girls in both our group of friends and in my list of hero's, even Emma Peel, Marina or Pussy Galore failed to float my boat.

I recall walking down the road with my Mum and a girl from our school, Fiona Winterbottom was coming the other way. She said 'hello John' but I just grunted and dipped my head, declaring to my Mum that 'I don't like girls'.

My first recollection of Horror also came at this time and it came during our regular visits to the Cinema. Two old but classic films and well ahead of their time sent shivers down my spine First of all the walking trees in Walt Disney's Fantasia and then the flying monkeys in Wizard of Oz. I was petrified.

Spot the difference, Haze and a Chimp. Answer on page 18
Photo credits, from Haze's personal collection

Tom Finney converts a penalty for Preston North End against Manchester United in front of "the Kop"
Photo credits, from Haze's personal collection

On the other side of the coin one of my best childhood memories was when Tom Finney came to Savick Infant School talk to us about football and give us a little coaching. Sir Tom was the greatest footballer of all time he played only for Preston North End an unbelievable 433 times and was capped 76 times for England scoring 30 goals and playing in all five forward positions along the way.

He got out a ball and showed us how to trap it, you could throw it at him and it wouldn't matter where on the body it hit him he could stop it dead before an amazing turn of pace and body swerve would send him leaving defenders for dead.

He displayed this for us and then chose a volunteer, to my amazement he chose me. He passed the ball to me and asked me to pass it back to the position he would run onto, so as to not slow his run. Instead I played it straight to his feet, not the general idea but who cares, here I was, nine years old and playing football with Tom Finney!

Sadly Tom had already retired before I started watching PNE so I only ever saw him play in charity games. Not only did I miss seeing Tom Finney play but my time supporting PNE in the 80's was when the team were on a downward spiral and I probably saw them lose as often as saw them win.

That ratio would have been worse had I gone to away games, the only one I attended was ironically a 1-0 away win at Blackburn.

Preston's decline started before they first received my support, so I can't, at least be held responsible for that one. It actually began shortly after Tom had retired. A year after he hung up his boots they were relegated from the old 1st Division (now The Premier League).

They did taste a degree of success in 1964 though when they finished 3rd in the old 2nd division (now the Championship) and as unlucky losing FA Cup finalists against West Ham.

I even missed that as well though, it was a year or two after the cup final defeat that I started going to Deepdale and supporting PNE, by which time their demise was well underway.

The 60's also saw the emergence of football violence. Often, away teams would come to Deepdale and 'take the Kop'. The Kop was an area for Preston fans but occasionally away supporters would turn up before the Preston fans and position themselves in the Preston Kop.

There was no segregation so a battle would ensue once the Preston fans arrived. I saw some terrible and bloody fights between Preston and Blackpool fans and once, when I was only nine years old, I turned round to see a dart stuck firmly in my coat only two inches from my head. It didn't put me off though, football was my game and PNE were my team.

Towards the end of the 60's I changed school to go to the newly opened Tulketh. It was nearer to Ingol than Savick but Basher and a bunch of friends from Savick agreed to maintain our group of "brothers" and they too went to Tulketh. I was soon though, unbeknown to me, about to break this special bond.

Most young boys want to grow up and be rock star, or footballer, train driver etc. Basher Briggs opted for a Solicitor, but he always was different.

I, however was no exception, not so much the train driving but more in my case emulating Ringo Starr on a biscuit tin drum or becoming the new Willie Irvine and scoring a hat trick for Preston North End or gunning Basher down in a Bondesque extravaganza.

My fate however was about to be taken out of my hands and change unrecognizably. Going from a stable home life and education to soon swap my house with an indoor bathroom for a caravan with a chemical toilet. My school to premature employment and my pet hamster for an alligator.

ANSWERS . . .
Page 13, Second row, far right, Doktor Haze. Third row, second left, Basher Briggs
Page 16, Haze is on the right of course

The Circus Supreme

FOSSETT BROS. CIRCUS

Langley Farm, Bishopton, Stratford-upon-Avon

Telephone: Stratford-upon-Avon 5408

Contract for 1970 Season

Mrs John Hayes — agrees to accept
an engagement with Fossett Bros Circus
as advance & Publicity agent.
The Show to Supply a Vehicle to
Pull trailer, also Fuel & Oil when
Being used for the advance.
Fossett Bros agrees to Pay
Mrs John Hayes Weekly Salary of
£20. (Twenty Pounds) Per Week

Sig Fossett & tossett

photo credits, from Haze's personal collection

Chapter Two
A Baptism of Fire

Man had landed on the Moon. The Beatles had split up. Manchester City had won the FA Cup. Preston North End were relegated into the old 3rd division for the first time in their illustrious history but the most unbelievable thing was about to happen. Mum was planning a reunion with my Dad.

It was unbeknown to me that my Mum had been trying to track down my Dad to seek maintenance, unexpected but totally justified. I have no idea how she did this but she was successful in tracking him down, gaining maintenance however, was going to prove an impossibility.

Not only was he completely skint but when she found him he was serving three years for fraud in Wandsworth Prison. In their time apart he had been in and out of prison, returned to the Circus and had a serious motorbike accident (one leg was now shorter than the other and bent around the thigh instead of at the knee). He also had at least five heart attacks, apparently three in one week.

He was coming to the end of his sentence and my Mum tried her maintenance claim only for a judge to unbelievably advise that they got back together 'and try again'. Even more unbelievable, my Mum agreed! The main reason for this was because she thought it was unfair for other kids to have Fathers and not me.

For the next few month's she travelled from Preston to London to visit my Dad in the nick, at first I did not know where she was going. After a few other visits though she owned up to seeing him. She did not tell me she was visiting him in prison though and I thought she was going to see him in hospital. I had no idea that my Dad was a jailbird.

She would bring letters back to me from him and I started writing back, my letters generally talking about Preston North End, he claimed to be a Spurs fan but he had no real interest in football.

My Mum planned the reconciliation and I had to swear to secrecy, I'm sure my Auntie Bessie Auntie Nell and Uncle Charles all knew we were going but no one else did. Not the rest of our family in Preston or in Portmadoc, not my friends and not even my best friend Basher Briggs

By this time Aunty Nell had moved out of Barry Avenue and at 62 got married for the first time to Frank, a widower from the other side of town. 5 Barry Ave was about to change from a house containing a family of five to one that just housed Auntie Bessie and Uncle Charles.

We packed our stuff into crates and moved to live with my Dad in London, I was 11 and we arrived on the day he was released. I was spared the embarrassment of our first remembered encounter being outside the prison gates by meeting him on the platform of Euston station.

My Mum had warned me of his accident and strange walk but made no mention of his encampment in Her Majesty's custody. I obviously did not recognize him but his accident meant he wore an orthopaedic shoe on one of his feet to level himself up. He hated it and one of the first things he did was throw his 'special shoe' away and replace it with a more conventional pair. We had nowhere to live and spent the first day traipsing around the streets of London looking for somewhere to call home. We eventually found two adjacent beds sits in Matheson Rd., Fulham and took them both. I felt quite at home when I found out it was off North End Road. I shortly afterwards enrolled in Henry Compton School in Fulham.

I lasted one and a half days.

This was a real culture shock, in Preston I never once saw anyone get the cane. In Henry Compton I saw five kids get the cane in my first hour there. It was a terrible school, the pupils were disruptive and the teachers thought the only way to deal with them was with corporal punishment. No one could ever learn anything under these conditions.

The premature end to my school days in London meant I spent most of my days accompanying my Dad as a door-to-door salesman. Vindictively, my Dad decided to tell me that my Aunty Bessie was in fact my Grandma. I don't think I was too shocked, it all seemed to make sense and I didn't feel the slightest anger despite being lied to all my life. Obviously this was not the reaction my Dad wanted, he was clearly trying to drive a wedge between my family and myself.

I did feel sorry though that the family thought it right to hide the truth, not just from me but also from everyone else. My Dad also decided to own up to being banged up for the past three years. I don't think that surprised me too much either. To get us on our feet my Dad's Mum had given us some money, now this did surprise me considering their hatred of each other. My Dad spent it on the deposit on the bedsits and on broken down cars.

The money was running out quickly, my Mum had taken a job in a factory and my Dad worked as a door-to-door salesman until he got fed up with that too. He sought salvation in the pages of The Worlds Fair (A Circus, Market Trader and Fair Ground magazine/paper). Moving directly to Motley, the Circus page, he saw an advert for acts wanted in a new Irish Circus, Circus Beck.

My Dad rang Jim Beck, a former Circus fan and supermarket owner. He continued to run his chain of supermarket stores but also fulfilled his ambition and started his own Circus. Dad told him we did a Fakir, Fire Eating and Mind Reading act and consequently got the job.

Great, we had a job, but no act. My Mum never allowed me to light a match let alone eat fire. So here we go, a crash course in fire eating, walking on broken glass, being strangled alive and mind reading. I had one day to learn.

The sad side to this was we had to leave my Mum behind, I still remember her crying so much when we had to leave, proclaiming that my Dad was taking me away from her.

We drove through the night to Liverpool, close on the tails of a large lorry, as the lights on our Morris Minor did not work. I was carsick. We made it to Liverpool, sold the car to pay for the ferry to Ireland. I was seasick. When we arrived in Belfast we were picked up in an American pick-up and taken to the Circus winter quarters. I was carsick again.

This certainly was another culture shock for me, a tiny caravan, a portaloo, sawdust and corn beef hash - my Dads favourite and an everyday delight!

We had joined the show well into their tour and stayed until the end of the season which was only about six weeks but at least my first Circus performances were about to begin.

We were replacing half of the Garcia Family. A brilliant multi talented family from Spain. We certainly were not worthy. They were led by two Spanish brothers who married two Irish sisters from the famous Fossett family.

I say half because the two sides of the family decided to split up with Antonio, Mary and her family, which included Carmen and Mona (friends of mine to this day) leaving Circus Beck.

Louis and Amy were to stay and he performed a lightning fast juggling act, and their two boys Losito and Roberto performing a roller balancing and a wire-walking act.

It was this split which had caused the show to close down and in turn the placement of the advert in The Worlds Fair, which led to our employment.

I quickly settled into Circus life but one thing I did not expect was to be questioned by local Northern Irish eleven year old kids as to whether I was Protestant or Catholic. It was early days in the Irish conflict and you would see barricades built down side streets, the kids who lived there seemed used to it but it was a real shock to me.

I was of course, even in my tender years, forever the diplomat and swerved around the question with the aplomb of a hardened politician.

Luckily we did not directly see any of the troubles or get involved with it.

Circus Beck was a small but good show, it had performing Horses and Dogs, our Fire Eating, Fakir and Mind Reading acts, The Garcia Family plus a Magic Act and some Clowns.

They had a very unique tent where the two King Poles (the main poles that hold up the big top) were on the outside of the tent which was also in one piece, none of it needed lacing up. As a result of which, we could pull down and load it on the trucks and trailers in an amazing 25 minutes from the end of the show.

This all helped the one day stands to become much more bearable although getting up at seven am every day wasn't much fun.

The shows lighting was very basic but one day it was to become unbelievably basic. We were half way through our Fakir act when the generator broke down and all the lights went out. We quickly switched to our Fire Eating act to take up some time as the flames from our torches were enough to light us up, we went on for about 10 minutes and I was beginning to smell like a barbeque.

We were expecting the lights to come back on at some point but instead we saw Jim Beck driving his Land Rover into the tent and the rest of the show was completed under the headlights from his jeep. Jim then took a megaphone and hummed the Saber Dance until we finished.

It was a baptism of fire (excuse the pun) but an enjoyable one, I had become the world's youngest fire-eater, I had been strangled by two members of the audience twice daily and had met lots of new friends some of which I still see to this day.

We also got paid a very splendid £30 per week, pretty good money for 1969.

After the six weeks run we returned to London, back to my Mum and back to being a door-to-door salesman. We sold everything from tea towels to cakes, all under the pretence of a fictitious company called 'The Disabled'.

Dad used to play on his disability and show the punters his dodgy leg, sometimes people would buy out of sympathy and sometimes not.

remember one day a guy refused to buy anything, my Dad turned around to leave and fell flat on his face, tea towels and cream cakes everywhere. The guy felt so guilty he spent about

£5 on our ware. I thought about tripping him up every day after that.

My life's ambitions never included being a door-to-door salesman but it certainly beat going back to Henry Compton School.

It was late September and as most Circuses finished at the end of October so there wouldn't be many openings to re-join a Circus at this time. There was however an advert for Billy Smarts who were in Finsbury Park and were looking for a fire-eater.

My Dad called them and we went over for an audition. The audition was with David Smart but we got there too early and got him out of bed, which probably wasn't the best of starts.

While we were waiting we went into the tent and the elephants were being put through their paces. It was totally amazing, the 20 fine ladies that I had seen walking through the streets of Preston some four years earlier where there right in front of me.

After they finished there routine they were rewarded with a large unsliced loaf of bread each.

The elephant trainer seemed to know my Dad and came over for a chat while we waited for David Smart. David did eventually arrive and it was our turn to take to this very famous sawdust ring. I've hardly ever auditioned for anything in my life and it certainly isn't easy. Our fire act did not contain fire blowing, I was too young and my Dad's false teeth once blew out when he tried it so he gave up that aspect of the act.

It was more the fakir type of act, body burning and eating the fire etc. Smarts were looking for a more cavalier approach to fit into their Wild West scene and we weren't right for that.

There was another option though, every Christmas Day straight after the Queen's speech the TV used to show Billy Smarts Circus and on boxing day Billy Smarts Children's Circus which contained Circus kids performing their acts.

David was very polite and let us down gently but he did ask my Dad if I would perform alone in their Children's Circus, which was to be shown on TV that year. I would have jumped at the chance but my Dad was so jealous he turned it down.

After this setback my Dad was starting to sound things out for the next summer and heard of a new show called Anglo - Danish Circus, it was to be run by a famous bear trainer called Hans Vogalbin and a theatrical agent.

We went to see the agent and he wasn't sure what acts they were going to use in their Circu but said he would talk to Hans and they would consider us. In the meantime he offered us job in Panto in Peterborough that winter and Dad accepted.

We were going to work our Fire Eating act in the panto but I could not get a child-performing license so Dad ended up as a stagehand instead, he hated it. He only worked there for about a week and then never went back.

We were again living in a caravan and the Theatre owned the land we were parked on so we had to move.

We had no money, no job and nowhere to park our caravan and I was about to see my Dad's dark side. My Mum had put up a Christmas tree and all our Christmas cards, it lasted about an hour, Dad came in and threw them all in the fire, declaring his hatred of Christmas.

Luckily we found a pub car park just down the road and got permission to park there for a few months, this eased the pain and I went back to school for the next three months. I had missed the last nine months but quickly got back in my stride, the only thing I seemed to be struggling with was Maths, this was strange as it was one of my best subjects at Tulketh.

The school was nice, Stanground Comprehensive, on the edge of Peterborough. It was very similar to Tulketh and poles apart from Henry Compton. The girls were pretty hot too and the skirts were getting shorter.

I was far to shy to do anything about it though but I was definitely beginning to show a liking for the finer sex.

My Dad went to work in London as a taxi driver and I would travel down to see him every weekend. I would come back most weeks with a new pet for my Mum to look after. He worked out of a cab office in Cable Street in London's East End. It was an area full of real characters but was nonetheless a seedy part of town.

From Victorian times through to the 1950's, Cable Street was famous for cheap lodgings, brothels, drinking inns and opium dens. It was supposedly the last occasion in England when a stake was hammered through a sinner's heart at an official burial. Cool Eh.

It was also close to Whitechapel, previously heavily populated by Irish and Jewish communities. There was terrible poverty and in the late 1800's this endemic poverty drove many women to prostitution. In October 1888 the Metropolitan Police estimated that there were 1,200 prostitutes and about 62 brothels. Such prostitutes were numbered amongst the eleven Whitechapel Murders (1888-91), some of which were committed by a legendary serial killer known as 'Jack the Ripper'.

) years later, it had certainly cleaned itself up from those days but the underworld were still prevalent there. The cab office seemed to be run by London's gangland, constantly at battle with the rival cab companies. So much so that a year after my Dad had left we read in the papers that the cab office had been burnt down in suspicious circumstances, killing a mentally disabled guy and his Mum who lived upstairs.

Nevertheless I enjoyed the experience of going down there each weekend and our menagerie of pets that I was slowly re-housing in our caravan in Peterborough now included a pet Alligator called Snappy.

On one weekend when Dad returned to our new but temporary Peterborough home we received some bad news. His Mum, my Grandma had died. I had only met her once so it didn't affect me. My Dad however burst into tears, I didn't get it, he always told me he hated her and I cruelly reminded him of this. He agreed that he did hate her but he reminded me, she was still his Mum. We didn't go to the funeral but she did leave me and my half brothers and sister some money in her will. This was in a trust until I was 18. The solicitors took ages telling us what our potential bounty might be, I thought I was going to be rich but ended up with 30 quid.

Spring was on its way though and time to start looking for a Circus to work for, so one weekend instead of heading to London we travelled to the Midlands to peddle our wares to anyone who wanted to look.

The Midlands was home to a number of Circus winterquarters, my Dad chose to go to Stratford-on-Avon and Henley-in-Arden. One part of the famous Fossett family were split up between the two towns, first of all we went to Henley-in-Arden to visit James Fossett and his family one of which was Gerry Cottle who had married James' youngest daughter Betty. Betty was away working with her sisters but a youthful Gerry was there.

They were really nice to us but didn't offer us a job. So on to Stratford to visit Claude and Sister Fossett. We drove into their farm to see a sort of Circus winterquarters cum scrap yard. It was hard to differentiate between the scrap vehicle and caravans and those inhabited by the Fossett family.

We knocked on the trailer that seemed to be lived in and Claude opened it. He recognized my Dad straightaway and said 'Ah Johnny Hayes, you did a great job as advance man for Winships' I was amazed that he remembered my Dad from 12 years earlier and equally amazed that he thought my Dad had done a good job for them, in my opinion Dad didn't do a good job of anything.

Our intention was to try and get a job with our Fire Eating and Fakir act but Claude had other ideas, he needed a new advance man and thought my Dad fitted the bill.

He offered us a job there and then with a wage of £20 per week. It was £10 per week less than we earned at Circus Beck but beggars can't be choosers, so Dad accepted.

We went back to Peterborough and told my Mum, there was a few more weeks before we left so I went back to school and Dad went back to the cab office in London. It turned out to be the last time I ever went to school and at the end of March we coupled up our trailer and left for Stratford.

The Fossett name is one of the oldest in the Circus business and can be traced back hundreds of years, lots of shows that were not directly called Fossett had traces of the Fossett bloodline in them. Chipperfields, Roberts and of course Gerry Cottle married a Fossett.

Some, such as James Brothers and Ringlands were actually Fossetts but chose to use a different name for their respective shows.

In the UK at the beginning of the 1970's there were three shows still using that famous name, plus one in Ireland. In Britain the largest was Sir Robert Fossett's, it had a troupe of baby elephants and a cage act of either lions or tigers, then there was Big Bob Fossett's Circus which was a smaller affair and smaller again Fossett Brothers Circus, run by Claude and Sister Fossett with their daughter Jessie.

Claude was already around 80 years old when we joined, he had a gammy leg after being shot in the leg during the war. An injury that put paid to his horse-riding act, he was still though a good horseman, the animals had great respect for him. He married his cousin Janet Fossett who was known as Sister, probably named by her four brothers. She was 20 years his junior and had performed many things throughout her life and she was a very accomplished trapeze artist. Many years earlier she also performed a sort of striptease act behind a gauze curtain lit from behind. Apparently it was amazingly sexy with her silhouette becoming less clothed without actually seeing anything. It was considered too steamy for children though and was only performed in the evening shows.

When we joined the show they were at the twilight of their career, although they both still performed, Claude occasionally Clowning and Sister showing the horses and dogs. They both still built up and pulled down the tent, Claude still swinging a sledge hammer in his 80's. They had a small tent which could be used as a one or two pole, music came from a record player on a table next to the ring doors and the box office was Sisters 18' caravan with the window open.

The rest of the show consisted of Jessie, Claude and Sister's lovely daughter and Valda Orry, who was Jessie's partner, with a Juggling and Rolling Globe act, a Double Trapeze and a Wild

West act, which included Jessie, throwing knifes around Valda.

Jessie or more precisely her hand became slightly famous after it was used as a body double when throwing a knife in one of the James Bond films.

In years gone by the show was larger, at one point they had an elephant and a cage act until one of the lions tragically killed the trainer in the ring.

I believe Jessie was sat in the ringside seats and witnessed this horrible event.

Fossett Brothers Circus in the 1970's was a much smaller affair with the house acts of Claude, Sister, Jessie and Valda augmented with Clown Brum and his comedy car and Low Wire act, a young Escapologist Jack Unell with his wife Yvonne and Dick Sandows family. Dick acting as Ringmaster, with his two kids Richard performing a Roller Roller act and Wiggy with a Hoops and Glasses act (this is sort of naff kids type contortion act for people who cannot do contortions).

We pulled onto their winter quarters in Stratford to meet Claude before going out and booking the grounds. Claude gave us a list of towns he would like to go to and my Dad would try and find grounds, book them and then do the publicity.

We worked about two weeks ahead of the show, I was doing a lot of the billing (putting up the posters), sometimes with my Dad and sometimes on my own while he went out to look for grounds.

We started the season in Tewkesbury before moving into South Wales, once a week returning to the show to get paid and usually to get a bollocking from Claude. The bollockings were generally because the business wasn't good enough and even if it was Claude would pretend it wasn't. It almost reached a head when the show was in Brecon and in our weekly dusting down Claude warned my Dad that things had to get better.

The show moved out of Wales, through the midlands and into Lancashire, my Dad didn't get on with Dick Sandow and for once my Dad was right. Dick, was a prick and was continuously shit stirring and my Dad had a huge row with him.

This led to us being hauled before the Fossetts with Claude saying things hadn't changed and he asked us to leave in a week. I sat in Claude's trailer and cried my eyes out, I just thought we had failed. My emotional outburst worked though and Sister felt so sorry for me she told Claude to give us another chance so he gave us a month's trial to prove ourselves.

A piece of light relief came when after a row between Jack Unel and his wife Yvonne, the performed the great trunk escape, more commonly known as the substitution trunk.

She would be wearing a long evening dress, get handcuffed put in a sack and then put into the trunk. The trunk would be chained and padlocked.

Normally he would jump on the trunk lift up a cover, when it dropped Yvonne would be stood on the trunk in a very small bikini. She would then unlock the trunk, sack etc and reveal Jack, in the handcuffs that she had on earlier coolly smoking a fag.

On this occasion, they had had a row prior to going in. Jack, handcuffed her, put her in the sack and then the trunk, chaining and padlocking it as normal before jumping on the top, she emerged in her bikini but instead of releasing him she swallowed the key and walked out of the ring. Jack stuck in the trunk until Brum and Dick Sandow carried it out with him inside.

The change that Claude was predicting did come but not in the shape we all expected and within two weeks Dick Sandow and his family had left. It was nothing to do with the row with my Dad, it was just Dick Sandow. Whatever show he worked for he never completed a season. His traditional way of leaving was to go up to the show's owner, in this case Claude, and hand them a blank post card.

He would then couple up his trailer and leave and this is exactly what he did. Claude limping, chasing him off the ground calling him a bleeding bastard and waving the blank postcard at him. Ironically on the same day, the 18th June, Edward Heath was elected as the new Conservative Prime Minister. A time for change for the country and a time for change for Fossett Brothers Circus.

We must have done OK in the next month as the bollockings were not as intense and our month to prove ourselves was never mentioned again. It may also have been the fact that the other artistes were jumping ship, next to go was Tommy Cooke AKA Clown Brum, so possibly Claude simply couldn't afford to lose any more people.

The show moved into North Wales and suddenly everything looked better, a beautiful part of the world and good business. I felt closer to home when the show stood on the Treath in Porthmadog (it was now cool to spell it in Welsh), the very site where I as a child I saw Lord George's Circus and the small town where my Mum was born.

I did a deal with Jack Unell and promised to teach him to eat fire and give him some fire torches. In return he offered to teach me to whip crack and give me a whip. I learnt to whip crack very quickly and was very proud of my new whip and new skill. Jack though, simply couldn't fire it, no matter how many times he tried he just didn't have the courage.

Shortly afterwards Jack Unell would become the next to leave, I don't know why, no big dramas I just think he had had enough, the good thing though I knew he was never going to rival me as a Fire Eater.

Claude brought in another Circus family, Valda's Mum Dot, with her husband Tom Eyers and her offspring from her first marriage to Eddie Orry, Karl and Dallas plus her kids with Tom, Sharon, Fred and Nicola.

Karl did a Fire Eating and Clown act, Dallas also clowned and did plate spinning and Sharon assisted them both as well as rope spinning with Jessie and Valda.

Their other main asset was the fact that Tom was a mechanic and helped to move the show.

Surprisingly, Valda aside we had remained the longest serving employees that season. That was until towards the end of the tour my Dad had the normal attack of itchy feet and bizarrely, with less than a month of the season to go he decided we should all do a runner, so we coupled up our trailer and scarpered.

My Dad sent a 'Dear John' letter to Claude, no blank postcard but a letter with some sort of explanation, probably blaming ill health. We left from Stratton-St-Margaret near Swindon and drove up towards Bristol, we found a caravan site across the Severn Bridge and stayed there for the first part of the winter.

We returned to our Fire Eating, Fakir and Mind Reading acts, briefly, performing in working men's clubs around Bristol. My Dad though had an idea and an ambition to start our own small show, Gala Promotions Mini Circus. Great Showmen would always oversell their acts and exaggerate the size of the show and the content within it. You would never see P T Barnum waxing lyrical about his 'Mini Circus'.

I used to design my own Circus programmes with magnificent and wondrous acts from all over the world, Gala Promotions, the worlds largest Circus.

Using the word 'mini' before Circus was never going to be an inspiration for people to come and Dad was certainly no great showman and his 'Mini Circus' was to prove to be a major disaster.

Well perhaps not a major disaster but certainly a mini one and more to the point it to prove the difference between my Dad and me.

He could not go about his great, all be it 'Mini' adventure on his own so he set about finding Tom and Dot. He knew Claude had pulled in and that they would have gone back to their own winter quarters in Stoke on Trent.

There were no mobile phones in those days and they didn't have a landline phone, furthermore we didn't even know their address. All we knew is that they lived in Stoke on Trent.

We drove up and down the M5/M6, pulling off at junction 14 in search for them. The search was not without it's own dramas. One night after a failed hunt we travelled home, it was about 1am and my Dad fell asleep at the wheel with me in the passenger seat.

The car swerved onto the wrong side of the road and up a grass bank before grinding to a halt on its side. Although not wearing seat belts, neither of us were hurt and we were picked up by the Police who drove us back to the Police Station and allowed us to sleep in the cells. The iron barred door remained open, which must have felt strange for my Dad.

The car was a write off so I had to withdraw all my childhood savings from my Post Office account to buy another. Mum was really mad with me for telling my Dad I had savings.

Dad didn't give up hope of finding Tom and Dot and after a few more trips and lots of secret detective style sorties we went to the Potteries and we somehow found them.

My Dad told them of his grand idea to create a 'Mini' Circus and he persuaded them to join us as partners. This meant we had to move again, this time to a caravan site in Stone near Stoke on Trent.

We booked a couple of village halls and put up our 'mini' posters and put on our 'mini' show. It consisted of our Mind Reading, Fire Eating and Fakir acts plus a magic act that I had been badly perfecting. Plus the entire acts of Tom and Dot's family now expanded to include Dot's oldest Daughter Bonny.

We didn't actually lose any money, just about broke even so I suppose you could call it a 'mini' success.

As 1970 began to draw to a close we had to start thinking about the next year and the next season. Would we continue to run our 'mini' Circus, would we possibly expand it to a small Circus?

Alternatively, we could seek employment with another Circus.

One thing was for sure, it was to prove possibly the most significant and influential years of my life, I was to discover Girls, I was to lose one influential character, although a rogue and a rotter, certainly an influence and I was about to gain a substantial other.

Marc Bolan, photo credit Masayoshi Sukita

CHAPTER THREE
GET IT ON!

Puberty was beginning to set in and my mind was playing all sorts of tricks on me. The mini skirts would only make things worse and many a time I had to sit with a book on my lap to avoid the embarrassment of teenage girls realizing my attraction to them.

The spring however took a rather familiar turn.

My Dad had travelled down to London a few times with the aim of joining a show that was to open in Battersea Park for the summer, Circus Astral. It looked quite promising but it appeared we were surplus to requirements.

Tom, Dot and their family had decided to return to Fossett Bros Circus again and after meeting Claude Fossett he suggested that we returned too.

So we went back to the show we had scarpered from six months earlier, arriving a little gingerly and with our tails between our legs. I was a little older and wiser and certainly a lot more confident, we were doing the publicity again and despite my tender years I was beginning to get a real feel for it. We also got a pay rise, now on £25 per week.

In the meantime Preston North End had gained promotion from the 3rd division at the first attempt. In great style too. With two games left for North End to play, they were in second place and had to go to the leaders Fulham. If Fulham had won they would have been promoted and been crowned Champions, the tension was amazing. Of course I missed this great occasion again as we had moved away from Fulham long before Ricky Heppolette scored a brilliant flying header earning PNE a 1-0 win. Preston also won their last game 3-0 against Rotherham.

I not only missed these games but every game in that magnificent season. Nevertheless Preston were back.

My Dad was becoming more useless and I pretty well took over running the publicity unit. He also became far too strict and stubborn. I lost a lot of my childhood because of this, where other kids were out playing and listening to music I was working.

Having said that this sort of on the road life style was a great education in it's own right.

I may not have ended up with qualifications but I learned to stand on my own two feet far quicker than most kids. I had loads of confidence and an abundance of common sense. Most of all though, I enjoyed it.

Fossett Brothers Circus started with a similar programme to how it ended the year before, Tom and Dot's family with their acts, the Fossett Family with their acts and a Fire Eater / Fakir called Hanloe. Hanloe did a few reasonable tricks but was a poor showman, I did though, learn a few more fire tricks just by watching him.

The main difference this year was the up turn in business, we were in South Wales again and going to many of the places we had been to the year before. The big change was the publicity and as my Dad got worse at it, I got better, so much so I was more than compensating for his ineptness.

I actually think decimalization helped too. The change had apparently, somehow, taken the Decimal Currency Board five years to plan and the first decimal coins in Britain started to be exchanged across the nation on 15 February 1971.

It was the end of the tanners, bobs and half-crowns of the old system, which was phased out over the next 18 months and replaced by 5p, 10p and 50p coins. Most businesses rounded up their prices to fit the new currency and Circuses were no exception.

I wouldn't say my Dad was a violent man, I can only remember one pretty small physical fight between my Mum and Dad, a bit of pushing really but he clearly had mental problems. My Mum always told me that when she met him he was charismatic and fun but in the two years I knew him he was pretty horrible and totally addicted to prescription drugs.

Allegedly anxiety attacks could potentially bring on another heart attack, so the solution for this seemed to be a concoction of drugs, mainly Valium.

My Mum believed it was the addiction to these drugs that was causing his irrational behaviour. As the year progressed I was becoming more interested in girls and my Dad always tried to keep me away from the finer sex, calling them poison.

The summer months were spent in North Wales again and it was there that I experienced my first kiss, it was in Caernarfon with a girl called Sue. She was older than me and quite attractive. I don't remember the kiss being particularly great but we all have to start somewhere.

My Dad's efforts to control my avalanche into adolescence were proving to be to be a waste of time and when the Circus rolled into Uttoxeter I was about to meet my first love. She turn was about to introduce me to a Rock 'n' Roll God and an influence whose legend would prove to guide me through my life.

The show had started and a friend of mine Robert Avery and I spotted two gorgeous chicks sitting in the seats, somehow I had this urge of self-belief and we went and sat next to them.

One of the girls, Heather Miller, was a total corker and I was smitten.

She was about a year older than me so I lied about my age and we spoke about horses etc, of course Fossett's had horses, she was admiring them and told me how she had just returned from the New Forest and how she adored horses. The word 'adore' tickled me and I commented on how posh she was, she quickly backtracked and told me she 'bloody liked them then'.

She went on to ask me what my favourite music was - I was suddenly scuppered, I didn't know, music had passed me by, my stupid Dad's fault again. I quickly said Chirpy Chirpy Cheep Cheep.

Chirpy Chirpy Fucking Cheep Cheep! What the fuck did I say that for?

I only even slightly liked it because of the short-skirted bird who was the singer in aptly named Middle of the Road.

Heather was into what she described as progressive music, loved the musical Hair and her favourite band were T-Rex. She told me to listen to their current number one 'Get it on'.

Every Sunday, Alan Freeman introduced the Pop Parade on Radio 1, I think it kicked off at about 5pm, it played the entire top 30 and climaxed with the number 1.

Climax was certainly the correct word to describe that particular number 1, Get it On, an absolute classic to loose your Rock 'n' Roll virginity to, a song that sounds as fresh today as it did then on our cheap transistor radio in 1971.

I sneaked out of my caravan that night, tuned into Radio Luxemburg until I heard it again, it was like being punched in the face, it was amazing, I was smitten again, this time with Rock 'n' Roll, this time with Marc Bolan.

Now was my time to make a move on Heather, luckily she seemed to have the same idea, the show was pulling down and she was hanging around, I went over to her and we just fell into each other's arms.

The kiss was fantastic and I couldn't resist rubbing my hand against her gorgeous breasts. We didn't move from Uttoxeter for a couple of days so I saw Heather a few more times.

All in all, we were only in Uttoxeter for four days and from the day we left town I never saw Heather again but I'll never forget her, she was the first girl I properly kissed, her's were the first breasts I touched and most of all she turned me into a T-Rex fan.

The show then headed into Mid-Wales, into Welshpool, Newtown, then onto the coast in Aberystwyth and Aberaeron.

It was there that my Dad decided to scarper again, this time on his own. He took the van and left us stranded in a caravan in the middle of nowhere. Yet again he'd fucked off, couldn't face up to his responsibilities, complete deja vu and I was glad. The Dad I never had as a kid turned out to be the parent from Hell but at last he had gone and I was free. I now knew what it was like having a Dad and quite frankly I was better off without him.

The first things I did was to tune the radio permanently onto Radio 1, we had been forced to listen to Radio 2 for the last two years but now it was the brilliant sounds of Santana, The Stones, Badfinger, CCS, The Faces and of course T-Rex.

Out came the Subbuteo and my Preston North End beat Robert Avery's Wolverhampton Wanderers. Suddenly life became fun again.

I also wrote to Heather Miller. I had written to her previously but did not give her my address due to the possible hostilities I would have faced from my Dad. Now he'd gone I could write and give her a return address. I gave her my Grandma's address in Preston.

I waited with anticipation for my letter to get delivered, for her to write back via my Grandma who would in turn forwarded it onto me.

I didn't have to wait too long, it was a pleasant letter and I was over the moon that she had replied, I hastily wrote back to her and waited again for her to answer.

The whole rigmarole of the letter getting to her, her response via my Grandma and the hastil opening of the letter when it arrived with me kept me on tenterhooks.

This time Heather had turned nasty, probably in an attempt to make me jealous, it worked.

Graphically telling me about this guy she had met and the fun they had in the long grass. was pretty cruel and although hurt and jealous I wasn't put off. I wrote a few more letters b this time she didn't reply.

The show had moved onto Carmarthen and we had to go to see Claude and Sister Fossett ar tell them my Dad had gone again. It was September and we only had two months until t season ended. They agreed to keep us on to the end of the season but would cut our wag from £25, to £15 per week. We agreed and despite my tender years I became the Advan Manager.

I managed to pull another girl in Carmarthen, we kissed, I felt her breasts and stroked her thighs up to her extremely short mini skirt. It wasn't the same though. She was very attractive but she was no Heather Miller. The girls may have been a pleasant diversion but I now had a job to do and the whole weight of running the advance was now on my 14 year old shoulders.

In those days an advance manager would book the sites for the Circus to appear on, arrange for the printing of posters and putting them up and placing adverts and editorial in the local newspapers. Although only 14 it was my job and would do it to the best of my ability.

Karl Orry, one of Dot's sons was given the job of moving our caravan from site to site, Robert Avery and myself would thumb lifts from town to town with a pile of posters under our arms and a paste bucket.

I remember, the surprise on newspaper editors faces when I turned up to place an advert in their paper and then blag some editorial space in their paper. A lot of them found it difficult to cope with the fact that someone so young was performing such a mature job.

Judgment day did come however at the end of the season, we were in Brosley, a small village on the edge of the new town of Telford.

We did not really know what was going to become our fate when the season ended until one day from the show's closure. At the start of the season, Claude had agreed to lend us a caravan, he told us we would be allowed us to stay in it and told us we could borrow it but could not pull onto their farm and would have to find somewhere to put it.

I did actually think about getting the trailer pulled to Uttoxeter and seeing if we could stay on the Racecourse, it would certainly have meant I could have been closer to Heather. I'm sure though it would have ended in tears so luckily that didn't turn out to be an option. Instead I found a piece of land to rent. It was a small yard with a shed behind a shop in the village centre and we agreed to pay £5 per week.

Karl Orry again pulled us in to what was going to be our private winter quarters and Robert Avery stayed with us for a while. It was a cold winter and just before Christmas I would return to Preston to visit my Grandma.

This was the first time that I had met her knowing she was my Gran' and not my Auntie. It didn't worry me at all and although she knew that I now knew her secret it was never mentioned. Out of respect I continued to call her Auntie Bessie.

While in Preston I met up with my former school friend Basher Briggs. Of course I went to see my beloved Preston North End demolish Millwall 4-0 and move into 4th place in Division Two.

I also bought my first record, appropriately Jeepster by T-Rex. All I needed now was a record player to play it on. The record player eventually came, bought from my cousin, Trevor, who lived at the other side of Preston with his Mum and Dad, Vera and Denis and his brother Julian.

I completely wore the record out. Ironically despite my love of T-Rex it took me 30 years to record my first ever Marc Bolan song, undoubtedly it had to be Jeepster.

Surprisingly though Jeepster only made number two in the charts, partly due to Marc's reluctance to promote it and partly at the expense of one of those awful novelty songs, Benny Hill's, Ernie - the fastest milkman in the west.

Benny Hill Vs T-Rex, and Benny Hill fucking won! What the fuck was going on?

I returned to Brosley and spent the rest of the winter as a virtual recluse with just me and my Mum and my increasing record collection. It now included my second T-Rex classic 'Telegram Sam'. Not realizing it was about Marc's drug dealer, but even if I had, it would have added to the song's notoriety. With the word's 'Me I fuck but I don't care cos I ain't no square with my corkscrew hair' disguised by Marc's explanation that he was saying 'Me I funk'. Of course, as with Get It On it went to number 1.

Around February we received a letter from Claude Fossett telling us that he needed the caravan back, he said he could find me a little job on the shows next tour but suggested my Mum went back to live with my Gran in Preston.

We rejected his offer and I wrote to his brother-in-law Dennis Fossett who had re-opened his Ringland's Circus, seeking a job for both my Mum and me.

Two days later there was a knock at the door, it was Sister and Jessie Fossett telling us to ignore Claude's letter and come back to Fossett Bros Circus, we agreed and joined for a third year.

This time I was to travel in advance as assistant to their new advance manager Bert Starmer and my Mum would stay on the show to work in the canteen.

Tom, Dot and family also returned and again their family, Sharon, Dallas and Karl along with the Fossetts formed the majority of the show. It also included Clown and Fire Eater Trevor Bailey, it was ironic that the last time I saw Trevor was when he was travelling with his family on Winships some 13 years earlier. My Dad had just scarpered then too.

It's fair to say Trevor was a poseur, if he was a musician he could have been in The Sweet, sort of pretty boy builder look but instead he ate fire and was a very fine Clown.

Jackie Unell and Yvonne returned for a short while. Jackie had got a job on a big Italian Circus

Enis Togni which was run by Mary Chipperfield. Enis Togni included an escapologist called Alan Alan who was chained and suspended upside-down from a burning rope over a cage of lions, the idea was he had to free himself from the chains and undo his feet that were attached to the rope before it burnt through.

Alan was going away for two months and Jackie was to take his place, so prior to his contract with Enis Togni he tried out the burning rope escapology act on Fossett Brothers. It was a great act and Jackie was unscathed by the stunt whilst with Fossett Brothers.

His performances at Enis Togni did not go so smoothly though and one day he escaped from the chains and was just undoing his legs when he slipped and fell 30' into the lion's cage.

Luckily the lions were ushered out before they could attack him and he survived with just a broken arm.

Tom and Dot's daughter Sharon was beginning to turn peoples head's, mine certainly included.

She was a little older than me and certainly sexually more mature, she always wore incredibly short skirts, as did most of the girls in the early 70's.

On one occasion while the show was on she asked me to collect a pair of hot pants for her from Jessie and deliver them to her trailer. She said when you get there don't knock just come straight in. I had a good idea what I was going to expect.

Nevertheless, forever the gentleman I did knock, she shouted come in. She was sat on the bed in her bra and knickers, although I was prepared for this I was still shocked, she stood up and handed her the hot pants and embarrassingly left.

The closing act in the show was the 'incredible riding machine', a harness was lowered from the roof of the tent and tied round a volunteer's waist, and they would then try trick riding round the ring on a beautiful and well-tempered white horse.

Mister used to ask for volunteers and always asked for a girl in a short skirt, there were always some genuine volunteers but also two stooges, Sharon and her younger brother Fred.

Fred would fly round and lose his trousers and Sharon's short skirts left nothing to the imagination, in fact all the guys on the show would regularly have a bet on what colour knickers she would be wearing.

My rendezvous in Sharon's caravan was different though, on that occasion, it was a private show and put on just for me. I knew Sharon for quite a few years, we never went out with each other and we never did get it on. We had a little snog on one occasion but that was as far as it went.

While we were still in Wales, we received some bad news from Preston, my Auntie Nell had fallen and was taken to hospital, three day's later she died. She was always very jolly and was great to me as a kid, it was very sad.

My Mum and I travelled to Preston for the funeral, in fact a cremation. Over the next few years the route from my Grandmas house in Barry Ave, Ingol to the crematorium would sadly become more and more familiar.

Shortly after we returned to the show and after only three months Bert Starmer had a row with Claude and Sister and left the show, this left me thumbing around the country with a paste bucket and piles of posters under my arm again. A pattern was beginning to form.

So here I was still travelling ahead of the show, booking the sites and publicizing it. Claude obviously wasn't sure that I could cope though and brought in yet another new advance man.

It turned out to be a record for the shortest time an advance manager stayed on the show. Peter Featherstone joined from Sir Robert Fossett's Circus, a much larger version of the famous Fossett dynasty. He must have wondered what he had let himself in for, he lasted precisely three days. He joined in Llanidoloes and Claude asked him to go to Machynellth to book the site, what Claude didn't give him though was any expenses so Peter Featherstone coupled up his trailer supposedly to go to Machynellth never to be seen again, or at least never with Fossett Bros Circus.

Peter did continue his career in Circus and successfully managed many large Circuses and still does at the age of 72, he simply, and quite correctly found Fossett Brothers Circus too disorganized. For me. I knew nothing else.

My unique way of travelling around booking the sites and doing the publicity was restored and it would stay this way for the rest of the season.

Again that summer, as the last two summers were spent touring North Wales. It was great, it a beautiful part of the country and my Mum came from there too. The farmers and land owner got to know me and booking the sites was easy,

I got to know the shop keepers who I displayed the posters with and on one occasion I eve got a lift off the same guy in the same car on the same road a year later.

There were lots of girls too, so I always enjoyed the summer in North Wales.

When we were in or near Porthmadog I would go and stay with Les who was actually n second cousin, and Charles, Dennis and Will's sister. My Mum and Les were like sisters although Les would prefer people to think they were brother and sister.

In many ways she suffered from small town syndrome in the same way as my Grandma did trying to come to terms with her unwanted and secret motherhood.

In Les's case it was her sexuality, she was undoubtedly a lesbian but as far as I know not a practicing one. She was a man in a woman's body. She dressed as a man, had her hair cut like a man and abbreviated her name from Elsie to Les. To us she was just Les, but to the people of Port she was a freak, this was also a term she would use to describe herself to me. It was really tragic that almost all her life she lived as a recluse in a big house built onto the side of a cliff with her cat's and dogs.

She clearly wanted more and I am sure if she had moved to a larger town or city she would have been accepted.

Business throughout that summer had been good but as the nights began to grow shorter we moved out of North Wales and towards the North Midlands.

Autumn was setting in, a time the Circus community would call 'the back end'. Generally its pretty grim, dark nights along with cold and wet weather and the resulting muddy fields. In those days we rarely had electric in the caravans, so we had battery powered TV's until the battery ran out.

even had a battery-powered record player to play my expanding record collection, I had started buying a single every week but very rarely albums. My collection was, of course, still favouring and bulging with T-Rex classics. Other bands had started creeping in their though, with Slade, he Sweet and David Bowie being the pick of the crop.

As Autumn came to an end and the show pulled in this time Claude allowed us to pull onto the winter quarters as long as I fed and watered the horses, ponies and newly acquired llama alled Larry.

Most of the horses were fine, one stallion however, Denbigh, was more than a little dangerous ut most of my caution was aimed at Larry the Llama after I saw him mount Sister and try and hag her in the ring in front of a packed house. My new long golden locks could have become n attraction and I certainly didn't want to lose my virginity to a fucking Llama.

pent about a month back in Preston, visited Basher Briggs and saw PNE. The rest of the time as spent in the Fossett Farm in Stratford on Avon.Still a sort of Circus scrap yard with two tting aircraft hangers and lines of old Circus caravans and vehicles, most of which didn't go.

After Christmas I took some part time work in a shop and somehow managed to persuade pubs to sell me drinks, there was no I.D. in those days, the landlords either believed you or they didn't, but as long as you were buying drinks they generally didn't care.

This winter I also bought my first electric Guitar.

I looked around various second hand shops in Birmingham but in the end decided to spend £12 on a purple and black offering from Woolworths. I didn't realize at the time, but later discovered that Marc Bolan also bought his first guitar from Woolworths so I was in good company. I started to teach my self how to play all the T-Rex tunes and started to write my own songs.

The winter came and went and it was time to pull out, Claude again failed to trust me as advance manager and recruited a former schoolteacher who I would work with, he was a nice guy and very right on.

He was to complete the age-old adage and run away from home to join the Circus. I don't think it helped him that he befriended Dick Sandow who, with his family, had rejoined the show to take the place of Tom and Dot who decided not to tour with Fossetts this year.

Dick became the Clown while son Richard performed a fine Roller Roller act, his sister Wiggy had outgrown her hoops and glasses act and become a Wirewalker.

Also on the show were a Czechoslovakian brother and sister Hand Balancing act, suddenly Fossett Brothers had a bit of culture.

Of course with Dick Sandow on the show the chances of the programme remaining the same were slim and true to form he did his blank post card trick again and after three months he had gone.

The curse of the advance manager was also about to strike again. This time sacked, by Claude leaving me to cope on my own.

He lasted until around June and was forced to leave. I took over again - still thumbing aroun but again on familiar territory in North Wales.

With Dick Sandown's family wow gone, Claude had to recruit some more acts quickl He brought in Dot's first husband and Valda's Dad Eddie Orry, who took over the Clownin A rookie Fire Eater called John Radanovich joined, as did a strange Fakir act Gus and Mirand

Gus's act was a bizarre affair, a sort of low budget Fakir act. Bizarre because instead of lyir on a bed of nails he laid on a bed of drawing pins, he also did the human blockhead ar hammered a nail into his nose. On one occasion he inhaled and the nail got stuck. We leaned him forward and banged and banged on the back of his head until it fell out.

I was falling about laughing so much I forgot to call an ambulance, Gus recovered with just a bloody nose but his confidence was forever dented.

John also started having an affair with Valda. This caused ructions with the Fossett family. Valda had been with them for many years, they considered her a daughter and did not believe John was good enough.

Sister also thought Valda was losing concentration although Valda's Dad, Eddie Orry was fine with the situation. Sister could however have been right as one day Valda fell off the trapeze, she was performing a hang from her toes on one foot and her foot seemed to just slip off.

I remember watching it, it was as though it was in slow motion. There were no safety harnesses in those days so if you fell you really did fall.

She landed in a lump on her side in the ring. There was an amazing groan from the audience but no screams, Jessie came down and helped Valda out of the ring.

Amazingly Eddie Orry had to come in as a Clown to fill in until the next act was ready. I cannot even begin to think how that must have felt. Watching your daughter fall then having to try and make people laugh while she was being carried out in front of you.

Valda recovered in time to carry on in the same performance and after half an hour returned to the ring to perform her rope-spinning act, the audience went wild.

It seemed to be a summer of near misses as far as accidents were concerned, Gus with his nail stuck up his nose, Valda's fall from the trapeze and the one that could have been, without doubt the most tragic for me.

One particular day, I was, as normal, ahead of the show putting up posters in South Wales when various shop keepers started asking me if this was the Circus who's tent had blown down? I obviously said no, or at least I hope not, and carried on putting up the posters. More and more shopkeepers were asking me about this and said it had been reported on the radio.

That evening I returned to the show which had been built up on a slag heap in Ferndale to see no tent, the shop keepers were right. Fossett Brothers was the show where the tent had blown down and to my horror my Mum was inside it on her own at the time.

Ferndale is on the edge of one of the Welsh Valleys and it seemed the wind just came from nowhere, gusted down the valley and took our tent with it, the soft undersoil of the slag heap not hard enough to hold the tent stakes in place.

My Mum had been picking up the rubbish in the tent from the packed shows of the night before, she described the noise as amazing with the wind sounding like the soundtrack from a biblical epic.

Luckily she was next to the raised seats which did not collapse and managed to claw her way to the walling before Karl Orry heard her cries for help and pulled her out.

It was certainly a lucky escape for my Mum but even luckier that it didn't happen the night before when the tent was packed with 600 people.

Once again, this eventful season was drawing to a close, again a season of change for Fossett Brothers Circus considered with a year of change for the country. There had been an oil crisis which also forced up the price of coal, a stock market crash was predicted.

Inflation had increased to 6.8% and despite this, the Heath government tried to impose a wage freeze to combat the subsequent recession.

Times of unrest were looming.

My other passions were also facing change, Alan Ball Senior had been sacked by Preston North End to be replaced as manager by Manchester United and England world cup winner Bobby Charlton.

Change too for T-Rex, the glory years were seemingly over, 1972 mega classics Telegram Sam, Metal Guru, Children of the Revolution and Solid Gold Easy Action were followed up in '73 by 20th Century Boy and The Groover reaching only Number three and four in the charts respectfully.

The T-Rex phenomenon was beginning to wane.

Ever since Heather Miller had encouraged me to start listening to Radio 1, tuning into the single charts on a Sunday evening was like listening to the football results and I was willin T-Rex to enter the charts higher than Slade, but Slade were slowly beginning to move ahead

I bought the Slade records, they were great but I couldn't help in feeling very guilty doing s every time I did it I felt like I was scoring an own goal.

This may have been a little over the top but I know a lot of T-Rex fans who felt the same a me.

Even with the decline of T-Rex It was still a golden period for music, particularly for Glam Ro and Top of the Pops. The charts would be packed with great tunes by The Sweet, Gary Glitter, Slade, David Bowie, Rod Stewart and, although not quite as potent as before, T-Rex.

Top of the Pops was the perfect vehicle for Glam Rock and the most classic Top of the Pops memories were from the Glam Rock era.

I bought all the glam records and prayed that Bolan would forgive me. Ironically I would work with both Gary Glitter and Dave Hill from Slade in years to come.

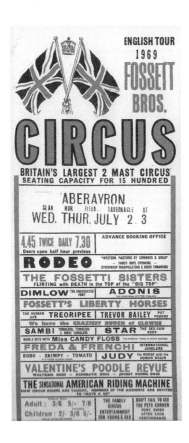

Despite the fact that the poster sates '1969', it was actually used in 1970,
Claude was saving money using last years' posters.
Photo credits, from Haze's personal collection

ALLAN GORDON PROMOTIONS LTD.

presents . . .

CIRCUS APOLLO

The Family Show – for all the Family

VAT No. 279 6698 75

Reg. in England No. 1087364

Directors:
ALLAN McPHERSON
B. J. McPHERSON

Registered Office:
APOLLO HOUSE,
HAFOD FARM,
RUABON,
WREXHAM LL14 6HF
Telephone (0978) 840364

Larry Gavette Esq.,

4080 Ledgestone,
Waterford,
MICHIGAN 48095.
U. S. A.

27th. March 1980.

Dear sir,

        re. Electro/Mechanical Elephant.

      I have been given your address by the Editor of the Brighton and Hove Gazette, in which they printed an artical on a Mechanical Elephant that went to America.

      Some years ago I purchased a Mechanical Elephant and I wrote to the B.B.C. Television. Later they featured it on their Childrens programme 'BLUE PETER' in December 1975. The response was so great to the Elephant that they asked for the Elephant to apear again on the programme on the 5th. April 1976. This time they managed to get hold of one of the original engineers who built the Elephant. I learned from him that only 6 of these elephants were built, 5 of them had a FORD 8hp. engine to power them and One only was built to go to America but this had to have an electric drive. This was built and sent to the U.S.A. but on the journey it was dropped and the chassis was damaged, so it was sent back to England. I bought this Elephant in 1973 and had the chassis repaired, I have since used it for publicity on my circus. Last year Vandalls tore the skin of the elephant and it is now being renovated by EXIDE BATTERIES.

      Enclosed please find a photograph of the elephant on parade and one without its skin.

      Yours faithfully,

                    Allan McPherson.

Photo credits, from Haze's personal collection

CHAPTER FOUR
A DEATH IN THE FAMILY

The winters seemed to be coming around quicker and quicker. Once again Claude and Sister allowed us to park on their winter quarters on the usual proviso that I would feed and water the horses, ponies and llama.

This winter I took part time work in a garage and become a petrol pump attendant in Stratford. You'd be amazed what bored housewives would do for a few extra green shield stamps.

Amazed too that the history and culture of Stratford passed me by, of course I knew about William Shakespeare and would drive past Ann Hathaway's Cottage but never even attempted to do any sight seeing. Stratford itself has Anglo-Saxon origins, and grew up as a market town in medieval times, it's name is a mixture straet, meaning "street", and ford, meaning that a Roman road forded the River Avon in the town.

Although officially too young to go to the pub I would still go regularly, occasionally getting drunk but hating the spinning room, and vowing never to drink again, that is until the next time. The main reason for frequenting bars though was the social aspect, mainly I would go with one of Fossett's tent men, a guy called Raymond.

Like me he had taken a job in town, his, as a kitchen porter in a hotel, which meant he could live in. Raymond was a really strong guy and would earn us free drinks by challenging the locals to arm wrestling competitions.

On one occasion though the competition went horribly wrong, both Raymond and his challenger were locked in combat and seemed to be equally matched until Raymond found another burst of strength. That is until we heard a large crack and the guy's arm crashed down on the table.

The guy was screaming and you could see the bone sticking out of his forearm. Raymond not realizing what he had done was dancing around the pub proclaiming his status as arm wrestling champion demanding that the guy was faking it to avoid buying us a drink.

I pointed to the bone sticking out of his arm and we did a runner before the Ambulance arrived.

We laid low for the next couple of weeks until it was time for me and my Mum to go to Preston again, it was the first time we had gone home together for Christmas in four years.

Things had changed in 5 Barry Avenue since we left. Frank who was briefly married to Nell until she died had moved into our house, it was a platonic situation but Frank turned out to be a serial proposer and consequently asked my Grandma to marry him, luckily she declined his offer.

My Mum used my Gran's room, I shared with Charles and we had a nice Christmas. I caught a North End game or two, saw my cousins Trevor and Julian and my mate Basher Briggs.

It was to become ironic that the first Christmas we spent with the rest of the family since we left would turn out to be our last together. We returned to Stratford on the 29th December.

A day after we arrived back at Fossett's winter quarters we received a knock at the door. It was a policeman and Sister Fossett and we knew something was wrong,

My Grandma had died, it was a real shock.

It was particularly strange for my Mum, she always resented my Gran for not acknowledging that she was in fact her Mum and telling her that she was considering sending her to an orphanage /workhouse.

I saw it a differently though, she clearly loved us both but could not show her emotions, there was always a house to go back to and you knew there would always be a roof over our heads. If my Mum had been born in another age, I'm sure things would have been different.

Despite their differences, neither of them spoke about them to me while my Grandma was alive. The funeral took the route from Barry Avenue to the crematorium, the same route my Auntie Nell had taken, the same words came from my Auntie Blodwin's lips as the hearse arrived outside our house, 'Here she goes, the final journey', words I would hear far too often.

After the funeral it was decided that my Mum would leave the Circus and return to live 5 Barry Ave, the council house in Preston that my Grandma had lived in. She became the lady of the house she was to share with my Uncle Charles and Uncle Frank. I decided to stay with the Circus.

I returned to Fossett Brothers Circus alone. I was still too young to drive but was now an established advance manager in my own right.

This year Claude did trust me with the job, this year there would be no Bert Starmer, Pete Featherstone or absent school teacher, this year I was the front man, I was the advance agent, I was the publicist.

Prior to starting the season, Claude and myself decided we needed to book some grounds in advance, it was normally done at the last minute but not this year, not on my watch.

I still couldn't drive so I persuaded Claude to drive us to Wales and we would go ground hunting. You would think we would have known every nook and cranny by now but you never really do.

We had a good day and booked quite a few grounds, we decided to leave it for the night and start again the next day. We stopped in a bed and breakfast in Bridgend and Claude suggested we go to the Cinema.

To my delight it was showing the T-Rex film 'Born to Boogie', I don't know why I hadn't seen it earlier and I have certainly made up for it now.

I said to Claude that it looked good and as the poster had a picture of Marc riding a Tiger, I think he thought he was going to see a wild life film, you've got to remember Claude was 84 years old by now.

The Cinema was packed, mainly with 14 to 16 year olds, most of which were screaming girls, and then there was Claude. The B movie came on first and Claude chuckled a bit.

Then came the main feature and after about three minutes T-Rex launched into Jeepster, I was in my element, it was like being at a gig and the crowd were screaming and cheering at Marc's every move. Claude thought he had landed on Mars and kept saying 'what the bleeding hell is this', is this bloke one of them there poofters?' After about 10 minutes he was saying 'I think I'm going back to the bleeding digs'.

He then started calling me a bleeding bastard and accusing me of conning him, I pleaded my innocence. An hour later the film had ended and we went back to the digs, me still boogying and reliving all of Marc's moves and grooves, Claude still Mumbling 'bleeding poofter' under his breath.

We booked a few more grounds the next day and drove back to Stratford. Even that wasn't without incident though. We stopped in a car park in Llandeilo, the car park was on a hill with a set of 20 steps leading into a recreation ground.

I left Claude in the car while I went to see the council to book the ground, when I got back the car was in a different place and there were some Tulips rammed into the front bumper, I asked him why he had moved it and what was with the flowers? He explained that he had forgotten to put the hand brake on. The car went freewheeling down the 20 steps and into a flowerbed in the recreation ground. Claude had to go and bribe the park keeper to let him out.

A productive and eventful couple of days out. When we got back I told Jessie of our adventure worrying that she may think I was corrupting her Dad but she just pissed herself.

The changes at the end of the previous season where nothing compared with the changes the next 12 months would bring.

First of all Fossett Brothers had a number of enforced changes Eddie Orry did not return, nor did the Czechoslovakian couple. The biggest shock though was Valda, who after 10 years with the family left with John Pravanavich to live in Redditch.

Karl Orry did return though with his new wife Sue. Tex and Anita Gibson also joined the show with their son Sandro plus another elderly couple Albert and Rositta who at 60 years old performed a hand-balancing act.

Sister at, 67 was still showing the horses and dogs, it is also fair to say that Tex and Anita were in the twilight of their career. On top of all this and due to the lack of performers 87 year old Claude was forced to don the motley again and return to the ring as the Clown.

It must have been the oldest Circus on earth. Jessie at 35 tipped the balance a little as did 22 year olds Karl and Sue with their Fire Eating act.

I suppose it was inevitable that the average age on the show had to reduce, that inevitability became a reality when Albert dropped dead in the ring, we all knew he was getting on a bit and he was doing a strenuous act but none of us expected this. All our hearts went out to his wife, Rositta, who was performing in the ring with him at the time.

A strange after shock happened when shortly after the accident the flag on the king pole unexpectedly and without explanation became unattached and fell on it's own to half-mast.

The tragedy forced me to mix my duties as advance man with various performances in the ring. I was coping without my Mum quite well if a little untidily, at least I could bring girls back now. My Mum would still come and visit though, she had taken a job in a factory in Preston but spent all her holidays with me at the Circus.

When my Mum wasn't around I revelled in my privacy and I generally had a lot of one-night stands. We were moving all the time and it made having a relationship very difficult, not that I wanted a long time relationship yet though.

I did however meet a girl called Peggy Teague while the show was in Brynmaw.

She was a pretty Welsh girl and an obligatory T-Rex fan. I saw her a few times during the season and we kept in touch by letter.

Apart from the accident to Albert, the summer was quite uneventful and it was beginning to become too routine for me, I was getting bored and stale.

I decided that this would be my last year with Fossett Brothers Circus.

If 1973 was a year of change it was nothing compared with 1974.

The second miners' strike during Ted Heath's premiership led to the Three-Day Week. Heath tried to bolster his government and called a general election for 28 February 1974. The result was inconclusive, the Conservative Party won the majority of votes cast but the Labour Party won the majority of parliamentary seats.

Edward Heath then tried to negotiate with Jeremy Thorpe, leader of the Liberal Party, this failed and on the 4th March 1974, he resigned as Prime Minister and was replaced by Harold Wilson. First of all in a coalition with the death defying 'Lib Lab Pact' and when that collapsed Mr. Wilson attempted to rule with a minority Labour government.

This forced a second general election, which took place in October of the same year when the Labour Party gained a slightly larger majority.

In addition to all this, and despite the appointment of Bobby Charlton as manager nine months earlier, Preston North End were relegated to division three again. T-Rex biggest hit of the year was Teenage Dream, which only reached a measly Number 12 in the charts.

What the fuck was going on in this world of mine?

I needed a fresh challenge and started to look around and found a new small Circus called Circus Apollo, it was run by Allan and Babbs McPherson who had two daughters, Debbie and Gina.

I went to see them with Karl Orry who was also contemplating jumping ship, they had heard of me and quickly we started to talk of joining them for the next season. I liked them both and this could be the new challenge I was looking for. Karl also agreed to leave with me.

The only thing I had to do now was tell Claude.

I was in his caravan one evening in October with about a month to go to the end of the season.

He started talking about the next year so I took my opportunity and told him I was going to move on. He was quite calm but his daughter Jessie really took it personally and accused me of deserting them 'after all they had done for me'. They had apparently looked after me when my Dad had gone, the usual clichés were pouring out etc, etc, etc.

It was true they did give my Mum and me a job but I did that job well and I was a cheap option for them too.

When their succession of advance men and artistes did a runner, it was me who picked up the pieces. At least I was not going to run away, not going to hand over any blank postcards, at least I gave proper notice. I pulled into the Stratford winter quarters with them and left the next day.

I remember struggling up the drive with all my possessions and they didn't even come out to say good bye. Instead Clive one of Sister's nephews helped me carry my stuff to the main road where I got a bus to Birmingham.

I spent one week with Apollo and then went to live in Preston for the winter prior to joining Apollo for the next season.

Even that wasn't as clear-cut as I had expected. First of all I had the option of sleeping in a freezing trailer with no heating or with this other guy called Rupert Dorgon. I tried both until Rupert tried to bugger me so I quickly buggered off into a trailer that resembled a deep-freeze, preferring to freeze my bollocks off as opposed to having a hot cock shoved up my arse.

With Apollo at that time was a guy called Ricky Deloro, a multi-talented Irish Circus performer with his family. He was starting his own show the next season and attempted to gazump Allan and Babbs and get me to join them for the following season for more money.

I declined, but Karl who was also offered a job with Circus Deloro did accept their offer, his career with Circus Apollo was consequently very short lived. I suppose, although not knowing them for long I felt loyal to Allan and Babbs. Loyalty is always something I have valued throughout my life, whether it be to my friends, my employers, PNE or Marc Bolan. I don't think Claude and Sister would agree, but I was particularly loyal to them too.

That winter was enjoyable but certainly strange. Strange because it was a long time since I had lived in any one town for a while, strange because it was a long time since I lived in a house and strange because it was the first time I had got a proper job.

T-Rex were struggling to sell records and Bolan was drinking heavily and taking far too many drugs, obviously I would stick by him though and kept buying everything he did.

Thankfully Preston North End, although now in the 3rd division, were having a good season and Bobby Charlton was the player manager so I went to lots of games and saw lots of wins

He had signed fellow, former England World cup winner Nobby Stiles and his former Utd. team mates Frances Burns and David Sadler, so PNE were now brimming with vintage football gentry, mainly ex Man Utd.

Near the end of my time with Fossett's I went to the cinema and saw The Exorcist. Horror films were definitely changing and the 1970's became a classic era for the birth of new horror with films such as The Wicker Man, The Texas Chain Saw Massacre, Carrie and Clockwork Orange etc.

Prior to this, horror films would consist of remakes of Frankenstein or Dracula but The Exorcist was a completely new direction, it scared me to death. I would go home and imagine my bed was shaking.

Unemployment was rising and against all odds I got a job in Preston in a Brewery, possibly the perfect job for me particularly as the girls outnumbered the guys by six to one, the trouble was I had suddenly and stupidly become teetotal and celibate.

Not only did this spoil my chances with the chicks in the brewery but also with my girl friend Peggy Teague. The culprit for this was my life long friend Basher Briggs, he had become a Born Again Christian and persuaded me to go to church.

I reluctantly went. It was an amazing feeling, I felt the whole service was about me and I openly blushed with embarrassment as the Pastor read out his sermon, it felt like God was talking directly to me through the pastor. Could this be so or is it a clever marketing ploy carried out by religious types, aimed to reel in sinners like me, or could it really be the hand of God reaching out to touch me?

Ploy or not, it worked, and my religious experience made me become a Born Again Christian. The plus side of this was that when I went to bed and got my Exorcist flashbacks I would pray and my dark thoughts diminished. I was not a bad person, didn't steal or treat people badly but as all guys of my age I had bodily urges, so I found myself not only praying for forgiveness to Marc Bolan for buying Slade records but also seeking forgiveness from God for wanking too much.

The winter came and went and as spring was just starting to flourish, I had a stroke of luck. It was about a month before I was to join Circus Apollo and I was made redundant from the brewery and received a pay off which paid for a new trailer to live in. Could this be God working in a strange way?

I joined Apollo in February, although still a small show it was a little larger than Fossett's and certainly better organized.

I was doing the advance and Allan gave me a car, a neat little Morris Minor, reminding me of the car, that my Dad drove through the night from London to Liverpool, with no lights, en route for Circus Beck. This was a much smarter version though, but not for long. It certainly beat thumbing around the country with a paste bucket in my hand, now I had wheels. Not that I had passed my driving test mind you, that just seemed like another complication.

Unfortunately I wrote it off by falling asleep at the wheel.

Allan decided that I would be safer on two wheels, little did he know. Allan bought me a scooter, a gleaming red Lambretta with a huge plastic flyscreen, so no more thumbing around for me. I painted it in Apollo livery and took my first ride. No one told me though that the throttle was fierce and my maiden voyage ended up in a heap at the end of the road after doing a 30-mile per hour wheelie. The flyscreen was in pieces and had to be glued together.

Nevertheless I brushed myself down and rode like a demon for the next eight months, although I did fall off and almost kill myself on at least two more occasions.

We spent the spring in South Wales and I went and visited Fossett Brothers Circus who were also in the area, our reunion was to last about 10 minutes as Claude accused me of stealing their grounds and he ordered Allan and myself off the ground.

It's fair to say that Allan and Babbs did not have the Circus pedigree of the Fossetts, Claude would refer to them as 'bleeding jossers' (a Circus term for someone not born and bred in the Circus). Allan had run away from his Southampton home and joined the Circus where he learned to be an acrobat, he met Babbs who was a dancer. At one time they performed a very good Adagio Balancing act. Unfortunately they had an almost fatal car crash which put paid to their acrobatic career. Rumour had it that the insurance pay out they received helped to buy Circus Apollo, I was always too polite to ask.

The show consisted of former Fossett Brothers artistes, John and Valda Pradanovich, who came out of temporary retirement and Tex and Anita, plus, Pete and Jayne with an Illusion Act and Gorilla skin and a Clown called Leon Lawrence who also had a comedy bear suit, 'Barney the TV Bear'.

The house acts of Allan Clowning and showing the shows three ponies. Babbs with her performing dogs and their daughter Debbie on an Arial Ladder and Rope Spinning with Valda

We had ventured into the top of the Welsh valleys and while we were in Seven Sisters we stood on a piece of common land. It was similar to the Hampshire's New Forest and horses would just wander free. We thought as they roamed free then they must not have an owner so we took two of them. Simply loaded them into the horse box and went onto the next town.

A week later while the show was in Llantwit Major we had a visit from the Police, the show was on and Allan was in the ring and they came up to me and asked to see the boss, 'you can't I said he's the Clown'. 'He's a Clown all right' they replied, where is he'.

No 'he really is a Clown' I said and took them into the tent and pointed into the ring, 'there he is' I said, they threatened to walk into the ring and arrest him. The publicist in me almost encouraged them to do it, imagine the headlines 'Clown arrested in Circus ring' but my more humane side made me persuade them to wait until the show was over.

Allan was nevertheless arrested and taken to the Police station in his full Clown make up, God I wish I'd had a camera. He was charged with horse rustling and ordered to take them back and let them loose again.

We did this and Allan ended up getting fined, we had great fun in the interim telling him the that people still got hung for horse rustling.

The rest of the year was spent in the Midlands, so a change from the normal North Wales route. I was still going out with Peggy but never did the dirty deed due to my new stupid religious beliefs. I split up with her in August, she didn't take it to well but I just didn't have any feelings for her.

Peggy was not the only thing I discarded and as the year progressed I realized I was not cut out for this Christian malarkey.

I could not stand the hypocrisy of it. So I dumped Peggy and dumped God, both in a matter of weeks and normal service was resumed.

Apollo pulled in at the end of November after a pretty successful season and for the first time was offered winter work at Granby Halls, Leicester. Originally reunited with Bert Starmer on the publicity team and then as lighting director.

Both Fossett's and Apollo were small shows, their only performing animals were horses, ponies, dogs and a llama. The Granby Halls show was a different beast altogether.

It was run by a Zoo owner, lion trainer and Circus enthusiast Martin Lacey and it contained some great acts, including Sir Robert Fossett's five elephants and six tigers, horses and ponies, Scotts sea lions, a Cossack riding troupe, loads of great acts and even the original Black Beauty.

Animal Circuses often get a rough ride from the media but I can honestly say that in all my years in Circus I saw nothing but kindness and often Circus proprietors cared more for their animals than they did for their artistes.

It was a great experience and I was really inspired by Horse Trainer Johnny Keys, he came from an old Circus family and was a great horseman and even greater showman, he gave me a few tips on horse training and I had a new challenge.

The season in Leicester ended on a sour note though as Martin Lacy ran out of money and did not pay many of the acts, I was lucky, Allan and Babbs McPherson were also on the show and had the Candy Floss concession, they paid me out of that. Most of the other acts weren't so fortunate.

Apollo had winter quarters in Rugley, Staffs and in-between the winter and summer seasons I went to live there. I helped them with admin for the next season but also started horse training. We had this great little spotted pony called Freckles and I trained him to do all sorts of things including leaping over a burning fence.

He was amazingly intelligent, one day during our training sessions I dropped some bread on he floor, he obviously liked the look of it and started gently kicking me on the leg with one of his front hooves until I noticed it on the floor. Of course I picked it up and gave it to him.

I still found time to return to Preston and combined my visit with a trip to Southport with Basher Briggs to see, for the first time, the almighty T-Rex.

It was during Marc's less popular period. He still looked great, a little overweight maybe and sadly totally off his face, but still a rock god, my rock god.

He was on the Futuristic Dragon tour, named after his current album but he did little from the new album and concentrated mainly on his Greatest Hits.

The drinking and drugs had taken their toll but not as much as the damage done to his ego by lower than expected ticket sales, this combined with his highest chart position of the previous year, a modest, by his standard number 12, with New York City.

Between songs he would stroll into the wings have a chat and a drink, come back on stag swear a little and launch into the next song.

In future years I would return to Southport and play the same venue with The Circus of Horror Unbelievably on one occasion I played on exactly the same day as I saw T-Rex in the sam venue. The stage manager and some of the usherettes were still there and we reminisced abou the day T-Rex came to town. They were working there and I was grooving to the Bolan boogi

Once the next season had started I was not only doing the advance but also showing the ponies including Freckles and acted as ringmaster, it was the hot summer of 1976 and we toured the south coast.

I was playing guitar more and writing songs, the best of which was tune I wrote called Jivin'.

Jivin' in many ways was a flash back to the Glam Rock years which by 1976 were all but gone. Not only had Marc Bolan's crown slipped but so had the popularity of his glam rivals, Gary Glitter, Slade and the Sweet. Bolan did have a great summer hit though with I Love to Boogie.

David Bowie and Queen were reinventing themselves and kept coming up with gems but there were some shocking bands that were dominating the charts. The tartan clad Bay City Rollers and the secretaries' favourites Abba competed with the dreadful drones of 70's disco. Change had to come.

Circus Apollo had more house acts now, if you included me. Allan and Bab's other daughter Gina started performing, with a hoops and glasses act, (I've already stated my contempt of this act). They also had a French illusionist and puppeteer Marc Christian.

The south coast, like North Wales, is a beautiful place to be during the hot summer months and I got lot of new friends. As my religious experience was behind me I could become at least a little promiscuous again.

During the tour we performed at Stourpaine, now known as The Great Dorset Steam Fair and had a little fling with a snake charmer who was working in a side show that was pitched next to us. This however would not be the last time would have a reptile in my bed.

We paid for the hot summer once autumn set in and the weather changed and we had a horrible and muddy back end.

During the season Allan McPherson had offered me the chance to become a director of Circus Apollo, along with his wife Babbs, of course I was flattered and accepted.

I had been getting more and more into music and started seeing as many bands as I could fit in, Marc Bolan had been championing the new Punk scene that was beginning to take root. It really interested me.

Music had become stale and it needed a kick up the arse, the choices seemed to be Prog rock, the Bay City Rollers and various clones of them such as Kenny or Abba and 70's disco, Vs Bolan and Punk. No competition.

The great thing about Punk was it was so accessible to everyone, the look was easily and cheaply achievable, it was shocking and it seemed that you didn't have to be that good a musician to make it so it gave me great hope.

In the winter I spent half of it in Preston and half in Rugley, I didn't get a job and chose instead to work with Allan getting the show ready for the next year. Allan and Babbs took Debbie and Gina on their annual holiday to Benidorm and I was left to hold the fort. I did this effortlessly and had the pleasant and unexpected bonus of shagging the stable girl in Allan and Babb's bed.

As usual I spent time with my Mum in Preston. I saw PNE who were still in the 3rd Division but were now managed by Nobby Stiles after Bobby Charlton had walked out after a row with the club about selling players.

Charles was still there and still working on the bins, my Mum was still working in the factory and Frank was still the lodger. Frank had other plans though and asked my Mum to marry him, the serial proposer strikes again.

We had now known him for eight years, in which time he had married and was widowed by my Aunty Nell. He then moved in with her sister, my gran and asked her to marry him. After she died he stayed in the house which my Mum took over and now asked my Mum to marry him. Luckily my Mum was not divorced from my Dad so she turned him down.

After returning to Rugley I went to see Status Quo in Bingley Hall, Stafford and hated it, they seemed old hat. I thought that even though I was only 18, I was too old to go to gigs and vowed to give up my interest in Rock 'n' Roll.

When my Dad used to force us to listen to Radio 2 I thought that's what happened to you when you get older, you have wear beige cloths (which I could never understand, surely i would show the piss stains more) and you have to listen to middle of the road drivel on Radio 2. It felt like my Radio 2 days were looming.

The very next day I bought Record Mirror and saw T-Rex were touring. I bought ticket immediately (my vow to dump Rock 'n' Roll lasted 12 hours). I saw T-Rex for the second time at The Birmingham Odeon, a young Punk band, the Damned, supported them. Marc says h chose the Damned to support him because when he met them Captain Sensible, the bass playe had the good taste to wear a Marc Bolan T-shirt. If listening to Get It On for the first tim in1971, it was like getting smashed in the face so too was seeing Bolan in 1977.

Still called T-Rex, but really it was Marc Bolan with a group of great musicians playing wi him. He had recruited two of Bowie's former band, Herbie Flowers on Bass and Tony Newma on drums plus long-term T-Rex keyboard player Dino Dines and his friend Miller Anderson on second guitar and backing vocals.

I regret never seeing the original T-Rex line up of Mickey Finn, Steve Curry, Bill Legend and Marc but the new band were awesome. Marc looked brilliant, he'd lost loads of weight, his voice now a little deeper and his guitar playing was tremendous, most of all, he knew it.

Birmingham Odeon was sold out and the fans rushed to the front of the seated venue when The Damned came on and stayed there. Once Bolan took to the stage they went wild, I had never seen hysteria like it. People were literally climbing on top of one another to get onto the stage. Bolan was back.

It was, and still is by far the best gig I have ever seen.

I had my hair corkscrewed like Marcs but a blond version and I became a sort of Glam Punk and started visiting the Punk clubs and watching the punk bands including a young Clash. Not only was Bolan back, so were PNE who were promoted back into division 2, things were definitely looking up in my little world.

Circus Apollo had grown in 1977 and now included, Billy Wild's Wild West act, Trevor and Bonnie Delmar with a Juggling and Balancing act, Bonnies son Ricky Clowning and Plate Spinning with his sister Yoland. There was also a bizarre farmyard act with goats and chickens presented by another Preston lad George Fey, dressed as a farmer.

The show also included Gwen and Maggie with a Revolving Balancing act. This was the very same Gwyn who hailed from Porthmadog and I saw performing his Trapeze act in Lord George

The original Bionic Bertha before it was rescued from a scrap yard

Sanger's Circus in the mid 1960's. Gwyn had had a bad fall from the trapeze while he was on Billy Smarts Circus and had to devise a new act, he came up with a revolving carousel with him precariously balanced on one end and Maggie on the other.

The show also included a mechanical Elephant that Allan had bought from a scrap yard, it was the year of The Six Million Dollar Man. AKA Steve Austin, AKA The Bionic Man.

I had the idea to call the Elephant Bionic Bertha and I got it on Blue Peter. We would also parade it around the towns and cities we played in and it couldn't fail to get us great publicity wherever we went.

We were about to get even more exotic and I drove to London to buy a monkey called Ramous, he came with two performing dogs. We bought him from Hans Vogalbine, former bear trainer and he of The Anglo Danish Circus that we nearly joined in 1971. I volunteered for the journey with the vague intention of bumping into Marc Bolan as I drove around the South Circular to Han's home in Streatham.

You'd have thought I had more chance of winning the lottery than meeting Marc on this trip but without even knowing it I drove right past his house. The route I chose, took me on The Lower Richmond Rd, Sheen's past his home, at the time on the corner of Kings Road.

We travelled to and from London in a horsebox with Circus Apollo written on the side. I went with a tent man called Snudge and after collecting the dogs and the monkey we stopped in a service station on the way back to the Midlands. I had the bright idea of giving Ramous a drink of water and got him out of his travelling cage.

He was a Rhesus monkey, grey in colour and only stood about 18" tall and a right little bastard. I gave him his water and then tried to persuade him to go back in his travelling cage. Would he go in, would he fuck.

Snudge was hiding around the corner and we had a large crowd watching me trying to tame this 18" tall wild beast. Two hours later and I eventually persuaded him to go back with the help of some dog biscuits.

I never did get on with Ramous, it was a mutual dislike really and he would try and humiliate me at every opportunity. He took to Allan like a father though and he would sit on top of him picking salt from his arm. Ramous soon joined in the show and was presented by Debbie, Gin and Yoland, along with the dogs.

That summer saw Apollo tour North Wales, the old stomping ground for Fossett's, myself and of course Gwyn.

We were not alone in North Wales that summer, as Fossett Brothers were already up there. The last I had seen of Claude and his sister was when they ordered me off the ground, so I plucked up courage and I went to see them and this time they were a lot less hostile.

In fact they tried to lure me away from Apollo by offering to double my money. My loyalty again, got the better of me and as a director of Apollo I stayed put.

Although friends again we were also in competition and they tried to cover up our posters whilst in Anglesey, I had no option but to cover all of theirs up, luckily they quit before it got out of hand.

During August and early September we travelled across the top of Wales from North to South. I was travelling ahead of the show again, booking the grounds and organizing the publicity, I had an elderly couple called Charlie and Marge Isaac billing for me and we had arrived in Port Talbot when disaster struck.

It was the 16th September 1977 and I was woken by Marge, banging on my trailer door and shouting 'get up, Marc Bolan has been killed'. I quickly arose and went into their trailer, I couldn't believe it. "Been killed", I asked what do you mean, 'he's been killed in a road accident' she said. Sure enough the TV bulletins were leading with the terrible news, Marc Bolan, my hero, was dead.

He was travelling back from a night out in the West End with Gloria Jones, his girlfriend and mother of his son Rolan. She was at the wheel when, at 5am, the car hit a tree on Barnes Common, London. He died instantly.

He was only 29, two weeks away from his 30th birthday, definitely on his way back to superstardom but it all ended at 5am on that September morning. Although a terrible tragedy it was also Marc Bolan's greatest means of holding onto fame, he was now forever immortalized along with his heros, Eddie Cochran, Buddy Holly and only a month earlier, Elvis Presley.

Marc joked on the 16th August, the day that Elvis died that he was glad he hadn't died on the same day, otherwise there would only have been a few column inches written about him. A month later though and Marc's death, like Elvis's hit the front pages.

There were many conspiracy theories about his death, allegedly his mini was in the garage that very day and he was been driven round in his Bentley with a Rolls Royce grill by his chauffeur/body guard Alfi. When the mini was ready he gave the Bentley/Rolls back to his Dad and he and Gloria went out in the Mini. After the inquest it was discovered that at the time of the accident two of the wheels were underinflated and three of the wheels had loose wheel nuts.

All this combined with the fact that Gloria was over the allowed alcohol limit and the treacherous road home allegedly conspired to this terrible tragedy.

I went back to the show a few days later, one or two people offered their condolences but I don't think they genuinely could believe how losing an idol was like losing a member of your family.

Debbie had recorded a tribute to him that was played on Radio 1 and offered to sell it to me, sell it to me! I told her to Fuck Off.

I didn't go to the funeral, I had know idea where or when it was but Marc's legacy, drive and influence would help to guide me through my life.

Photo credits, Masayoshi Sukita

Chapter Five
The Curtain Comes Down

People always say things come in threes, I'm not sure about that, but when changes happen in life they do all seem to happen around the same time.

The next 18 months were about to have profound changes not only to my life, but also to Circus Apollo, the British music scene and the country in general.

Labour's small majority in the House of Commons and their inept new leader James Callaghan were causing chaos. Inflation had been raging at a staggering 23%, even more than interest rates, so the interest you earned on your savings was actually depreciating. Everybody was on strike, including gravediggers, the country was in one hell of a mess.

In '77 Marc Bolan did not have any hit singles, he did produce a great album though in Dandy the Underworld, his tour was amazing and at the time of his death he was starring in and hosting his own TV show.

The trendsetters though were the punks, The Damned, The Clash, The Ramones and the frontrunners of the new movement The Sex Pistols. The Pistols had produced four great singles, and a great album, Never Mind the Bollocks. The country was in decay and anarchy certainly was in the UK.

During the time I had known Allan we had very few cross words but in the winter of 1977 our working relationship was going to take a nasty turn. He had been having digs at me throughout the season, claiming 'my head was in the clouds' etc. True I had a Rock 'n' Roll dream, what kid doesn't, I just wanted to follow that dream.

I had masses of ambition and still have, I think it's important to have drive and ambition and I don't think, as you get older you should lose your ambitions. Allan's dream was to own his own Circus, he fulfilled it, the fact that I had more lavish dreams didn't mean my head was any more in the clouds than his. A lot of the problems stemmed from Billy Wild, don't get me wrong I liked Billy, he did a good western act was a good showman and was a reasonable Advance Agent. The trouble was he got into Allan's head and was often too critical and, forever telling Allan how he thought things could have been done better.

Allan was so taken in by him that he also made him a Director of Circus Apollo, not that that really meant anything, I was a director but it was just a title on a piece of paper.

Billy had a brainwave that we should do a Christmas show on a field in the middle of the Isle of Anglesey for the Christmas period! Anglesey is a small holiday island in North Wales, it had a population of only 66,000. We had toured three of its towns that summer so all the population who wanted to see us would have done so then, not in the middle of winter, additionally of course, there wouldn't be any holiday makers to boost attendances.

It was a fucking stupid idea and had no chance of succeeding.

I was taken off the advance, gambler and petty thief Charlie Isaac and his wife Marge were entrusted with the job of billing under the supervision of Billy Wild.

At the same time Allan and Babbs sold their house cum winter quarters in Rugley and bought an old farm near Wrexham, I was given the job of helping them move from Rugley to Wrexham.

I use the term 'job' lightly as I didn't get paid, in fact I never got paid for the work I did in the winter. I got free parking and sometimes got fed, that was it.

Charlie Isaac did get paid however, but that wouldn't be enough, not enough for our Charlie. He was also given expenses in advance. Instead of billing he went to the bookies and squandered those expenses then did a runner.

The billing he had done was shit and there were still loads of posters left. Billy asked me if I would go and finish them off. I should have told him to "Fuck Off" and do it himself, if I wasn't good enough three weeks ago why should I be good enough now. I didn't, and went out billing.

When I got back Allan confronted me, I thought he was going to say thanks for standing in at the last minute, how wrong could I be.

Apparently when I helped move things from Rugley to Wrexham I forgot to pack the dog food, kid you not, the fucking dog food. I had left four bags of the stuff in Wrexham and despite being out billing for the day Allan insisted I drove from Anglesey to Wrexham and back to collect the dog food.

I offered to buy some locally but he was adamant, 'it was my fault I would have to rectify it' driving the 140 mile round trip to his farm and back to pick up the fucking dog food'. We had a huge row and I went back to my trailer. I was really fucked off and upset and almost walked out.

I did repent though and drove to Wrexham for the dog food but obviously under duress, not only had I worked for nothing during my day and nights excursions, it was also my birthday.

The show in Anglesey was reasonable and included, Debbie, Gina and Yoland with the dogs and monkey, Billy Wild with his Western act, Trevor and Bonnie Juggling and Hand Balancing, Ricky Clowning. Plus the Roller Balancing Stilt Walking and Fire Eating of Neville Campbell.

I was Ringmaster, showed the ponies which had now increased to six after the acquisition of two strawberry roans from Dennis Fossett. In addition we brought in a Crocodile act that had previously come from Chipperfields Circus, but even that failed to bring in the crowds.

Despite the bad business on Anglesey, the parties were great, we had a licensed bar and Ricky and myself would sit on bar stools right next to the optics. Every night on several occasions we would send Neville out to unplug the electric for a few seconds when he did, it went totally black and we leant over and filled up our glasses, it was like the "emperors new clothes", every time the lights came back on our glasses were miraculously full again. I also had a couple of flings, first of all with Yolland then with a local girl Michelle Hell.

One evening I threw a party in the tent and it later moved into my caravan, there was a heavy wind getting up outside and me and Ricky were drinking equally as heavy inside my trailer there was a knock at the door, it was Neville.

He said we've got to go out – the tents blowing down, we said "fuck it" and thrust a drink into his hand and he got pissed too. We then locked my Mum in the bedroom and had an almighty food fight. About half an hour later, totally bladdered, we went out to 'save the tent'.

Billy, Allan and Snudge were already there, we shouted 'fear not the cavalry has arrived', even if the cavalry were completely pissed. We quickly put all the lorries tight into the tent and pulled out the ropes making sure the stakes weren't pulling. The floor of one of the trailer blew right up in the air over our heads and landed on the tent.

Amazingly it didn't rip it and we clambered up there and got it down, I'd never had so much fun pulling out the tent even though I could hardly stand up.

Aside from the parties, Anglesey was as expected, a waste of time and the show closed early most of us went back to Wrexham except Billy Wild who left to join Gerry Cottles Circus, which was in Cardiff.

I don't know if my argument with Allan had anything to do with it, but I was becoming really disillusioned with Circus and my Rock 'n' Roll urge was definitely getting the better of me, I knew if I didn't make a move soon I never would.

I was writing more songs and generally they were getting better, I knew though that I could never fulfil my dream and join a band while I was trekking around the country with a Circus, something had to give.

The season started reasonable enough and I organized a christening in the tent for The Campbell Boys, I managed to get a priest to perform the ceremony and got a story and picture in the Daily Mirror. I was asked by the Campbells if I would like to become the Godfather to one of their boys and gave me the choice of which one, I chose Neville Jnr.

The Christening was a success, the priest sprinkled holy water onto the boy's heads and we sprinkled sawdust.

The party afterwards though ended with an almighty fight, Neville Snr. left home and moved in across the other side of the ground into my trailer. That didn't last long though, I locked him in the bedroom until he wanted a piss so much he had to climb out of the window. I still remember his cries, 'let me out John, I want a wee'. He moved back in with Pauline and the rest of his family –I'd done my bit for marriage guidance.

The show was smaller again this year, Trevor and Bonny were still there as was Ricky and Yolland. I was showing the ponies and sometimes acting as Ringmaster as well as doing the publicity. The Campbells did their acts, Gina had started Wire Walking and did that in addition to the dreaded Hoops and Glasses.

I had a pretty regular but I emphasize, safe, sex life, not with anyone in particular but relatively often. There was one situation though when I thought I had got myself into a spot of bother.

I pulled a girl in a pub in Smethwick, Birmingham and brought her back to my trailer. We started kissing and touching each other until she stopped me to take her wig off, I thought strange, I didn't even realize she had a wig on.

We started getting more into it and my hand headed south, then she stopped me again and went into the other room, allegedly to take her all in one corset off and it suddenly dawned on me this girl was like no other I had pulled . . . Was I about to get it on with a man?

I was trembling and wondered what the fuck to do as she got back into bed and then I thought, oh fuck it, so I did. To my relief, she certainly was a she, so my wandering south bound hand didn't end up clutching anything other than I had originally intended.

That wasn't the end of the dramas of Smethwick though and after a row with Allan. Neville and his family left. I had to fill in and for most of the season I did my Fire Eating act along with all my other duties.

We returned to North Wales for the summer, only six months since our disastrous Christmas season and for the third time in 14 months. This time the weather was shit and it wasn't particularly enjoyable.

The best fun that Summer was when a rival Circus tried to take us on, first of all Fossett Brothers were also heading towards Wales with my Dad, of all people, back with them and running their advance.

It wasn't Fossett's that we ran into though it was Charlie Weights, a small show, about the same size as Apollo but with some exotic animals such as a Zebra and a couple of Camels.

We were on Anglesey and they billed a town we were in, I wasn't too happy but sometimes that happens, they then jumped into Pwllheli a week before we were due there, now it had become personal.

I drove into Pwllheli, I knew that when their show was on they would all be a working, so I stole about 100 of their posters from the shops, simply telling the shopkeepers that the show had been cancelled.

I then returned to the town the next morning at five am. I pasted their posters all over the town centre banks with quick drying paste. It was the days before CCTV so as long as I was quick I knew I would get away with it.

In addition I had a load of slips printed that would fit the overprint section of Weights poster (the section that contains the Venue, Dates and Box office).

Once the shops opened I went around all the shops and told the shopkeeper the show was back on and put the posters back up, now overprinted with the slips containing our dates and venue.

The Weights were so busy trying to deal with the angry bank managers that they didn't notice the date change on their posters and wondered why nobody was going to see them.

I bumped into their advance agent in the town, I was stood right next to a poster displaying one of their posters with our dates on, luckily he didn't notice. He told me about the incident with the banks, he thought the animal rights demonstrators did it and I helped him believe that.

The next few days I went back to Pwllheli and billed it with our posters.

At the end of the week we pulled onto the ground that was right across the road from the ground where Weights were standing.

They put up huge boards on the main road pointing to their site so we parked our trucks on the grass verge so no-one could see them.

We were winning the battle hands down and we had a huge queue waiting to get in until The Weights turned up with all their men, they put chains on our trucks and pulled them into the road, I tried to pull one of them out of the cab of a truck and he came at me with a sledge hammer.

The battle continued for about 10 minutes until Allan McPherson and Charlie Weight called a truce and they agreed to pull down and move.

Amazingly no one got hurt but Weights did get the last laugh, first of all by finding a better site and then by stealing almost all of our staff.

Everyone seemed to be jumping ship, Ricky had a row with Yolland after she had gone off with some gypsy boys and she left. Ricky himself was the next to go, he fell in love with someone he shouldn't have and scarpered (not me I hasten to add). Another of our tent man left and joined Weights and two weeks later Trevor and Bonnie scarpered too, obviously to Weights.

Apollo was down to bare bones and Allan just shrunk into his shell while I tried but failed to find some replacement artistes.

Artistes at this time were hard to come by at short notice,

We had just about enough people to run the show ourselves. Myself showing the horses and fire Eating, Debbie and Gina with the dogs, monkey, Wire and Arial Ladder acts, Allan Clowning and Bobbie Gaylord as Ringmaster.

In total there was six of us in the ring. That figure was going to temporarily shrink to five for week of so.

We were in Prestatyn and a friend of mine from Preston, Bruce Carter had come to visit and watch the show. In the fire act I used to do this huge blowout, I would pack my mouth with paraffin, run, jump and land right in front of the ringside seats then blow the fire as I was running backwards, it looked great, the flame seemed 20' long.

The trouble was my cockiness had got the better of me and I wanted to show off to Bruce. I had a cold and consequently a blocked nose. To do a blow out you need to breath in through your nose, fill your lungs with air and then do an almighty blow. When I breathed in my nose was blocked and I ended up inhaling the paraffin.

What I would have given for a Vicks nasal spray.

I carried on with the act despite coughing violently.

I was working with Debbie and Gina as Chief Crazy Haze and The Mac Sisters. Debbie and Gina thought it was hilarious and were pissing themselves. After the show I felt terrible and had a really bad nights sleep.

The next morning I went to Southport billing with Steve, the tent man cum biller. I still felt shit so I went to Liverpool hospital on the way back to Prestatyn. I explained what had happened and they gave me an x-ray, at first they found nothing until I started coughing up blood and then they discovered a clot on one of my lungs.

I was kept in for about a week, Apollo tried to carry on without me but after a day they decided to pull down and move to Southport and wait for my recovery. In hospital I felt like the Elephant Man, all the student doctors would come round to see me due to my strange injury. The only similar thing they had seen was when someone was admitted after syphening petrol out of parked cars (we were in Liverpool after all).

When I was discharged the doctor told me not to fire eat for a while, we had a show that night and of course I ignored him and did my Fire Eating that evening. Strangely, despite the amount of performers in Apollo the show was actually going down well and business was good during the back end, the atmosphere on the show was much better too.

The season ended and we pulled into Wrexham. Allan, Babbs Debbie and Gina went on their annual pilgrimage to Benidorm and I was left to look after the fort. No stable girl to shag in their bed this time but plenty of animals to look after including that fucking monkey.

At first I used to go and sit with the monkey at night to keep him company and feed him. The little bastard though, used to jump on my knee and give himself a wank and blowjob. Every time I tried to stop him he would try and bite me and start again until I was covered in monkey spunk.

I felt totally violated by an animal, it was like bestiality in reverse, back at Fossett's it was Larry the Llama who made me keep my back against the wall now it's Ramous the fucking monkey getting his rocks off on my knee.

I soon reverted to just feeding him, getting out quick and leaving him to pleasure himself alone.

While the show was in Prestatyn I met the guy called

Ramous the Rhesis Monkey – the little war

Pete, we would often go for a drink in the pub behind the Circus site until I had my Fire Eating accident. I bumped into Pete in Wrexham, he told me it was his home town and he had moved back there, he invited me to a Butane party just outside town.

I was to meet him in a pub then we would go onto the party, I took Tentman Steve with me. I was in a pub waiting when this guy called Monty introduced himself to me and said he was going to the same party. He suddenly flashed a container of Butane in my direction. I asked him 'where's Purple Pie Pete' he said 'his lips are like lightning' and I replied 'girls melt in the heat'. Immortal words from Telegram Sam the T-Rex classic.

I knew from that moment on he would be a friend for life.

I thought I'd test his gullibility and when he asked me if I would like a drink I said, 'yes please a Molotov cocktail'. He promptly went to the bar and ordered one. He certainly passed my gullibility test and we became instant friends and still are to this day although he had to change his name, we couldn't have any of this daft Monty malarkey, he was re-christened a much more sensible Paul Peculiar.

A few days later we travelled together to Southport to a T-Rex convention and again took tentman Steve with us. At this point I had a little Simca car strangely sprayed orange and most definitely the worse for wear.

It was a freezing day and snowing heavily, the windscreen wipers did not work so I had attached a rope to each of them wound the windows down and pulled the rope from side to side while driving. The back door didn't close either and Paul had to sit there with a ships rope holding it shut. We first went to my Mum's house in Preston, we all got changed into our glam gear and went out into town prior to our trip to Southport.

Snow was all over the ground and there we were, I wore an inside out sheepskin waist coat with no shirt underneath, Paul Peculiar in his Mum's purple satin dressing gown with a Dandy in the Underworld sticker on the back, Steve with bovver boots on with automatic written on one and shoes on the other and my Mum with her beige coat on and shopping basket on wheels.

The convention was great and the next day we all travelled to Manchester. We dropped Steve at his Aunties, who lived in a sort of pre-Shameless, shameless house, the kids were peeling wallpaper off the walls and she sat there smoking a fag, can of lager in hand, her jeans wide open and her fat belly hanging over the top of them. Paul and I went to see Peter Tosh at the Apollo. Neither of us was into Reggae but Mick Jagger and Keith Richards had just recorded a song with him, we were there really with the vain hope of Mick and Keef turning up.

They didn't.

So it was back to reality and time for my last stand in the Circus.

Both Allan and myself were going to work over the Christmas season with Circus Hoffman, he would go to Birmingham in one unit and I would go to Stoke with the other.

In the last decade all the big three in the British Circus world had closed down, Bertrum Mills, then Smarts and finally Chipperfields, although other members of the Chipperfield family were still touring big shows. The mantle of 'the big show' though had been handed over to Gerry Cottle, Austen Brothers, Sir Robert Fossett's, Robert Brothers and Circus Hoffman.

Hoffman's was run by brothers Peter, Jeffrey and, to a lesser degree, Gerald.

They had a good Circus pedigree, their father Billy Mack once worked as advance agent for two different shows at the same time without either of the shows knowing about the other.

In the 1960's Billy started Circus Hoffman, originally a small show that advertised lots of animals that they either didn't have or if they did they weren't performing.

After Billy's death and under the control of the brothers it was a chaotic rise to fame, the show rapidly got bigger. Hoffman was a big show with elephants, tigers and bears.

I was with Jeffrey, I joined them originally to do the billing and to act as publicist but ended up doing everything including buying the cash and carry and putting up the tiger cage.

It was a really cold winter and we got loads of publicity when we used one of the elephants to push a car out of the snow in front of a mass of photographers. The story got in almost every national newspaper the next day. Certainly a great stunt if this was to be my last hurrah in the traditional Circus industry?

During that winter North End were having a pretty good run and were steadily climbing the 2nd division table, I drove to Preston from Stoke to see a few games, all wins too, including 6-1 demolition of Charlton.

Back in 1977 I met a journalist called Mike Gilmore, who lived in Llandeilo, South Wales, we kept in touch and I had told him of my Rock n' Roll dream. He offered to help me get a band together but to do this I had to leave the Circus. Mike had visited me a few times that winter and we decided the time had come to give my Rock 'n' Roll dream a go.

At the end of the run with Hoffman I decided that enough was enough. I rang Allan and told him I wouldn't be pulling back onto Wrexham and I wouldn't be coming back the next season

Allan started the season without me and Apollo now had a lion act, it didn't last though and by the summer most of the artistes left and Allan had a heart attack. Thankfully Allan was OK but that turned out to be the end of Circus Apollo

My Circus career was all but over and now it was time at long last to try my luck at Rock 'n' Roll.

Presenting the Strawberry Roans at Circus Apollo
Photo credits, from Haze's personal collection

The first Flash Harry lineup. Llandeilo 1979. Photo credits, from Haze's personal collection

Chapter Six
Flash Harry and a Close Encounter

Early 1979 and I had decided to make my break, I'd wanted to join a band but found it impossible to do so when you are in a different town every three days.

I called Mike Gilmore and told him I was ready to move on, he, like me was keen to start a band, in his case though, he wanted to be the manager.

Mike said he had some musicians waiting to meet me in a small village called Llandeilo, South Wales. He also told me he had somewhere to park my caravan.

Of course I had been to Llandeilo many times, this was the very place where Claude Fossett had an unexpected rendezvous with a bed of tulips after careering down 20 steps into the recreation ground in his car.

I had my own caravan and car but foolishly the car was nowhere near big enough to pull the caravan, my calamity Simca could only just about pull itself let alone a caravan. Consequently I got a friend of mine, Trevor Delmar to help with my great escape. The weather was still awful and the trek to Wales was blighted by heavy snowstorms. We eventually arrived, knocked on the door, met the band and asked Gilmore where I was to park the caravan.

Of course, I quickly realized his incredible management skills when he told me he had not arranged anywhere for me to park my trailer and advised me to leave it in the council car park. Suddenly I had gone from a bona fide Circus Artiste into a gypsy with Rock 'n' Roll ambitions.

I took the situation into my own hands and found a space to park at the back of a pub until I could find something more permanent.

The band he had lined up were far from perfect either. RELIC, great name eh (not). They thought they would be a sort of prog, folk, rock thing with me a Glam Punk fronting it. It would never work, they had one good musician, guitarist Alan Burgess.

I did however record my first song with Relic on a four track, it was a version of the Santana song 'Black Magic Woman'. I remember it being pretty cool but don't know what has happened to that recording.

It soon became clear that I wouldn't fit in and I was beginning to think I had made a huge mistake. Gilmore, however persuaded me that everything would work out OK and suggested we put adverts in the local paper for musicians to join a new 'new wave band'.

The adverts proved quite fruitful and we recruited a guitarist, Gordon Gonad and Bassist Chris Cleen, we also auditioned a drummer who couldn't really play, sadly he committed suicide, hanging himself from a tree before we had the chance to turn him down.

The drummer from Relic, Animal Jones decided to jump ship and bat for the other side, we burnt his fairisle jumpers and put him in a torn T-shirt and Flash Harry was born.

In the meantime, I drove back to Preston for a week to take my driving test. I had already failed twice, the first time for driving into a tree. The second for putting a whoopee cushion under the inspectors seat, I thought he would see the funny side as a large fart incurred while he told me to do an emergency stop.

Not that any of this had stopped me driving though, while with Apollo I drove a large Commer lorry, pulling two trailers with a total length of 85'.

Thankfully this time, no trees jumped out in front of me and I resisted a trip to the joke shop prior to my test and passed with flying colours. Third time lucky. From now on I could drive my Simca with pride and not break into cold sweats every time I saw a Police car in my rear view mirror.

I returned to Wales and we started rehearsing, I had written loads of songs, obviously including 'ivin' but none were considered worthy by the rest of the band. We therefore compiled a set of Punk classics with songs by The Sex Pistols, The Damned, Clash etc. I begged for a T-Rex tune though and we choose Jeepster, I also insisted on some original songs and we wrote four new tunes between us.

I needed to earn a crust until I became a rock star and earning a crust is exactly what I did when I took a job delivering bread for a bakery, you'd be amazed what a bored housewife would do for a hard-crusted cob. The job in the bakery gave me a few bob and when not rehearsing and delivering bread Chris Cleen and myself would hitch hike a lift to London for the weekend, we spent many a night

Me and Bruce in Barry Avenue, Ingol
Me with my corkscrew hair
Photo credits, from Haze's personal collection

under a motorway bridge on the M4 when we simply couldn't get anyone to stop.

I was still being courted by Circuses to make a return, first of all an advert appeared in the Worlds Fair 'Can John Haze contact Colin Enos', Colin was running a show the size of Apollo but it included Martin Lacy's Lions.

He tried to get me to drop my Rock 'n' Roll idea and join his show, I politely declined.

Chris Cleen quite liked the idea of running away and joining a Circus. So four months after I gave up Circus for good, I was back, not only in the Circus but also back with Fossett Brothers as advance agent with Chris Cleen as my assistant.

Claude had contacted me and asked if I would run their advance on a part time basis, travelling back to Llandeilo to rehearse with the band. As Fossett's normally went to Wales I thought we could do the advance during the week and return to rehearse with Flash Harry at weekends. I guessed that it was better than delivering bread.

Every year Fossett's would tour Wales, the south in the spring and the north in the summer so my plan had to work. That was until I joined the show and Claude announced they wouldn't be going to Wales this spring and summer and would instead go the Midlands and the North. Fucking hell I'd only just returned to the Circus and I was already being fucked over.

I had committed myself to Claude though so I joined Fossett's again, with Chris Cleen as my deputy. Before we went I spotted an opportunity to get Flash Harry on the map, there was a general election and Margaret Thatcher was about to sweep the Labour party aside and become Britain's first female Prime Minister.

There is a strange byelaw that states if you are a political party you can fly post legally during an election, I therefore decided to call Flash Harry a political party (although I didn't actually stand as a candidate) and in the best traditions of Screaming Lord Sutch I had hundreds of posters printed. The posters proclaimed 'VOTE FLASH HARRY' to confuse everyone even more had some printed in red and some in blue. We plastered them everywhere, the back of road signs, telegraph poles and even on the side of a cow in a field while it was sleeping.

Everyone in or around Llandeilo had certainly heard of Flash Harry even if they didn't know what we were. I was gaining a strong friendship with Chris Cleen, I was a couple of years older and apart from one skirmish, where in true western fashion we pushed each other through van window (it was closed at the time), we have remained friends all of our lives.

There was no way my idea of doing the advance and gigging or rehearsing at the weeker would work so after three months, for the second time I told Claude Fossett I was leaving.

was now late July and the show was in Cleveleys near Blackpool for two weeks. He asked how long I needed to go for and I said I don't know.

There were very few artistes with Fossett's that year, of course the entire house acts, Jessie's Ariel, Juggling and Western act's, the horses and dogs, Larry the human fancying Llama. Plus Raymond former tent man, arm wrestler and now Fire Eater and Strongman – unbelievably again, Dick Sandow and his family.

Unfortunately within a week of me leaving Raymond did a runner and Dick Sandow did his usual blank postcard trick on Claude and left too.

Claude rang me and asked me to come back, I explained I could but not yet, I really didn't want to let him down but I knew if I had gone back it would have been the end of the band. He called me all the bleeding bastards under the sun.

I had sold my strange little orange Simca and bought an Austin Princess for £20. Cleen and myself travelled back to Wales and we started rehearsing with earnest, usually in the guitarist, Gordon Gonads shed.

Each day it was twice around the set then to the pub for a pint of beer, we were pretty poor and could only afford one pint per night. We managed to sell the Austin Princess for £120 and I split the profit with Cleen, this helped us pay for our daily pint.

We were getting a bit of a reputation, Llandeilo was a small village and had a healthy amount of exchange students from France, predominantly girls, visiting every summer, we were their band and for a while Llandeilo's claim to fame.

Once our £120 car sale windfall had run out we were all struggling for money and one day I was in a sweet shop with Chris Cleen when he showed me a Mars bar he had secretly slipped into his pocket.

immediately shouted 'That boy has stolen a Mars Bar' and the shopkeeper and myself chased him down the road shouting 'Stop Thief'. He got away and the shopkeeper and myself went back to the shop complaining about 'the youth of today'. The shopkeeper gave me a Mars bar for helping him to stop a shoplifter.

fter three weeks of intensive rehearsing and 21 pints of beer, spread out over 21 days, Flash Harry started gigging. The first gig was in Cardiff Top Rank, it was some sort of competition and we had to play three original songs. We took a coach load of fans/friends from Llandeio to cheer us on. We opted to go on early because the bus driver threatened to leave all our fans behind if we went on after 11pm.

We were in the wings and seconds before we got on the stage Chris Cleen whispered in my ear 'How does the first song go'. I had a mouth full of Paraffin that I was about to spit out in a ball of flames, I tried to mime the tune of he song by rolling my eyes.

I then lit my fire torch only for a voice to come down the monitors 'put that fire out' I gestured to Animal to quickly start the song and away we went.

I got to centre stage, blew a huge ball of fire and Chris Cleen played a completely different song to the rest of us. Our friends and fans surged to the front and we were rock stars for 10 minutes.

We didn't win but definitely left an impression, most of all, I was on the way, I had taken my fist step and climbed the first rung on the ladder of my Rock 'n' Roll dream.

We did five more gigs that summer in clubs and pubs in North and South Wales. The first of which after Cardiff was in Ammanford Welfare club, it was only down the road from Llandeilo so we had a good turn out and lots of tasty cakes, kindly donated by Animal and Chris Cleen's Mums.

The next was a shit gig with a group of Mods in Bridgend, in between songs they would chant 'get involved'. Apparently it was some sort of term of endearment but we were not sure what they wanted us to get involved with, so we didn't.

We then travelled to North Wales to play a club on my old stomping ground of Anglesey and finally a gig in the White Horse in Llandeilo. I kicked over a microphone stand and the crowd went wild, they were so easily pleased.

Flash Harry's Welsh adventure was to be short lived as Gordon Gonad decided to persue a career with the milk marketing board and the rest of us would go our separate ways.

There was no stopping me now though, I decided to move to London to try my luck there. To whet my appetite I thumbed to London to visit Golders Green, the cemetery where Marc Bolan was cremated on the anniversary of his death.

I met loads of fellow Bolan fans and although Marc was no longer around I knew I would be closer to him and to his legend if I moved to London. If I hadn't made my mind up before t move to the smoke then I certainly had now.

Just before my trek to the south I had a really strange thing happen to me.

I was about to thumb a lift back to my caravan with Gilmore, it was around midnight and w had all been out drinking, I still remember the date it was August 31st 1979.

I had met a girl, Pinkie Parnell and went for a snog, so I left Gilmore to head back to my caravan first. After I had finished I started to walk down the hill and saw Gilmore getting into a car, he was no more the 20 meters ahead of me. I shouted but he didn't seem to hear me, he didn't even look round.

Annoyed, I decided to thumb a lift on my own but not one car came. I had no option but to walk the 10 miles back to my caravan, Mumbling and swearing about Gilmore along the way. The sky was completely clear, not a single cloud.

All of a sudden I looked up and saw a strange object flying across the sky, once it disappeared it doubled back on itself in a flash. This happened about 40 times during my long walk home and I was totally terrified. The hairs on the back of my neck were standing up.

Once back at the caravan I tore into Gilmore and told him he had deserted me at the mercy of a multitude of aliens, he quite rightly just laughed at me.

In hindsight I can understand his sceptical stance. To prove my point though, I took him out at precisely the same time the next night and there they were again. I knew they would be, but how could I know that? Gilmore couldn't explain what he too was seeing but still remained sceptical. He simply couldn't believe his own eyes.

The time had finally come to move to London, I thumbed down and went to a T-Rex convention in Henley-on-Thames. After the convention I, and a load of fellow Bolan fans slept in a workman's hut. This was a luxury to me. Generally on my soirees to London I would sleep under bridges, in toilets, under park benches, even on the train embankment under Earls Court. Basically anywhere that had some sort of roof over my head.

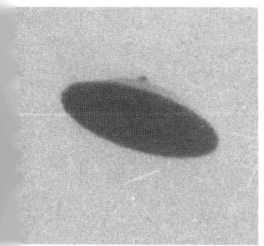

Of course this tramp like existence was only temporary as I was soon to find a bed-sit to rent in Fulham, London.

At the Henley T-Rex convention I met a beautiful girl who amazingly and co-incidentally lived only 500 yards from my newly found accommodation. I travelled back to Wales, hired a van put all my stuff in it and moved to London.

The strange sequence of co-incidences and alien encounters had not finished yet though.

I took the van back to Wales. Animal had travelled to London with me and was going to stay in my bed-sit while I took the hire van back.

Something in the bed-sit scared him though, to this day he won't say what. He refused to stay and instead he went back to Wales with me. The next day I thumbed back to London alone, it was to be my final voyage on this boomerang adventure.

I got to the M4, there was at least 10 other hitchhikers already there. I was pissed off and had visions of me being stuck there for hours, I did the honourable thing though and walked to the end of the queue.

The very first car amazingly stopped, it drove passed all the other hitchhikers and picked me up. I jumped in and headed south. The driver was a woman and after a while she asked me if I had had any strange things happen to me. I thought this was a weird thing to say, I told her of my alien encounter. She said she knew all about it and that is why she picked me up, that is why she drove past all the other hitchhikers.

The hairs on the back of my neck began to stand up again. She assured me they would not harm me but were interested in me.

She took me as far as Cardiff but arranged to meet me at the Aetherius Society in Fulham Rd, London the following Thursday. The Aetherius Societies offices were almost across the road from my new girlfriend, Denise's flat and about 500 yards from my bed-sit.

Was I picked up by an alien? Was I having a close encounter of the third kind? Or was she just a believer? Her assurances that my potential Alien abductors were only here to protect us seemed to add up, we were after all in the middle of the cold war and on the verge of sending Mother Earth into Armageddon.

The following quote was taken from the Aetherius Society website in 2010. 31 years after my encounter, reading it now still sends a shiver down my spine, the words of the lady/alien who gave me a lift still ringing in my ear.

The similarity of what she told about spirituality and other worlds are echoed in this paragraph

'The Cosmic Masters, our spiritual elders from other worlds, have come again to help us in our time of need. They have delivered their messages to the political and religious leaders, and have been ignored. They come now to you, with compassion and desire to help. They come with great hope'.

In years to come I have not had any other encounters but various people have felt I possesse a spirituality, what sort of spirituality I don't know but these people have included Marc Bolan's girlfriend, Gloria Jones.

I arrived in London and met Denise, I was still thinking about my encounter when Denise told me that the Marc Bolan film 'Born to Boogie' was being shown in the West End on Thursday, this was on the same day that I had agreed to meet the lady/alien, who had given me a lift. I decided that a night watching Bolan with Denise was more interesting than learning about my possible alien abductors so Marc got the nod.

The flat I had rented in Fulham was awful, overpriced, cold and dirty.

No. 5 Waldemar Ave. in Fulham. I wrote quite a number of songs while I was in this shitty bed-sit, often inspired either by the flat or by my neighbour.

One of them was 'Dive 5' about No. five Waldermar Avenue and another was called 'Insane' and dedicated it to my neighbour who would bang on my door asking me to keep quiet, to try and prove his point he would play classical music at full volume causing every other resident of five Waldermar Ave. to bang on his door asking him to turn Debussy down.

Now encamped in the Metropolis it was time to start recruiting new blood for Flash Harry and the hunt had begun.

Flash Harry (mark 3) Haze, Chris Cleen and two builders, photo credits, from Haze's personal collection

CHAPTER SEVEN
LONDON CALLING

I went to London to find fame and fortune and ended up driving a lorry for a Textile Rental Company! A laundry by any other name.

I could possibly have signed on and let the state fund my ambitions in the same way that many other budding musicians do but that's not me.

I would feel I was sponging from the nation and my self-pride wouldn't have allowed it.

I've always been a hard worker and realized that although I had a dream I also had to earn a crust while I started to resurrect my brief musical career.

Mike Gilmore moved down a week or so later quickly followed by Chris Cleen and we decided to re-launch Flash Harry with a new line up in London.

It took us a while to get going in the Capital, I was enjoying it though, loads of gigs to go to see and the crappie job I had at least gave me more money than I ever had before.

It was 1980 and the new romantics were starting to rear there heavily made up and often-ugly heads, generally a flash back to 70's Glam Rock but without the songs. Adam Ant and Blondie were exceptions to this and created a good new sound and looked great too.

I would go and see North End every time they came to London, they were now a mid-table 2nd division team. Chelsea, West Ham and QPR were in the same league so I got the chance to see them at Stamford Bridge, Upton Park and Loftus Road.

I began to look very flamboyant, with pink, stripped or leopard skin, skintight trousers often with matching jackets. I regularly wore make up to go out. Generally this was OK if I was going to the Embassy or Gossips but didn't go down to well on the football terraces.

I had to persuade the Police at Stamford Bridge that I was a PNE fan before they would let me in, how could a boy who looked like a girl support North End. Fair comment I suppose.

The worst situation though was at Upton Park, the Preston Fans got surrounded by West Ham fans and I got singled out, I was pulled out of the throng by the Police. They thought I looked strange, again, I didn't look like a typical football fan or more precisely a PNE fan.

Pulling me out of the crowd in fact pointed me out to the Hammers fans, so too though, did my bright pink trousers. The Police searched me on the terraces as Preston scored a goal, it was promptly disallowed. They let me go back into the baying crowd, the West Ham fans were gesturing to me but somehow I got away unscathed, to make matters worse PNE lost 2-0.

My image may not have gone down to well on football terraces but it was perfect for my new venture, it was time to work on my music, searching for new recruits and bringing in fresh blood into Flash Harry.

I used to frequent a record shop called Roman Records in Fulham, it was owned by a Glam fan and mate of mine Jim Roman.

I called in there one day and met two fellow Bolan Fans, Colm and Kim Jackson, Colm was a guitarist, a little overweight but looked good. Kim had no musical abilities but looked gorgeous.

Quickly we installed Colm as guitarist into Flash Harry and I moved from Waldemar Avenue into a nicer and cheaper bed-sit in Southfields that happened to be the next flat to Colm and Kim. Chris Cleen moved into a bed-sit downstairs too.

327 Wimbledon Park Rd. was just down the road from Wimbledon Tennis Courts, I hated Tennis and the fact that the nearest pub was a mile away, it wasn't the most exciting area to live in.

It was though, the new HQ for Flash Harry. We set about writing our own songs and recruiting a drummer. We placed an advert in the NME and found a guy called Colin Atkin, to be honest he wasn't our first choice and although a nice guy he wasn't really good enough.

Mike Gilmore got us a recording session with former Relic guitarist and now budding producer Alan Burgess, who had also left Llandeilo and was now studying music at Surrey University in Guildford. Surrey Uni had its own recording studio and Alan smuggled us in to record there We recorded three tracks with the new Flash Harry with Alan at the desk. Gilmore also brough in a guy called Brian Evens who was a friend of his and very capable engineer. The tracks were Carving up the Corpses, Barbiturate and Dive Five.

The songs turned out ok but we got kicked out of the studio by the security before we had time to mix them properly. It was very much Flash Harry - warts an all and at this point those warts were pretty significant.

We started taking the recordings around record companies. Knowing their inadequacies we came up with a cunning plot, every time we played them to a record company if we came t a dodgy part of the song we would drop something on the floor and Kim wearing her mi skirt would bend over and pick it up. It was a poor attempt to distract the Record Compar

A and R man from noticing the musical mistakes.

Kim's distractions didn't prove enough and no record deal was forthcoming but we had at least recorded our own songs, we were on the next rung of the ladder and it was time to start booking gigs.

The first gig for the new Flash Harry, ironically, took us back to South Wales to play a University gig at Trinity College, Carmarthen. We now had a Swiss sax player Takka Yungo amongst our ranks. It made no difference, we were shit and most of the audience walked out.

We got a wake up call, sacked drummer Colin Aitkin and shortly afterwards Takka left too.

Gilmore also did a runner, taking with him our merchandise money, his Dad stepped in though and paid us back the dosh that Mike had "accidentally" borrowed.

I don't really know why Gilmore did a runner, I suppose he was the whipping boy of the band and subject to our frequent practical jokes, we possibly bullied him a little, for me though, my ambitions were profound.

We needed a manager who would help us achieve these ambitions, whereas, I thought Gilmore hindered them. Unperturbed we took a number of gigs in London, first an awful gig in a Crystal Palace pub then a residence in a club called Gossips in the West End.

The gig in Gossips turned out to be a lot more than just a gig and we actually ended up running a Glam Rock night there. Jim Roman would DJ and generally we were the live act. We also showed music videos on the various screens around the venue.

It was the dawning of the Video era, Colm would record our favourite videos of the time off the TV and we would show them. It was probably illegal but who cares. I think we invented the term 'Video Jockey'.

Our Glam night ran every Wednesday, we played most weeks and generally went down well, occasionally though we would put a guest band on such as friends of ours, The Cuddly Toys or the Dumb Blonds. It was our night though so we were the resident 'Glam Night' band.

We had replaced Colin with a drummer called John Gaster, who was much better, he had auditioned for the Glitter Band but was turned down because he looked too butch.

I could understand that, but we weren't the Glitter Band and beggars can't be choosers, John Gastor in fact looked more like a builder than a drummer, possibly because he was a builder. His thick beard didn't help and I thought that when I bought him a razor for Christmas he would get the hint, he didn't.

Colm also left and was replaced by another good-looking guitarist Steve Zodiac (named after one of my favourite puppet heroes).

Steve, sadly, didn't last too long and joined punk band Chelsea. Chelsea's singer Gene October would be a regular at 'Glam Night' and we even let Chelsea play there one week (even though they were a hard core punk band). Gene probably saw Steve playing with us and poached him.

We didn't advertise our new vacancy for a guitarist in the NME, instead chose 'Builders News'. Steve was replaced by a friend of John Gastor and fellow builder Dirk Forum, half the band were beginning to look like builder drag queens, I suppose the Sweet got away with looking like that for long enough though, so why couldn't we.

It was strange really, despite my Circus upbringing I very rarely went to see Circuses and would only go and see a Circus if I had friend working there. Hoffman were in and around London so I would pop over and see Sean McPherson. Neville Campbell and his family were with Jimmy Chipperfields Circus World so I went to see them and Allan McPherson, Babbs, Debbie and Gina were with a human only show, Circus Hasanni.

On one of my visits to see Allan I bought a car from him, another old banger, a grey Morris 1300. A day after I got the car I pulled out of a road and was driven into by an oncoming van, it caused a lot of cosmetic damage to my front wing. When I got home I got some grey parcel tape and basically taped all the wing back together, it looked strange, a bit Blue Peter and I doubt if it would pass its next MOT, but hey, I'd driven worse, an orange Simca to name one. The crash also damaged the radiator and despite adding rad weld there was still a leak.

That Christmas I drove to Preston to see my Mum in my new patched up car. It was a nightmare journey and I gave a lift to a friend of mine Penny who was also going home, in her case to Manchester. It took forever and my car was overheating. I was busting for a piss so I decided to kill two birds with one stone and ended up pulling on the hard shoulder of the M1 and pissing in the radiator.

Eventually we arrived in Manchester and dropped Penny off at her brother Steve's. I went inside and spent a while with them. Steve, at the time was going out with Joanne Whalley, she was there too, looking absolutely gorgeous as always. I had met Joanne a few weeks earlier, she was only around 17 but looked stunning, she had turned down a permanent part in Coronation Street, preferring not to be type cast, instead taking a small recurring part in the soap. You just knew she was going to be a star.

It was no surprise to see her rapid raise to fame in a huge amount of TV and film parts including 'The Singing Detective'. She then appeared in her first Hollywood movie Willow and in turn left Steve and met her soon to be Hollywood husband Val Kilmer. Willow also introduced her to future Circus of Horrors star Captain Dan. He was one of the many Dwarfs to appear in the film. It's probably fair to say Joanne's most memorable role though was as Christine Keeler in Scandal.

After leaving Penny, Steve and Joanne, I continued the journey to Preston.

I was ill all that Christmas and Bruce Carter and a friend of his, Graham Seed, kindly repaired my car. I didn't see the newly married Basher Briggs and I didn't even see my beloved PNE. What sort of Christmas was this!

Having said that, I didn't miss much, North End were going through a bad time, they had been relegated to Division Three, Nobby Stiles had been sacked and replaced by Tommy Docherty who in turn had been sacked and replaced by Gordon Lee. All within the space of nine months.

327 suddenly had more room though as while I was away Colm and Kim had moved out and into a council flat in Clapham. This gave us the chance to take over the whole house. My good friend Paul Peculiar was moving to London from his Wrexham home and needed somewhere to live. He moved in and within a few weeks, a couple of his friends moved in too.

I had kept in touch with Paul by letter since our visit to The Marc Bolan convention two years earlier.

He arrived at 7am on a Sunday morning and his arrival wasn't without controversy, it was a cold but dry morning, somehow he turned up soaking wet and looking somewhat bedraggled, I asked him if it was raining and he begged me to let him inside quickly to explain.

We lived at 327 Wimbledon Park Road but the Christmas card I sent to Paul had the corner ripped and he read the address as 27 Wimbledon Park Rd. He vigorously banged on the wrong door at 6.30 on a Sunday morning. A guy looked out of the window and Paul thought he was one of us and shouted up to him 'Hey man are you a child of the revolution', the guy shouted back 'child of the revolution, its 6.30 in the morning', 'I'll give you child of the fuckin' revolution' and threw a bucket of water over him.

Paul, dripping wet, then rechecked the address realized the mistake and rang the phone number on the card, a guy called Damian Damage, our temporary new manager answered and wearily gave him the correct address. Damian a hippy punk had taken over as our manager after Imore ran off with our merchandise money.

Once Paul found us, we dried him off and the rest of the day he helped us making props with borrowed pair of scissors and some oil drums. I'm sure you realize by now I watched far too many Blue Peters as a kid.

Paul soon came to understand there was no such thing as a free lunch in the Haze household.

It was the pages of Melody Maker that introduced us to our next, and again temporary manager. I saw an ad placed by a guy call Peter Skull who was looking for bands to manage, he heard our music but wasn't convinced.

Despite this he booked us a couple of gigs in Putney, both were well attended, mainly with my mates from Brooks Textiles, and both went down well. Peter Skull still wasn't convinced. When I asked him what he thought was wrong he said his girlfriend didn't like it, I said good, she's a fuckin' hippy, she's not supposed to like it. Suddenly he was convinced.

I decided though that Peter Skull or Psycho, as I christened him didn't have the know-how to manage us and retained Damian for the time being. I did agree to allow Psycho to act as our agent and book us some gigs.

Shortly afterwards we all went for a drink in The Windmill pub in Clapham and a chance meeting with Brian Evan helped us to secure another chunk of recording time. Brian was the mate of Gilmore's who had engineered the Carving up the Corpses session in the recording studio in Surrey Uni. He spotted me and re-introduced himself. He now worked as engineer in a posh 24 track-recording studio in Clapham called Majestic.

I quickly signed a production deal with him and the new Flash Harry recorded two tracks 'The Exorcist' and 'Flash Harry'.

We were certainly beginning to move in better circles, our new producer Brian Evans was being tipped for bigger things and our temporary new manager Damian Damage was introducing me to the likes of Joanne Whalley and various drugs, we now even had an agent Peter 'Psycho' Skull.

Damian Damage didn't last long though and was replaced by another manger, Peter Coombe he looked the part and went on to con a lot more famous people than me.

It was my job delivering laundry that introduced me to Coombsey, I was delivering laundry t a Christian hostel and he was the warden who used to take in the deliveries.

Like me, Coombsey had ambitions but took a day job to pay his way. He had been working wi a Christian band called 'Famous Names' and New Romantic, music, mime, dance and pop grou Shock.

In the early 1980's they supported Gary Numan at Wembley, Adam and the Ants and Depec

Mode. Through these liaisons Coombsey had become a friend of Gary Numan.

Coombsey started to get us some really tasty gigs including the Venue in Victoria with Depeche Mode. The Venue was the biggest gig we had played and was packed out, we actually went on after Detached Mode but the timing was bad, they were very much the new kids on the block, they had a new very 80's electro sound and unfortunately for us we played with them on the week 'Just can't get enough' entered the charts. They stormed it and despite us being very tight we were in the wrong place at the wrong time and bombed, soon emptying the auditorium.

We played another three gigs however, in smaller but non the less historic venues such as The Rock Garden in Covent Garden and Café De Paris.

All of which as a contrast to the venue we went down a storm.

The Venue gig though, as humiliating as it was made us realize our sound wasn't right, if we wanted to progress from The Rock Gardens to The 2000 capacity 'Venue' we needed to change. I liked the rock edge but it was a little too 70's, I felt we needed to fill out the sound and to modernize so initially we advertised for a keyboard player.

I tended to stay in London most of the time but Chris Cleen still travelled back to Wales occasionally, sometimes to Llandeilo and sometimes to see his Mum in Swansea. He still used our normal mode of transport, his thumb.

On one occasion he was picked up by a wine merchant come keyboard player from Hungerford called Nick Neutron. Chris invited Nick to audition for us and was given the job, this solved our first problem and filled out the sound. At the same time a guy called Ian Ritchie came to see me, he was an astounding musical arranger, sax player and also former member of Def School, who happened to be one of Paul Peculiar's favourite bands.

I introduced him to the band and invited him to come and see us rehearse. Once we met Ian we could see he was clearly amazingly talented, the main problem was, he liked my music and me but he didn't like the band. He pulled me to one side and said 'they look like builders' I said 'that's because they are builders'. We all thought though, that bringing Ian into the fold would move us in a new direction. We agreed to bring him on board.

We were right, he took all our music and gave it a very modern feel.

We had gone out to a party to celebrate our new expanding line up and the potential new sound when Paul Peculiar accidentally head butted me and broke my nose, apparently it was bent at a right angle and was flat on my face, I grabbed hold of it and yanked it straight again. I was taken to hospital and had to have it re broken and re set. I was still working for Brooks

Textile Rentals as a driver and had two weeks off to allow my nose and the consequential black eyes to repair.

I used this unexpected time off to write a rock musical called 'The Adventures of Shock Rock' based on my alien encounter.

Chris Cleen was also involved in a strange occurrence around this time. In his case a touch of arson. His day job was in a paint factory and somehow he managed to burn it down after smoking in the stock room. He swears it was actually a work colleague who had caused the fire but as Chris was there and was smoking he was accused, framed but thankfully, acquitted. Not until after a gruelling three day trial in The Old Bailey though. Good to be able to add suspected arsonist to his CV though.

Ian Ritchie lived in Kilburn and I travelled over to see him and played him the Adventures of Shock Rock. I recorded the tracks on his Fostex four track and he started work, he gave my songs completely new arrangements. We played this to the band and although originally shocked they went along with it. They appreciated the quality and the modernism of the new arrangements but it would mean them thinking completely out of the box.

To be fair they tried, but unfortunately, the new electro sound meant that slowly but surely the rocky members of the band left, first Dreg Forum then sadly but understandably so did Chris Cleen, I was soon to find out why.

Brian Evans had heard the rough mixes of the new sound and really liked it and offered us more time in Majestic Studios, this time to record two tracks from my new musical 'The Adventures of Shock Rock", Neutron Daze and Shock Rock. We recorded the backing and I did a guide vocal.

I then went to France on holiday with former drummer Animal Jones, although not currently in the band he agreed to play percussion on Shock Rock and after his session we left for Paris.

It was my first time abroad and we had a great time, starting in Paris, then to Lyon to stay with Animals girlfriend Tina and then onto Nice.

Chris Cleen had laid down his bass track before I went but had unexpectedly visited the studio while I was away. He saw Nick Neutron overdubbing his bass parts on Shock Rock. Pete Coombes took Chris to one side and told him his playing didn't fit the new sound.

Of course this was a double whammy for Chris, he had introduced Nick to the band only find him re-recoding the bass tracks without anybody even telling him, or even telling me for that matter.

On our return Cleen told me of this, I felt terrible and when I went back into the studio, I secretly deleted Nick Neutron's bass lines and changed the name on the desk of Chris Cleen's track, so when the mix happened it was actually Cleen playing on Nick Neutrons channel, no one realized or knew except me, but I felt better.

Chris was completely justified in leaving the band, it was like losing a member of the family, he had been with me from the beginning. The divorce settlement quickly ensued however.

Originally, we had run the band like a co-operative, we would all chip in and buy the different equipment and split the proceeds of the gigs and merchandise sales.

Chris was part of this so it was only logical that we started dividing everything up. I kept the Dry Ice Machine and the strobe Chris Cleen kept the homemade oil drum lights. Seemed fair? Well perhaps not but he could always use them as scrap yard table lights.

The fact is though I had lost not only a band member but also a true friend, suddenly I was the only survivor from the original Flash Harry.

Psycho Skull and Paul Peculiar
Photo credits, from Haze's personal collection

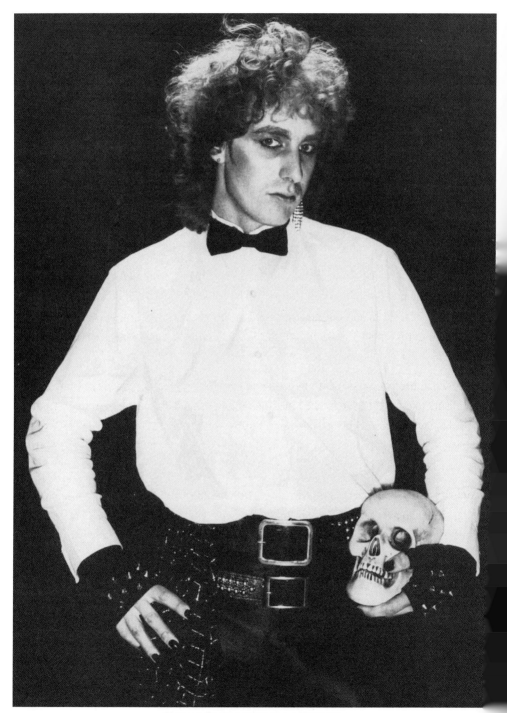

Photo credits, from Haze's personal collection

CHAPTER EIGHT
VERGING ON THE VERGE

Despite the progression of my music career I had been having a bit of a drought with the fairer sex, a few flings but nothing substantial, it wouldn't be long though before our new New Romantic sound would help to bring a new romance.

After our recent visit to Majestic studios I now had two new recordings of the new sound but only half a band, not that it mattered too much at this point as we had stopped playing live.

With these new beginnings the logical thing was to drop the name Flash Harry and simply called it Haze.

Pete Coombes started taking our new recordings around the record companies and we were beginning to get interest. Thanks to another Peter Coombes contact my love life started to bloom too.

Coombsey had been going out with a stunning blond Nottingham girl, Janey Le Grace and he had foolishly told me that she fancied me. Their relationship didn't last long though and they split up. I really liked her and I also fancied her like mad so I made a move and we soon started seeing each other (Coombsey wasn't too pleased). She had just left Uni and started work as a singer and sang backing vocals on Shock Rock.

To complicate my personal affairs even more, In November, I moved out of Southfields and into Bayswater to share a flat with Pete Coombes, Tim Dry and various other floor dwelling inmates one of which was Coombsey's new girlfriend Andrea and a Canadian poet called Biff.

We all shared the basement flat, 66 Princess Sq., ironically the same Square that my Mum moved into when she first came to London and where she was living when she met my Dad.

Bayswater is one of London's more cosmopolitan areas, architecturally, the biggest part of the area is made up of Georgian stucco terraces and garden squares, and Princess Sq. is one of those.

Princes Sq. was certainly a happening address, lots of budding pop stars would visit and most everyone who crossed the threshold at 66 Princes Sq. were either in the music biz or wanted to shag someone who was. I certainly didn't want to disappoint.

Tim Dry had a head start on us, he had perfected a really cool Robot act with his partner Sean Crawford and as Tik and Tok performed in various clubs around town. They also formed part of a techno dance band called Shock.

They had a record deal with RCA and recorded the Glitterband song Angle Face, it was ahead of it's time and a good version of the song although I don't think Tim or Shock had too much to do with playing on it, Robert Pereno possibly sang on it but it looked as though Tik and Tok just did their Robot impressions on the video and maybe some BV's. It was produced by Rusty Egan of Visage and Richard Burgess of Landscape.

As far as I could see, Shock's main attribute was the fetish look and the three gorgeous girls in the band, Barbie Wilde, LA and this amazing red Bolan haired creature called Carol Caplin.

It was live that Shock excelled, in addition to their shows With Gary Newman, Depeche Mode and Adam Ant, Shock co-starred with Ultravox at 'People's Palace Valentine's Ball' at the Rainbow Theatre. This was possibly the moment when the New Romantic scene exploded and went from being an obscure cult to a global trend. They eventually broke up and reformed as a foursome with Barbie, Tim, Sean and Carole and released another single for RCA 'Dynamo Beat'.

LA, Barbie and Carole also appeared on Top of the Pops with Landscape miming to Einstein A Go Go. Tim's girlfriend was Barbie so she was often around but I always looked forward to Carole's visits most.

Shock, although not really a band, certainly had the right look and right sound for the time it's a shame they couldn't capitalize on it and turn their media appeal into hit records.

Around November, while Coombsey was touting our recordings around the record companies he became friendly with the A and R man from Innervision Records and he was asked to meet a new band who needed management. That band turned out to be two guys who called themselves Wham!

In addition to playing with us Ian Ritchie also had a deal with Innervision to record in his own right and to arrange the brass parts for Wham! Coombsey would bring home these amazing songs such as 'Careless Whisper' and Wham Rap.

There was no doubt that they were going to be massive. George Michael obviously realized this too and quickly told Coombsey that he wouldn't be signing with him and chose to instead to go with millionaire music mogul Simon Napier Bell. A wise move George.

Despite the lack of commitment from record companies Coombsey did get us a couple brilliant gigs, to perform my new show 'The Adventures of Shock Rock'.

First, a New Year's all-dayer (as opposed to all-nighter) in the Lyceum and then a couple of weeks later at the Embassy.

Great, we had two very prestigious gigs lined up. The only problem, I didn't have a band.

I quickly got on the phone and started contacting people, Brian Evans said he would take over guitar, our next door neighbour and part-time brain surgeon Phil O'Sophical agreed to join on bass with Ian Ritchie on Sax.

Pete Coombes girlfriend Andrea Slopa on BVs, Nick Neutron played Keyboards and we re-recruited former Flasher and builder John Gastor on Drums. We still needed another musician, a second keyboard player and narrator to tell the tale during our new show. Again I found someone thanks to my laundry deliveries.

I would deliver table linen to the trendy restaurants in Knightsbridge and in one of those, Parkes, the headwaiter was a fellow Glam fan (in his case Roxy Music). Jon Rinous, he was a keyboard player and actor. He had an excellent English ascent and had a penchant for cocaine. He was perfect.

The only problem was his lack of a keyboard. I soon rectified that though and lent him the money to buy a Korg Vocoder.

I spent Christmas with my Mum in Preston and travelled back on Boxing Day, no dramatic car journeys this time, I let the train take the strain. We started the rehearsals in the front room of 66 Princes Sq., all the new band were there except for John Gastor.

To be honest, the band were technically not that good but Ian Ritchie made us sound great, he stripped the songs down to bare bones and then added layers of well constructed rhythms to run below my melodies, his arrangements were phenomenal.

The next evening and the eve of our all-dayer gig we hired a rehearsal room in Chelsea, again everyone was there except John Gastor, despite endless assurances that he was 'on his way', he never turned up. I got so fucked off with him and told him to shove his drumsticks up his arse and rang up Animal who swiftly came to our rescue.

The Lyceum gig was scary, the biggest venue we had played and the debut of my new band and my new show 'The Adventures of Shock Rock'.

I was treading the same boards that Marc Bolan performed on, with The Futuristic Dragon tour and where John Lennon played his last UK gig with the Plastic Ono band.

In addition to the music we incorporated a couple of wannabe actors, they were to be Biff who would play a Neo Nazi type character and an Alien and Paul Peculiar was to be his accomplice.

The problem was Biff got drunk the night before (I suppose it was New Year's Eve) and arrived two hours after we finished. Animal's girlfriend Tina had to stand in, it-looked ridiculous Paul and Biff were 6 '2" foot tall whereas Tina stood a mere 4'11". Our Neo Nazis suddenly looked like the Slumberland ad with the Hippo and the duck with neo swastikas.

We had a really strange end to the show, it would just finish sharply mid song and a huge Neutron Bomb pyrotechnic would go off, the lights would snap off too. When they came back on, the stage was empty. It was actually very clever, the audience didn't react, just silence, not realizing if we had finished. After a moment though people started to applaud.

The next show was at The Embassy Club in Bond St, it was extremely good, the band were tight, Animal had found his groove and a new image as a rampant reverend. We reduced the acting so Biff played all the parts and we didn't let him out of our sight until after the gig.

We rehearsed two extra songs, one for Andrea to sing 'Neon Dungeon', and a song I wrote five years earlier 'Jivin'. We slotted Neon Dungeon into the set to allow me to do a costume change and saved Jivin' for the expected encore.

The venue was packed, all of Shock were there, as was Joanne Whalley, Richard Burgess o Landscape and Lemmie from Motorhead (although I'm not sure that he watched us, he seeme more interested in playing on the fruit machine in the bar). Kim and Janey were also there until Kim stormed out in tears – read on.

At the end of the set, the audience erupted and of course we did the encore, Jivin'. We wer definitely on the right tracks, a modern sound, a shit tight band, a very glammy 80's look an loads of people in the audience who didn't walk out.

Shortly afterwards we returned to Majestic studio to recorded two more songs, at long la Jivin' and a new song I had written 'Dance Dance'. Once again Janey sang backing vocals.

During all this time I was still working during the day as a driver for Brooks Textile Rentals. wasn't however only my working life that was getting busy and complicated so too was r personal life. Colm and Kim had split up and I started seeing Kim, first of all as a friend b shortly afterwards as a girl friend. So I now had at least two girl friends, Janey and Kim plus couple of other flings and for a couple of months I never slept alone.

If I wasn't with Janey or Kim I would have other bed buddies who dared to enter the lair th was 66 Princess Sq. I was certainly more than making up for the drought of the year befor

Kim obviously knew I was going out with Janey hence the storming out of the Embassy, Janey however didn't know about Kim, that was until Coombsey threatened to tell her. He didn't get the chance though as I beat him to it. She wasn't too happy but she, like Kim also had complicated relationships of their own.

Janey was in fact engaged to a guy who was living in Saudi Arabia and although Colm and Kim had gone their separate ways there was a time during the early part of our relationship that she left me and they got back together again. One thing was for sure. Something had to give.

The gigs were still going well and a month later we returned to The Embassy, another great gig, two encores this time Jivin' and Dance Dance.

Lots more record company A and R men were turning up at the shows and checking us out, partly due to Coombsey's hassling, partly due to Ian Ritchie's recommendations and partly due to the vibe we were creating. Would this buzz prove to be enough to secure a record deal, only time will tell.

I recall one gig at Legends when Gary Glitter turned up with his producer and co songwriter Mike Leander. He arrived before the show and an excited Coombsey came running down to my dressing room, 'guess who's upstairs', 'no idea' I said, he was nearly creaming himself "Gary fuckin Newman' I said, he said 'nearly, Gary Glitter'. I said 'fuck me, is he staying to watch us' Coombsey said 'he can't' but suggested we should go upstairs and meet him. I had in fact met Gary a year earlier when he did a failed Rock n' Roll Circus with Gerry Cottle, I got on really well with him and thankfully when we met again in Legends he remembered me.

I persuaded him to stay and it was great to see him dancing to my music instead, of as had previously happened, me dancing to his. After the show we all went to the bar for a drink and Mike Leander showed interest in us signing for his label. Mike was the co-writer with Gary Glitter of all those brilliant 70's anthems. In the 60's and 70's he had worked with Marianne Faithful, Billy Fury, Marc Bolan, Joe Cocker, The Small Faces, Van Morrison, Alan Price, Peter Frampton, Keith Richards, Shirley Bassey, Lulu, Jimmy Page, Roy Orbison, Brian Jones and Gene Pitney. It would have been great to add Haze to that list.

Gary said he really enjoyed the show and offered us a few words of wisdom, telling me to make the audience 'want to fuck me', he proclaimed that he 'wanted to fuck me' but said he wanted to 'fuck Kim too'.

We both, although flattered, obviously declined his offer but I knew what he meant, what does a guitarist need a guitar for if it's not to use it as a dick extension.

Around the same time another friend of mine Peter 'Psycho' Skull would regularly come to gigs, he still booked some of our shows and had now become a good friend albeit always a friend with a crisis. He would bring along a friend of his Chris Barrie. Chris was now an impressionist, on the Comedy circuit, and claimed he had perfected a great 'Haze' impression in readiness for my forthcoming star status.

Of course Chris beat me too it, becoming famous for one of the voices in Spitting Image, as Arnold Rimmer in the sci-fi sitcom Red Dwarf, as Gordon Brittas in the BBC sitcom The Brittas Empire and as Lara Croft's butler Hillary in Tomb Raider.

Coombsey was still touting our music around the record companies, one of those appointments turned out to be a management company B and E Management, I went with him. I'm not sure what the E stood for but the B stood for Bolan, Marc's wife, June Bolan in fact. We both went to see June, she looked great and turned out to be a really nice person.

Stupidly Coombsey arrived at B and E's offices without any of our recordings, the twat left them at home. We did send them to her later and she seemed to like them and gave me her home number, I would ring her occasionally for advice but neither of us ever mentioned Marc. She obviously knew though that I was a Marc Bolan fan and possibly that is why she was so supportive.

She recommended us to EG Records (could the E in EG be the same as the E in B and E Management? I certainly knew who the E in EG was, David Enthoven, former manager of T-Rex, Roxy Music, King Crimson and later to revive his career as manager of Robbie Williams.

The whole template was there, we had a good band, lots of gigs, were recording lots, and were getting more than our fair share of either upcoming or established celebrities coming to the shows. The one thing we lacked was a good manager, Coombsey talked the talk but he couldn't walk the walk, he seemed to have loads of appointments but as he did with June, once inside their offices he would, either forget the tape or take four or five tapes of different bands with him, there was no focus, it was more like a lucky dip.

June told us that E and G wanted to come and see us live, as did Mike Leander again, we quick went out to get another venue to book us, the one gig we needed actually and ended up being ten shows.

Myself and Coombsey went to see Gulliver's, a club in Down Street, Mayfair, they were keen put us on, but only, if we did a similar deal to Gossips where we run a specific night with video and a DJ. I wasn't so keen to do this but told Coombsey we would do every other Wednesd I honestly thought we'd end up doing two or three.

We called the night 'The Electric Music Hall', it turned out to be a great success and gave us the perfect showcase, and on one occasion five different record companies came to see us. We just needed that final push.

Although the Gullivers gigs were a success we still had our fair share of disasters, these disasters, often attributed to Paul Peculiar and often where he had kindly stood in for someone. Gullivers didn't have a house PA or lighting rig so we used to hire them in from a guy called Hugh Sadlier, Hugh would operate the PA and his brother would operate the lights. One week his brother didn't show up so Paul Peculiar offered to stand in. Oh oh, if Paul had been a Mr. Man he would have been Mr. Clumsy.

Paul said he'd operated the lights in a trendy club in Wrexham, in fact he worked as a bar man in a workingmans club in Wrexham and switched the house lights off when the main turn came on.

We were mid-way through the first song and Paul decided to push every fader to full, this drew too much power and not only sent the club into darkness but also the whole of Mayfair.

An hour later, the mains were put back on but Gulliver's wouldn't allow us to use the lights so we had to finish the gig in candle light, very romantic but hardly the neon look of the New Romantics.

Two weeks later Paul was back, the gig went without a hitch until the end of the evening, I asked him to throw away an unused piece of the dry ice. Dry ice is the solid form of carbon dioxide (chemical formula: CO_2), it is so cold you can't touch it with your bare hands or you will stick to it. Paul had the bright idea of emptying it down the toilet pan. The pan promptly shattered before our eyes and we all did a runner.

Another two weeks had passed and after getting a ticking off from Gulliver's manager for our unruly fans' breaking his toilet we were told that Biff had done it again, got pissed and got on the wrong train, ending up in Greenford instead of Green Park and missed the gig. It was apparent Biff wasn't going to arrive on time so we needed someone else to play the Neo Nazi and the Evil Alien, Paul Peculiar volunteered. Please no, its bound to end it tears, and it did.

Paul pulled off the Neo Nazi OK but when he donned the cape with huge padded shoulders and Darth Vader mask, he put the cape on inside out with the foam padding sticking out all over the place, talk about Darth Vader, this was Daft Vader. He came out from the wings and we all started laughing and I called him Steptoe. He suddenly got stage fright and ended up just pepping shyly round the corner in this stupid mask and foam rubber cape. John Rinous was laughing so much he fell off his raiser onto Animals drum kit, which in turn sent the drums rolling all over the stage. The Who would have been proud of us!

Aside from our live shows, a broader view of the world saw Britain at war with Argentina over the occupation of the Falklands, thankfully it ended quickly. Duran Duran were emerging as a major force and Coombsey was becoming more inept and the situation between Kim and Janey had come to a head, it was decision time.

We agreed to get John Rinous to start taking our music around the record labels and I decided to dump Janey and become the full-time boyfriend of Kim.

We hadn't actually sacked Coombsey but didn't give him exclusivity on hawking our music around. We did a couple more gigs around town and then I heard that Gary Glitter was going to play two summer shows in Great Yarmouth with the Radio 1 road show and at The Venue in London.

I had kept in touch with Mike Leander and sent him our recordings of Jivin' and Dance Dance, he still hadn't made up his mind as to whether to sign us. I asked him if he could arrange for us to support Garry Glitter at his two shows. He said 'I know Gary is a fan of yours, I'll ask him'. Again flattered by Gary's alleged comments, first of all he wanted to fuck me, this time he's a fan of mine. A few days later I received a call from Mike Leander telling me Gary Glitter had agreed to our offer to support him.

We opened for Gary Glitter in Gt. Yarmouth with the Radio 1 road show and once again he remembered me when we turned up for the sound check. His roadie though proved a little over zealous and wouldn't allow us to use our pyrotechnics that was until I had a hissy fit with him and demanded he consulted Gary. Gary of course allowed us to use them and in fact we lent them to him to use for his set too.

Both gigs were brilliant and my Mum and Animal's Mum turned up to see our London date with the Leader. I liked Gary Glitter, I was a fan in the 70's and I saw no signs of his infamy that was to curse his life later on.

John Rinous did have an inkling though and said to me he thought that Gary had the eyes of a pervert, I thought John had taken too much of the white stuff again but he turned out to be right.

Gary Glitter was definitely a real talent and a great showman with some good songs, sadly, he was obviously hiding other urges.

As I predicted Wham! had begun their run of incredible success, you couldn't knock the quality of the songs but they were typical of the time.

If you consider Paul McCartney and Stevie Wonder were number one for seven weeks with the awful Ebony and Ivory. This gives you an idea of the complete tosh that was now Top of the Pops.

A highlight of the year for me though was seeing The Rolling Stones at Wembley just as T-Rex had done five year's earlier, they restored my faith in Rock 'n' Roll.

John Rinous was doing well with his trips around the Record Companies and got interest from RAK Records, Mickey Most's company. The A and R person Brenda Brooker and Mickey Most's brother came along to a show in West Hampstead and really liked it.

As the year progressed, I took a holiday with Kim to Majorca, It was the first time either of us had flown, we were both nervous, in her case so much so she was crying. This made me see the funny side and I was fine.

It was a great budget holiday and supplied the much-needed rest and escape from what I thought was reality.

We did two more gigs that year and I felt we were losing momentum. I have always been a live performer, I find recording boring although I am generally pleased with my piece of art that comes out at the end of it.

Ian Ritchie tried to persuade me to give up the live shows and continue to record, he was totally wrong and in many ways the writing was on the wall.

RAK liked my songs but for a first release wanted me to record other peoples songs and paired me up with a producer, we sort of co-wrote a song with him and went into RAK Records to record it. They had a lovely studio in Swiss Cottage. The song 'Love Revolution' had a Culture Club feel about it and Ian played a blistering sax on the recording.

It didn't quite impress RAK enough and they asked us to go back in the studio and suggested we try a cover, the particular cover was Black is Black. Originally a 1966 hit for Los Bravos, it had already been covered in the 1980's as a disco track and I didn't see the point so I refused, was a mistake.

In the same tradition as London Buses, record deals all come along at once and while I was still in discussions with RAK I was offered a deal with a guy called Peter Calendar. He was predominantly a songwriter and had wrote, The Ballad of Bonny and Clyde and all of the Paper Lace hits. In all he had four Number Ones in both the UK and the States.

The good thing about the deal with Peter Calendar was he wanted to record my songs.

What complicated things though were that the publishing deal came in tandem with a management deal, this was offered by an agency called Thomas and Bender. Ian Ritchie was adamant that I shouldn't sign, he didn't see the value of signing a publishing deal unless it was going to pay you money.

I was in a real dilemma, I was sat in Thomas and Bender's office with this contract in front of me, signing it meant I would probably lose my deal with RAK and I would piss off our best musician, Ian Ritchie.

The thing was, this was what I had always wanted, what I had dreamed about, not quite a record deal, not yet, but a management and publishing deal that had a guaranteed record deal built into it. I rang Brenda Brooker at RAK and said, "are you definitely going to sign me", she said, "I think so, we just want you to record some more first". Her response didn't help. I needed her to be decisive.

The sequence of events that followed were straight out of Monty Python, I had travelled to Thomas and Bender's office in one of the Brooks vans and parked it on a single yellow line. I took my uniform off in the back of the van and replaced it with my Glam Punk look.

I was supposed to be out delivering laundry and instead I was signing a publishing deal, Ian Ritchie, left telling me and the management company that I was making a mistake. As he left I looked out of the window to see him leaving and saw a van lifting my Brooks van up and towing it away. I ran down the stairs and outside just in time to see it disappearing in the distance.

I shouted Noooo and Ian Ritchie looked back thought I was shouting at him and he shouted back 'oh good you've seen sense and changed your mind'. I hadn't I was just trying to get the van back.

I turned to go back into the offices when I saw Peter Coombes running down the road, I thought I was dreaming, I have no idea how he found out but he heard that I was about to sign the deal, unlike Ian he thought I should sign but he wanted a piece of the action.

I told him he was too late and had missed his chance, he then threatened to chain himself to the gates to stop me going back inside.

Peter Bender then persuaded Coombsey to come inside and discuss everything. Coombsey pleaded to be involved and offered his services to the management agency. They agreed, but would only put him on trial.

I signed the deal and then set about finding my van, which had been towed away, I took a tube to the pound in Hammersmith paid £20 and got it back.

I changed back into my Brooks uniform and drove back to the depot in Putney, they asked why it had taken me so long to make the delivery, I blamed the traffic,

As you can imagine, Coombes either wasn't up for the job or didn't try.

His trial didn't go well and he was soon omitted from the deal.

Shortly afterwards I moved out of Bayswater and into a council flat with Kim in Clapham. I didn't want to let anyone down in Princess Sq. and persuaded Paul Peculiar to take my room. I don't know why I felt at all obliged to not let Coombsey and Tim down but I did. It's a shame they didn't show me the same solidarity.

Despite Ian Ritchie's reluctance to me signing with Peter Calendar he still continued to record with us although he refused to do any live gigs.

We were booked into a really expensive studio in Finchley and we recorded Jivin' again and a new song called 'Lounge Lizard'.

For the first time budget wasn't an issue, Nick Neutron played keys, Ian programmed the drums, Phil played bass and played some strange recorder type thing and we brought in Kim Wilde's guitarist for the session.

I rated and still do rate Ian Ritchie very highly but this time he got our sound completely wrong and his arrangements on these tunes were rubbish.

The sound was weak, I was a rocker and between Ian Ritchie and Peter Calendar they were wrapping me up into naff bubble gum pop.

I was a lot happier with the recording at Majestic, they were modern but they had bollocks and cost a fraction of the price.

We travelled to Peter Calendar's mansion in Beaconsfield and recorded two video's, one for each song. We had completely stopped gigging to concentrate on this project and it looked like it was about to pay off.

We were offered a deal with Lamborghini Records, with an £20,000 advance and Jivin' was due for release in January 1984.

I was told of all the details of the contract and met the MD of Lamborghini for dinner in a hotel in Marble Arch.

I don't know what went wrong, I was told the deal was in the bag, I would have received a percentage of the £20,000 advance and I could, at last have given up my job at Brooks and all my concentration would have been on the music. Unfortunately it never happened and we were back to the drawing board.

With the Lamborghini deal now in tatters Peter Bender got us a gig at The Embassy to showcase our new tunes to more potential record companies.

I was OK with this, I liked gigging and had written some new tunes that we could play there.

Guitarist Brian Evans wasn't available and Ian Ritchie did not believe we should be doing showcases or any live gigs and refused to do it.

Without Ian's arrangements we were in the shit. We played reasonably well but went on far too late and most of the audience walked out before the end.

The next day I received a call from Peter Calendar who told me to sack the entire band and start again, he said they look crap and can't play. I couldn't do it, I felt drained and they were all my mates. So that was that, music had almost ruined my friendship with Chris Cleen and I didn't want that to happen again. I was so fucked off with the music industry and when I woke up on my 25th birthday I thought I was too old, I'd missed my chance and I decided to give up music altogether.

To rub salt in the wounds in 1984 Gary Glitter had a hit with a song called 'Dance Me Up' which was a complete rip off of my 'Dance Dance'. I had given tapes of Dance Dance and Jivin' to Mike Leander when he was interested in signing me, he had obviously kept them, nicked the chorus and melody of Dance Dance and added it to his song 'Dance me up'.

Brian Evans went onto become a very successful engineer with T-Rex and David Bowie produce Tony Visconti, he also became a producer in his own right.

Joanne Whalley became Joanne Whalley Kilmner, after she married Hollywood legend Val Kilmer while filming the fantasy adventure Willow. She continued filming in Hollywood, including the mystery noire, Shattered and, in 1989, the role of Christine Keeler in Scandal alongside star John Hurt and Sir Ian McKellen. In 1994 she became the second actress to play Gone with the Winds heroine, Scarlet O'Hara, when she appeared in a made-for-TV adaptation of the sequel novel, Scarlet.

After a break from filming to raise her two children with Val Kilmer, she filed divorce papers after he left to film The Island of Dr. Moreau in 1996. He found out about it from a CNN broadcast.

Janey Le Grace became backing vocalist with the Wilsations, Wham! Kim Wilde and Boy George, she was in Eurovision and went on to have her own top ten hit as Cola Boy with Seven Ways To Love. She has presented shows for Virgin Radio, BBC London and Radio 1. She wrote the best-selling book 'Imperfectly Natural Woman'. She also appears regularly on Radio 2's Steve Wright show.

Chris Barrie perfected his impressions and provided the voice of Ronald Reagan in the pop song "Two Tribes" by Frankie Goes to Hollywood and worked on Spitting Image before he played the character Arnold Rimmer in nine series of Red Dwarf. He also played Gordon Brittas, the well-meaning but incompetent manager in The Brittas Empire.

The show ran for seven series and 52 episodes – including two Christmas specials.

Ian Ritchie released a couple of singles in the 1980's under the name Miro Miroe. He played on "See the Day" by D. C. Lee, "Club Tropicana" by Wham, "C'est La Vie" by Robbie Nevil and more recently on his debut jazz album "Ian Ritchie's SOHO Project". He toured as the saxophonist with Roger Waters as part of the band on the Dark Side of the Moon Live tour.

Gary Glitter had a hit with Another Rock 'n' Roll Christmas and Dance Me Up, the rip off of my song Dance Dance. He completed large arena tours of the UK and was convicted and jailed for alleged child sex abuse.

Carol Caplin became Cherie Blair's style Guru. She hit the newspaper headlines in the scandal referred to as "Cheriegate" because of her involvement with Peter Foster, a convicted Australian conman, who assisted Cherie Blair in the purchase of two flats in Bristol.

George Michael became a superstar selling over 100 million records.

Depeche Mode continued their success and also sold over 100 million records

got promoted to transport manager with Brooks, big fucking deal.

Haze, the Brooks days, photo credits, from Haze's personal collection

CHAPTER NINE
PARALLEL LINES

I went to London to find fame and fortune and ended up driving a lorry for a Textile Rental Company! A laundry by any other name.

Sound's familiar, well allow me to take you on a second journey, not a journey of Rock 'n' Roll but a journey of a second life, a second job, a job that didn't matter, a job I didn't talk about, but ultimately the job that supported my Rock 'n' Roll ambitions.

After arriving in London I slept under a bridge in Hammersmith, I had found a shit hole of a bed-sit in Waldemar Ave, Fulham, I borrowed £50 off my Mum to pay the deposit and the first weeks rent.

I now needed to get a job, I had rent to pay and I needed to earn a crust until my Rock n' Roll dream was fulfilled. I signed onto a temp agency and they found me work driving a lorry.

The work was with a so called Textile Rental Company, 'Brooks Textiles', who's London depot was in Putney.

Calling a Laundry a Textile Rental Company somehow gives it a bit more credibility. True it did own the linen, sheets, pillow cases, towels, table clothes etc, they would rent them to restaurants or hotels and then collect them every week and wash them. So a Laundry basically.

I was offered one days work to deliver the clean laundry and collect the soiled linen from their various clients'. It was a pretty shit job but I wasn't really in a position to complain, I worked hard during my one day and was approached by the then Transport Manager, who said he could only give me a full time job if I left the agency I was with as Brooks would not pay the agency commission.

The next day the agency sent me to another job, this was to last four days and was in a cardboard factory in Park Royal, I have no idea what I did for those four days, moved a few cardboard boxes I think. The Agency offered me another days work in Brooks on the Saturday.

The night before however I met up with Billy Wild who was still working for Gerry Cottle's Circus, they were coming to Shepherd's Bush. I had a Chinese take away with Billy and he offered me a job billing.

I turned him down, I wasn't going to fall into that trap again, I returned home to Waldemar Ave. at around midnight and went to bed but forgot to set my alarm.

I woke up late and didn't go to Brooks for my work on the Saturday. On Monday I rang the agency and told them I was ill, they said I had let them down and couldn't work for them again. I then promptly walked to Brooks, told the transport supervisor I had left the agency and he gave me a full time job, ironically I had to let Brooks down in order to get a full time job with them.

I started my full time job with Brooks the next day, it was really disorganized and deliveries would regularly go out late, this basically meant you had to do overtime. I had no problem with this as long as it didn't affect my time as a wannabe Rock 'n' Roller or my personal life.

I can't say I enjoyed delivering laundry but I did enjoy earning more money. I would regularly buy outlandish clothes from Kings Road and would always be out watching bands such as The Damned, The Hunter Ronson Band, Iggy Pop and loads more. On the football front, in addition to watching PNE whenever they were in town I also took my first couple of trips to see England at Wembley.

There were nine drivers at Brooks, made up of London lads whereas the factory staff were a mixture of Asian workers who they drove in from Southwell and their Putney counterparts who generally lived in the council flats at the end of the road.

The factory was situated in Pentlow St., off Lower Richmond Rd. and only about a mile from Barns Common where Marc Bolan met his untimely death. I didn't even realize this when took the job. I did realize though that my walk to work each day across Putney Bridge would fill my mind with thoughts of HG Wells War of the Worlds and visions of Martians in their tripods coming the other way.

I didn't particularly hang out with anyone from Brooks although most of the drivers were nice guys. The Transport Supervisor though was a little strange, he bore a definite resemblance to Blakey from 'On the Buses' both in mannerisms and in looks. We all actually called him Blakey (behind his back of course). It's probably fair to say that I made more friends with my customers than with my work colleagues although everyone at Brooks supported my Rock 'n' Roll ambitions and would occasionally come to gigs and buy the merchandise.

Even the managers at Brooks were supportive; every so often they would lend me a van to move our gear around and for me to move house from Waldemear Rd. to 327 Wimbledon Park Rd. Nor did they ever complain about my vividly and often changing hair colour, one-week pink, one week blue, sometimes multi-colored but generally black and blond.

In my first Christmas in London I managed to get the train home to Preston to see my Mum, it was very much a fleeting visit though, leaving on the last train on Christmas Eve and returning on the first train on the 27th December.

As my time in the big smoke progressed I got more used to driving around London and consequently the job got easier. I still remember though, every Friday afternoon, whilst delivering to The Priory how I used to think to myself 'what the fuck am I doing this for'. I then reminded myself that it was Friday afternoon and a weekend off beckoned.

During my first year I didn't save much money and I was not there long enough to qualify for a paid holiday. Nevertheless I took two weeks unpaid holiday and went to Preston. Tommy Fossett had a new show called Fosserfields Circus, they were just down the road in Ormskirk and asked me if I would do a weeks work for them billing and getting some press in the local paper. I decided to do it but made it clear that it was a one off and I was returning home to London the next week.

The fact that most of Flash Harry lived in one house had its advantages, we rehearsed in the basement for example, it was always a problem though when people left the band. The first 327 dweller to leave was Gilmore but as he did a runner from the house and the band at the same time it didn't rock the boat too much.

When Colm left to join another band however it was different, he left the band but stayed in the house and became a rival as well as a housemate. His new band were pretentiously called Panache, they were better looking than our Glam builder look (although I exclude myself and Chris Cleen from that reference).

They were very glammy and to be fair they were reasonably good, they were quickly offered a record deal in Japan. Suddenly 327 Wimbledon Park Rd. had two budding and rival bands living here, one with a record deal and it wasn't us.

The rivalry didn't last long though as Colm and Kim moved out of 327 and into a council flat in Clapham.

A driver from Brooks called Bob and his girlfriend Kate took Colms room, they provided great entertainment with their often-heated domestics.

Always overstated and loudly executed to make sure we all heard Kate pulling a blunt kitchen knife on him.

As summer approached I started seeing Janey and she would come over and stay the night, we had to be quiet though as Chris Cleen was sleeping in the same room.

My first date with Janey was a leaving party for one of the drivers, it was in a pub in Chelsea. He had shocked the workforce when his resignation letter which stated:-

'I am reluctantly leaving my position as a driver as I am a transvestite.

I am undergoing hormone replacement and intend in a year or so to have a full sex change, during this period my breasts would grow and I would have to come to work wearing a bra' which would not match my uniform'.

He was clearly effeminate but no one knew about his secret until now, I was the more open minded of my butch driver comrades so you can only imagine what they all thought.

True to form, he turned up to his leaving do in full drag and was of course accompanied to the ladies toilets by the giggling factory girls. The drivers found it a bitter pill to swallow, one of their own was 'a bloody poofter' but nevertheless wished him well in his new found life.

Thankfully, Janey was also open minded, our only difference of opinion was the fact that she thought he made a convincing woman, I thought he looked like a builder in drag, in fact, if he could play guitar we would have given him a job in Flash Harry.

I managed to have quite a lot of time off this year, firstly my broken nose incident had given me two weeks off sick. This was swiftly followed by a sail-training course.

Brooks ran a scholarship scheme for some of its younger and less privileged employees and I qualified for this (although I'm not sure that it is actually a compliment). It was a sort of personal fulfillment training, it came in the shape of sail-training course on what I can only describe as a three-mast galleon.

It was a real time warp and a great experience, we set sail from Swansea hoping to turn left to France but instead turned right and headed for the Outer Hebrides, I was horrendously sick 11 times the first day and on various occasions during the trip.

Despite my motion sickness, it was amazing to see this beautiful replica of our seafaring year docked in the fabulous surroundings of Stornoway, I don't know if I gained anything from this but it sure beat delivering fucking laundry to The Priory.

My third and final break of the year was my first holiday abroad when Animal and myself spent two weeks in France, only to return home to see Flash Harry falling apart.

On a personal front I was still seeing Janey but started seeing Kim as well, this came about after going to see Panache, Colms new band. Kim was there but informed me that Colm had left her for another woman.

For the next few weeks I started seeing Kim, originally just as friends until we both attended a party with Paul Peculiar and we got it together. This was the beginning my unique love triangle that was resolved by splitting up with Janey and going the whole hog with Kim.

Back at Brooks, Blackey had been offered promotion to production manager and all the drivers were asked to apply for the job of Transport Manager. I declined and explained my involvement in Rock 'n' Roll could infringe on any extra responsibilities. I had been getting on really well with Kim and we decided to move in together.

She had a council flat in Clapham and it seemed logical that we lived together, I persuaded Paul Peculiar to move into my room in 66 Princes Sq. We didn't stay too long in Clapham though after Kim was attacked, our car was nicked and we were burgled, it was time to move again.

A couple of months before we left, to prevent further break ins, we nailed the windows shut. During our time in the flat we had also, painted one of the rooms black (very badly) and stored a coffin in the spare room. We moved out but left the coffin in the spare room, we also left the windows nailed shut and took all the light bulbs with us, although this was really just me being tight. After we had moved out Kim received a call from the Clapham Council saying the council workers refused to go in there to get it ready for the next tenant until it had been exorcised.

We found a small two bedroom flat in Colliers Wood and bought our first home for £18,000, we were there 18 months before I decided that my Rock 'n' Roll ambitions were over.

It just happened overnight really, I somehow thought I had missed my chance and decided that was that.

This is where my parallel life ended and I concentrated on my unwanted career in Brooks.

For the next five years I turned into Mr. Suburbia, gone were the blond and black corkscrew curls to be replaced by a side parting. Gone was the Glam gear to be substituted by a suit and gone was the fun.

had joined the free market revolution created by Margaret Thatcher who was in her second term as prime minister and on her way to winning a third. This all despite an assassination attempt by the IRA when they detonated a bomb in The Grand Hotel, Brighton during the Tory party Conference.

Everybody was encouraged to buy his or her own houses. We joined that revolution and purchased 64 Grove Rd, Colliers Wood. We stayed there two years and doubled the money we paid for it, selling it for £32,000, making £18,000 profit. We then bought a house in South

Wimbledon, again stayed two years and sold that to Peter Skull, this time making £30,000 profit. We then went on and bought a house in Wimbledon itself for £103,000 using our £30,000 profit as a deposit.

Musically the mid 80's were shit. In fact almost all of the music in the 80's was shit. The highlights were the Live Aid concerts at Wembley, Bowie but particular Queen were brilliant that night and proved there was life after Glam.

Despite my dislike of 80's music, there were a few exceptions to the rule, I really liked Sigue Siuge Sputnik and I went to see Duran Duran, Frankie Goes to Hollywood, who were suprisingly good as was Michael Jackson. I also saw David Bowie, two Queen gigs, one of which was Freddie Mercury's last ever performance. The one that would again restore may faith in Rock 'n' Roll for the third time, was Alice Cooper on his 'The Nightmare Returns' tour.

Now my Rock 'n' Roll dream had gone I started to accept promotions with Brooks, from transport manager to production manager, to factory manager, to operations manager and finally to general manager in a new factory they had bought in West Norwood.

I was sent on a six months course for senior management, I came first and won a scholarship in Denmark. I hated every minute of it. The only bit of excitement I got from my time at Brooks was when I saw one of our drivers on Crimewatch after he was wanted for abducting a 20 year old girl and the day we had a wages snatch.

The wages were delivered in cash to Brooks every Friday at 10am, someone must have either tipped the gang off or they simply staked out the factory for a couple of weeks and worked out what time to execute the raid. The Security Company had come and deposited the wages in the safe, they then left but before there was time to distribute the wages to the staff, they struck. Two stocky guys with full-face balaclavas on, burst into the office complex, I was in a separate office at the end and on the phone to our other branch.

I could hear all this commotion but ignored it thinking it as one of the drivers complaining about work. One of the office girls then ran into my office and said there was a hold up. She was followed by one of the guys carrying a sawn off shotgun covered in a plastic bag. immediately got up to confront him but soon realized it was not a good idea, he then told u to get on the floor and pointed the shotgun at my head.

Of course I did what he said, he then dragged us both into the hallway where he could see u His accomplice told the office manager Rita, to open the safe, she coolly told him, she woul open it if they didn't hurt anyone, he said he wouldn't hurt anyone if she hurried up. Not s cool though was the girl next to me who started screaming and crawling towards me, th prompted the first guy to wield his gun in our direction again, I told her to keep calm.

Within a few minutes they had collected their bounty and were gone, I jumped up, ran to my car and gave chase. At the gate, surprisingly was a police man, he was supervising a car clamping company picking up people's cars. The robbers must have run straight past him, he radioed for help and jumped in my car, we roared around West Norwood with the clamping lorry in hot pursuit, it felt just like The Sweeney.

We failed to find them and nor did the Police investigation. If only we had had CCTV.

In my private life Kim and I had bought three houses and sold two houses, had some great holidays together to Majorca, Greece, Turkey and America. I also gained some solace in Preston North End promotions but equal amounts of depression when they got relegated; they even had to seek re-election to the football league after finishing 91st out of the 92 professional teams.

A huge fall of grace for the once mighty PNE.

Despite their demise, as my music ambitions waned my love for Preston North End grew and I was going to quite a few games even though I often found myself standing on the terraces with only 3,000 to 5,000 other fans.

By the late 1980's, it was time for another change The Berlin Wall was torn down brick by brick as East and West Germany unified.

The Rave Culture and ecstasy were taking over the UK's club scene. The World was changing and thankfully music was changing for the better and my private life was also about to change fundamentally.

Kim and myself had moved into a new house in Wimbledon, we had a large mortgage but it didn't matter, we were both earning good money. The problem was she omitted to tell me that she was about to leave me.

Whether she knew she was going to leave me when we bought the house is unsure but what was about to transpire is she certainly knew there was a strong possibility of it.

It all came to a head on New Year's Eve 1989, It was a Saturday and that evening we were due to drive to Oxford to spend New Year's Eve with Kim's Sister and her Mum and Dad. Kim had gone out 'shopping' and I was watching the Preston North End goals fly in on teletext.

We were playing Sheffield United and winning 2-1 when the phone rang, it was a voice I didn't recognize and he claimed he had been having an affair with Kim for three years and told me they had just split up.

Somehow I knew it was true, I couldn't work out how I knew, it just made sense, the coming home late from work etc. I went crazy, threatening to kill him, at this point I heard the key going in the door, it was Kim arriving back from her 'shopping' expedition, I went crazy again this time with her and she just kept saying 'please don't hit me'.

Of course I had no intention of hitting her and luckily for her, my anger was lessened when from the corner of my eye I glanced at the teletext and saw Mark Patterson had just made it 3-1 for PNE. Surprising how a goal for North End can heal all wounds, well most of them anyway.

I have no idea if this guy's claims of a three year relationship were true, I certainly think whatever went on it couldn't have been for that long. One thing is for sure though is that Kim had betrayed me, she had cheated on me and definitely given me a false sense of security.

The timing of the purchase of our house in Wimbledon was particularly stupid of her, I had no way at that time of raising the money to buy her out. I'm sure she really did care for me and sure she wouldn't deliberately want to hurt me. She had well and truly fucked me in more ways than one.

Naturally we aborted our New Years Eve trip to Oxford and stayed in.

Surprisingly we still went to her sister's the next day and made passionate love on her sister's floor that night, the trouble was the damage was done.

The guy she had been having an affair with was a boring looking accountant for ITV and worked in the same building as her in the London Studios on the South Bank.

Although he told me she had left him I knew the fact that they worked together was going to cause more problems.

She continued to go to work everyday and I knew in my heart that our relationship was over. This guy had a lot more money than me and the lifestyle it brings with it made him a better prospect for Kim. I would never have believed Kim could have been so materialistic but I was proved wrong.

With Kim's imminent departure I thought I'd whet my whistle in the Rock 'n' Roll sea of debauchery again and called my mates Chris Cleen, Animal Jones and John Rinous. The idea was to do a 10-year anniversary gig 'just for fun', the thing is I take music far to seriously and can't do it 'just for fun'.

I found I had not lost my ability to write songs and set about writing a load of new tunes, the only survivors from the old set were Shock Rock and Jivin'. We brought in Mad Dog Ian James Gardner on guitar and Martin Bassett Jones who was a sales rep at Brooks to play second guitar.

Using the old boy network, I even stupidly recruited Peter Skull as our manager. We called the new band Haze II in the greatest traditions of the action movies.

It took Kim about six months to leave, I still loved her but I knew it was over and didn't see any reason to prolong the agony. I could never tell her to go though, instead I would return home each day hoping to find a 'Dear John' letter.

She eventually went and I was very upset at first but got over it. At least I had Rock 'n' Roll again. It took me a while to get my confidence with women back. You tend to forget how to chat someone up and when you get over that barrier you find it very hard to make the first move for fear of rejection.

After she left and for the next two years Kim did do the honourable thing and pay her half of the mortgage, it was an investment at first but once house prices dropped the investment wasn't so appealing. We came to an agreement that suited both sides, I would pay the mortgage and I would buy her out, but not until I could afford to do so. She couldn't have been fairer than that really.

So onwards and upwards, a reunion with the band to look forward to but would it be enough, would I be able to cope with playing 'just for fun' or would I want more. Only time would tell.

HAZE II

THE CRACK IS BACK

Photo credits, from Haze's personal collection

CHAPTER TEN
THE RESURRECTION

A few weeks after Kim left I decided to take a break and go on holiday to Vancouver. Peter Coombes had moved over there and although he had been an unreliable manager he was still my friend albeit an unreliable one of those too.

On the flight over to Vancouver I kept reminding myself about the occasion when I left Princess Square and I left one of my guitars behind.

Six months later I saw Tim Dry attempting to play it and I said 'oi, I'll take my guitar back' and he proclaimed that he had bought it for £50 from Coombsey. With this in mind I did worry that on my arrival in Vancouver he may not be there to greet me.

Thankfully, I needn't have worried, he was there and I had a great two weeks with him in the beautiful British Columbia.

I came home rightly refreshed and ready to continue my Rock n' Roll dream again.

Peter Skull booked our first gig in the Mean Fiddler for the 28th December.

By show time John Rinous had pulled out, it didn't help that he was our keyboard player and didn't have a keyboard. It was very much déja vu, the difference this time he was our main keyboard player so a Korg Oscoda wouldn't suffice. He kept assuring me he was buying a Korg M1 but realistically he didn't have a pot to piss in let alone a £1500 to buy a Korg M1. I decided to go ahead without a keyboard player.

We learned the songs in my house and then went to a rehearsal room to run through them. The rehearsals were awful, we were shitting ourselves.

We arrived at the Mean Fiddler at the allotted sound check time of 4pm, that is all of us except Ian James Gardner. Ian was so hideously late I had to convince the management at 'The Fiddler' that he had broken his leg. We were ready to do a runner. Our 10-year anniversary gig was about to collapse before it had begun when around the corner came Ian James Gardner, I quickly told him to limp and the show was back on.

We stormed it. We were back.

In addition to the ravers, the late 1980's also saw the emergence of Hair Rock or American Sleazy Glam with pioneers such as Motley Crue and Guns and Roses. Aerosmith had a brilliant album Pump and Alice Cooper too with Trash. Rock was back and so was I.

Animal Jones found the Mean Fiddler gig too stressful. Particularly the Ian James Gardner incident and left, Chris Cleen stayed for four more gigs before he found the travelling from Wales to London to do a gig for no money too much so he also left. We replaced Animal Jones with former Gary Newman drummer Barry Benn and brought in keyboard player James T Kirk.

Bass players though turned out to be our nemesis and we changed them regularly throughout the year. We were doing lots of gigs and building up a bit of a following and the shows were getting more and more theatrical.

If ever Spinal Tap needed inspiration then they need not look any further than our performances in the early 1990's. For a few shows Peter Skull persuaded a stripogramme to perform naked during a shower scene while we played another of my new songs 'Just so Psycho'. That was one of his more successful dealings and one that certainly put him in the good books with the rest of the band.

Although on stage I was a Rock 'n' Roll animal, off stage I still lacked confidence with the finer sex, that too was all about to change though. We were playing at The Grey Horse in Kingston and towards the end of the show I invited the audience to 'come and join the party' when we played in Fulham the following Tuesday.

Two girls came up to me after the show and asked me where the party was, I was obviously referring to the gig the following Tuesday but quickly said 'It's round my house', they said 'great can we come', of course I agreed but told them there was only going to be three people at this party. In actual fact most of the band came back too but one by one they left leaving me with the two girls and an instant cure for my lack of confidence. Most guys dream of a threesome and I was no exception, it did turn out a little strange though, I did the dirty deed with one of the girls but the other girl just lay next to us, she didn't even watch, which certainly was disappointment.

That summer I went on holiday with James Kirk and a friend of mine Ian Orron and his Uncle Jarvis, who was actually three years younger than him. We went to the Greek Island of Anti Paros. I'd been to Greece a few times, it was unspoilt during my first visits but I found generally the country was getting far too commercialized.

Anti Paros though was a lot less so, to get there you had to take a flight to Athens and then take a light aircraft to the island, it certainly was 'take a chance' airlines. There were no window in the plane, not that you needed them though as there was a large hole in the Fuselage and you could clearly see through it, in fact we had to walk around it when we disembarked.

In the days before the internet it was difficult to find out much about places like Anti Paros but I should have had a clue after I saw a picture of Ian standing on a beach stark naked.

Unbeknown to me Anti Paros was known as the island of Sex and Drugs and Rock 'n' Roll, of course it contained an unofficial nudist beach but it seemed to me that the whole island was one big nudist beach, so when in Rome.

I was a little worried that my willie would burn up in the sizzling sunshine while lying by the Aegean Sea but not worried enough to cover it in sun tan cream despite the many mock warnings from the more seasoned nudists.

I can't remember many drugs on the island but it was definitely the law to get shit faced every night, mainly on tequila, the idea then was to sleep it off while lying naked on the beach the next day. Not really my type of holiday but I thought I'd go along with it.

My newfound confidence allowed me to have a number of romantic interludes on Anti Paros, mostly harmless enough with the exception of one fling with the local gang leaders wife, particularly when he came looking for me with his Smith and Wesson 9mm semi-automatic.

Oh no not again, less than a year ago I had had a sawn off shotgun pointed at my head, now I had this armed lunatic chasing me around the island. I should have known better, only two days earlier he had rode his motorbike into the centre of a clubs dancefloor and shouted Malakas, Malakas, Malakas, pointing at all the holidaymakers. Malakas is the Greek word for Wanker. Uncle Jarvis knew what it meant and said to the guy on the bike "no you Malakas', that was it, it was like a western bar room scene, bar stools being broken over peoples heads, girls screaming. Brilliant.

Why oh why, with this guy's reputation did I try unsuccessfully to shag his wife. Thankfully I escaped the island in one piece and sporting a lovely all over tan.

On returning to the UK, it was back to work at Brooks and back to seeking Rock 'n' Roll stardom. Peter Skull had booked two gig's in Blackpool, it was the first time we had played outside London with the new band. The first night was a bit shit, a rock club called 'Le Tache but the second, in a venue called The Star on the Pleasure Beach was really good. This all whetted my appetite to go on tour and take our own brand of Glam punk on the road.

After that year we did a gig in a pub called The Wheatsheaf in Fulham, it was the 22nd December, my birthday. We had loads of pretty tacky stunts in the show one of which was where I would stab a hunchback on his hunch and he would fall to he floor. I would then kneel over him and sing 'The only sure thing'. We had done a gig two days earlier in The Cartoon in Croydon and I left my knife in its holder and when I went to remove it, the fake blood had congealed and it was well and truly stuck.

For some reason I looked behind me and saw a huge sword that bizarrely Ian James Gardner had brought along. I didn't think, I grabbed the sword and plunged it straight into the hunchbacks back.

It went straight through the padding, through the board that was strapped to his back and seemed to go into his spine. He collapsed to the ground like a sack of spuds, I didn't really know what to do, so I carried on, I knelt over him and sang 'The only sure thing in life is death'.

I remember thinking mid song 'Fuck me I'm singing the only sure thing is death over a corpse and I'm going to get arrested for murder on my birthday'. He got dragged off stage, still not moving and we went into our final song Fire with Fire, I kept glancing across, a lump firmly in my throat until I thankfully saw him get up.

It was a great relief to find out that it was the amount of whisky he had drunk and not Ian's sword that felled him so convincingly. We had a party back at my place after the show, it was pretty wild, loads of blow, loads of whisky and a few birds, I had taken one to my bed room only to find the hunchback, minus his hunch laying on my bedroom floor.

The girl grabbed his feet and dragged him into the other room leaving us to do the dirty deed

The next morning he came into my room complaining that his back was hurting, I said it must have been where we dragged you out of the room, somehow forgetting to mention the sword incident.

That Christmas like almost every previous Christmas I went to see my Mum and as always visited Basher Briggs who had now bought a house on his own after splitting up with his wife Preston North End were going through another of their lulls and were treading water in Division Three, of course I still went to see them and still, forever the optimist, believed that before long they would become a force in English football again.

As the New Year loomed I looked back at our partial success in Blackpool and my taste for taking the show on the road I decided to book a tour with the new band around the UK. The job of booking the tour was originally given to Peter Skull but he was pretty useless and ended up getting us just one or two gigs.

I quickly took over and managed to book another 12 venues, we now had a 14-night tour around the UK. Enough nights for me to take a two weeks holiday from work to do it.

I had become a real life Jeckel and Hyde. By day I was the booted and suited General Manager of Brooks Textiles and by night I was this leather clad Rock n' Roll monster.

To promote the shows, we had loads of large posters printed and took a quarter page ad in Melody Maker. I also spun loads of stories with various regional newspapers in the towns and cities we were visiting.

We changed the band around, Ian James Gardner decided to hang up his Glam rock boots and return to his folk rock band The Wyred and take up ventriloquism. We had a new Dutch drummer Dirk Sticks, new Bass Player Anthony Analio, and a new Guitarist Ed Furry.

Potentially it was a better band. Ed could play lots of widdly lead guitar until his tricks had run out, usually by the second song, he was then lost and would break a string or two. Dirk Sticks was fine until he got drunk which usually happened by the third song and Anthony was fine until he broke his fingernail, generally by song five when he looked as though he would burst into tears. Theatrically we were a little better and I had started using a few smallish illusions.

The tour went OK, some gigs were well attended and others such as The Horn of Plenty in St Albans had three men and a dog in the audience.

We didn't make any money and none of us got paid, I didn't actually lose money though. Basher's new abode proved very helpful as a free doss house while we were in the frozen north.

We did a number of gigs that summer, some in London and some in the towns and cites we had visited on the tour. The Railway Inn in Telford became a regular haunt.

My appetite for travelling was even stronger and that summer I went to Egypt for a holiday. My Mum, although a little worried, thought I was brave going to such an exotic country on my own, what I didn't tell her was that I would arrive in Cairo in the middle of the night with nowhere to stay.

On my arrival, the customs asked me where I was staying, I lied and said I had booked in a hotel called the Adelphia hotel I had read about in a guide book, I jumped into a Taxi and asked him to take me to The Adelphia and decided to take a chance.

He suggested another one that 'his brother owned', I took his advice and went instead to the cryptic 'his brothers hotel'.

It was a bit grim but by Cairo standards I suppose it was quite nice, I stayed there for three nights and took in as much sight seeing as you could fit in.

The Pyramids and Sphinx in Giza, a camel ride, The Museum of Cairo and the Tutankhamen exhibits within. There was even a Circus in town, I went to see it, it was a small show with poor acts but included a lion act. The lion trainer was like a superhero in a den of savage beasts.

I then took a train to the southern city of Luxor, which contains numerous ancient temples and burial grounds, the most famous were Karnack Temple, the Valley of the Kings and the Queens and the Temple of Hatshepsut.

The next day, moving further south to Aswan, then even further south to Abu Simbel. Abu Simbel is an archaeological site comprising two massive rock temples in southern Egypt on the western bank of Lake Nasser. It is about 290 km southwest of Aswan.

Unbelievably the temples were re-located to avoid them being submerged during the creation of Lake Nasser, a massive artificial water reservoir formed after the building of the Aswan High Dam on the River Nile.

The front of the Temple was huge, around 50 meters tall, inside though was a modern concrete structure that resembled a James Bond set.

To get to Abu Simbel I teamed up with three other people and took a taxi. The taxis in Egypt were like Flintstone cars with an engine, we left at 5am to avoid the heat of the Sahara on the 290km drive.

The obvious happened and the car had two punctures in the space of half an hour, even more obviously the taxi didn't have a spare tyre and on two occasions the driver flagged down two identical cars to borrow spare wheels off them.

After this epic trip I had culture overload, so I travelled across the Suez Canal to the Red Sea and stayed in a Bedouin village at the foot of Mount Sinai,

I resisted the dawn walk up the Biblical Mount Sinai in favour of wallowing on the beach although I do regret not visiting the place that allegedly hosted God's authorization of the Ten Commandments upon tablets of stone held by Moses. After all I have probably broken all of them. The last leg of my journey saw me return to Cairo for two nights and this time I did stay in the Adelphi. It was no better than Coptic. During my Egyptian adventure I had decided not to eat meat and avoided the legendary 'Pharaoh's Revenge', I survived until two days from the end, then it got me, fucking hell, Howard Carter's got a lot to answer for.

Back home things at Brooks had got worse, the senior managers were beginning to get culled and a year or so earlier two of my superiors were unceremoniously sacked on the same day and for no apparent reason.

I returned from my Egyptian trip to the UK and got a call from a friend of mine at Brooks Paddy Murphy tipping me off that I was going to be the next to get the sack, it seemed as though my time had come.

I arrived at work the next morning fired up and with intrepidation. I had not slept a wink and I was ready to tear the head off my potential assassin. It never happened, but there is no smoke without fire and my stay of execution had begun.

The next two evenings I went to Wembley to see my other hero (after Marc Bolan) Alice Cooper on the Hey Stoopid tour, as always he was awesome and I was inspired once again.

As autumn turned to winter all my spare time was spent doing gigs, we had changed bass player and drummers again, now with Ex Angle Witch bassist Pete Godzilla and Brian Bungo on drums.

After our UK tour earlier in the year we would embark on small weekend tours to the better venues. We also went into Hugh Saddler's studio which was squatting in a former public toilet in Fulham. We recorded a 12 inch version of Jivin' with the Sigue Sigue Sputnik inspired Jivin' goes Spunkmix and a short story 'The Samhain Saga' on the B side.

had agreed a distribution deal with Four Skin Records and a limited amount of the records were in the shops. Jivin' was released at Christmas 1992 and I went to my Mum's for Christmas and New Year. Long ball specialist John Beck now managed PNE and shortly after New Year I saw them narrowly lose to then Premiership team Sheffield Wednesday in the FA Cup.

got back to London worked as normal and got called into the office, the inevitable was about to happen. I had worked for Brooks for an unbelievable 12 years (mainly during my various rock incarnations). Talk about an endurance test. I took all the holidays I was entitled to but I did not have one day off sick in the past 10 years. The factory I was running was the only one in the whole group that at this point that was making money, they did the 'logical thing' and made me redundant.

Felt completely betrayed but relieved at the same time. I had only stayed there for the security so I now had to make my own security and vowed never to work for anyone ever again.

had a good case to sue for unfair dismissal and unfair selection for redundancy. I made my case clear to Brooks and the original offer of severance play of £8,000 was increased to £15,000 and I got a car thrown into the deal too.

The timing of my redundancy was perfect, I started plugging Jivin' and got quite a few radio stations to play it and even got it on the B play list on some stations, it sold reasonably well and I booked a tour a few weeks later.

At least I could now book a tour without the restraints of fitting it into a two-weeks holiday.

We were even starting to get paid for gigs and playing all over the UK and Ireland. Playing mainly in rock clubs but began to take a few gigs in Universities. The carousel of players continued though, Godzilla didn't like Kirk and left to be replaced by Bradley Bacon. He only lasted a few months, he wouldn't go to Ireland and he was replaced by Andy Higgins. We recruited a new drummer called Jess Johansson.

I had gone through a promiscuous patch until I met a girl called Joanna in the local record shop, she had seen the show in the Cartoon in Croydon a month or so earlier and her shop stocked Jivin'. We started going out with each other and she regularly stayed over at my house.

The band were now gigging regularly all over the UK, not just doing gigs at weekends but doing large tours, the show had improved and I had bought a number of large scale illusions. While we were in St. Andrews in Scotland we did a show one night then had a day off and a group of students agreed we could stay with them.

Their hospitality was amazing they gave us Haggis followed by mushroom tea made from the fresh crop they had picked on the golf course earlier. Most of the band had 50 each. I thought they wouldn't affect me so I took 100. About half an hour later I was floating on air, it was amazing, I'd never felt anything like it.

I took a walk down through a park by a river with one of the girl students. I just stopped and stared at the goal posts on the football pitch, saying wow, as if I had never seen goal post before. Everything seemed heightened, all the colours of the trees and bushes seemed day glo, the river seemed to be down a 100 foot ravine but I just had to try and touch it to see. A bird flew overhead and you could hear its wings flap and it looked like a pterodactyl.

Walking back to the house someone had set fire to the bins on the lampposts and they looked like giant candles, I could clearly hear a choir singing a requiem. Now I knew what it was like in Lewis Carroll's head.

The trip lasted about two hours until I kept falling in and out of it, not sure which was real life and which was drug induced. What a trip, I had never really been into drugs in a big way, blow didn't do much for me, coke was OK but I could take it or leave it but mushrooms were something special. A few years later Gerry Cottle informed me that whilst in rehab the doctor had told him 'everyone has a drug but thankfully most people never find it'. Gerry had found his with coke and I seemed to have found mine growing on St. Andrews golf course.

I did try mushrooms again in future years but they were never the same, I found if you were in the wrong frame of mind you can have a really bad trip, if you get it right though they are magic.

After the tour I returned home and started what would turn out to be a successful Management and Entertainment agency 'The Psycho Management Company', originally on my own but with the occasional help of Peter Skull then a year or so later with my current business partner Paddy Haveron.

I was booking more and more Universities for my band and the Student Union Entertainments Officers were asking me for more acts, I simply asked them what other acts they were booking and then went about contacting those acts directly and asking if I could represent them.

It was a very simple lesson in marketing, find out what people want, make sure you can supply it and make sure people know you can supply it. I was now making money from the agency and from the band and I didn't have to work for other people to do so.

Ed Furry left the band and was replaced by Steve Zenton, the band were now taking shape, the gigs were getting bigger and we had our first feature in a national paper, albeit The Daily Sport. We were also getting quite a few mentions in Kerrang!

Steve didn't last too long and we brought back Ian James Gardner on guitar. I suddenly realized what it was that made us appear to be a real life Spinal Tap, it was three word's 'Ian James Gardner'. In the times when he had left the band there was no 'Tap like' disasters, as soon as he rejoined they returned.

The first tour we did with him was in Ireland, we left London at 8pm, two hours late because Ian, as normal was late arriving. I drove a mini bus and trailer to Dumfries to get the 7am Ferry. Andy Higgins took a load of blow with him but was worried that he wouldn't get across the Irish borders with it, so he decided to try and smoke it all. He was so stoned that on the last few miles of the journey he was throwing up out of the van's window, shouting slow doooowwwn, I cocked a deaf un and continued to drive like a demon attempting to make our 7am deadline.

We arrived at the port just in time to see the ferry sail away. The problem was I had done a deal with the Ferry Company that we would get free travel if we played on the boat.

We got the next ferry, completely knackered, but still played a set minus Andy Higgins who was now being sick over the side of the boat, we tied a rope around his leg so he wouldn't fall while we were playing.

Once we got to Belfast we had to drive across Ireland to Galway. We eventually got there after driving for 24 hours, just in time to do the show.

Most of the shows went well in Ireland except for one that we had to do without James Kirk, as he was taken ill, we sounded like a punk band and got paid off after half an hour. We could see the students union entertainment manager waving a wad of Irish Punts at us from the wings bribing us to get off.

The most memorable shows though were in Belfast, we did one in The University of Ulster, which went OK. The next day we had a night off and Ian James Gardner talked someone into booking us in a club in the Falls Rd. on the pretence that we had a bazooka! Luckily that gig didn't go ahead.

The next day the reality of Northern Ireland at this time was clear after the IRA detonated a bomb in a chip shop in the Shankhill Rd, killing 10 people. The same night we were due to play the Catholic Queens University, I was foolishly determined that the show must go on and we played to a large but slightly hostile crowd. Once we moved out of Belfast things were less tense and after the show in Sligo we were given a bottle of Tequila as a bonus.

I remember being taken short during the show and pissing into a pint glass at the side of the stage. I left the glass on the floor and went back onto the stage. Half an hour later I glanced round and saw our Roadie Simon Harris completely pissed drinking my piss from the pint glass and mumbling that the lager was warm.

Although I didn't leave the glass of piss deliberately for Simon to consume I did feel the slightest twinge of guilt and decided to give the bottle of Tequila to Simon. It didn't last long though after our next gig in Waterford, we bet him to drink it down in one, he managed to down it i two. We couldn't believe it so decided to push each other into the shower to celebrate. The next morning the chambermaids called us in a panic to tell us that Simon was dead.

We all went downstairs and were just about to call the Police when Simon came stumblir down the stairs in his underpants, very much alive but still dead drunk, the chamberma started screaming as thought she'd seen a ghost. We all vowed never to drink again, all that except Simon who ordered a pint of Guinness.

The return to the UK was not quite as eventful as the journey to Ireland although it was anoth mammoth journey, we finished in Dublin at 11pm, packed our gear away drove through t' night to Belfast to get our free travel to Dumfries before the long drive to Guildford, aga arriving just in time to go on stage at Surrey University.

HAZE
Vs THE X FACTOR

WELCOME TO SIN CITY...

It is a futuristic metropolis set in the year 2020, where Mad Max dares to step into the House of Wax. A decrepit waxworks inside a broken-down funfair plays host to classic horror characters such as Frankenstein, Freddie Kruger and Vampires, as well as other heroes like Street Fighters, Fire Eaters, Illusionists, Escapologists and Jugglers. A unique musical and visual Xtravaganza... Dare you step into...

THE HOUSE OF WAX
A FUTURISTIC HORROR MUSICAL

HAZE ONSTAGE 8.30PM

marquee the club

105 CHARING CROSS RD, LONDON, WC2. Box Office: 071-437 6603

SAT 28 JAN

Photo credits, Sarah Photogirl

*The COH on the set of London's Burning
Photo credits, Haze's Personal Collection*

THE CIRCUS OF HORRORS
Bloedstollend Grappig!
Live Music By
Dr. HAZE
v the
X-FACTOR
VAN 12 MAART
RIJNHAL ARNHEM
T/M 16 MAART
INFO & RESERVEREN 026-3219060
RIJNHAL ONLINE: www.rijnhal.nl

Photo credits, Judy Totton, COH 2002

Photo credits, Haze Personal Collection, COH The roundhouse 1997

Photo credits, Haze Personal Collection

Photo credits, Haze Personal Collection

Haze & McAbre
Photo credit, Haze's Personal Collection

Photo credits, Sarah Photogirl

Photo credits, Sarah Photogirl

Garry Stretch
Photo credits, Seventhwave Imagery

El Grande Circo Rock de Londra

THE CIRCUS OF HORRORS

Directed by
PIERROT
BIDON

ROCK
en
VIVO!

Un Circo para
morirse de risa!

Design: TONY SHAKER

Photo credits, Sarah Photogirl

Day of the Dead cast 2009. Photo credits, Sarah Photogirl
I wouldn't say Sandro was ugly but this image looked much better once we had decapitated him.

The Cast outside the O2, 2010.
Photo credits, Sarah Photogirl

Circus of Horrors on Ross Lee's Goolies for Nickelodeon TV. With my old mate the horizonal Ross Lee.
Photo Credits Haze's personal collection

Circus of Horrors cast Asylum Tour 2008.   Photo Credits Haze's personal collection

Kirsty Nicholson joined us as a singer not knowing she would also be our topless girl in the bottle. She had to secretly overcome her claustrophobia by sitting in the laundry basket before she could become our new 'pickled person'. Photo credits, Sarah Photogirl

That Christmas, I, as normal went to my Mum's. I always had a good time in Preston but I could see my Uncle Charles was getting weaker, you could see that he didn't have long left.

I was glad to get back to London to resume my recording career where we laid down Girl, Destiny, The Only Sure Thing and Love Solution.

Unfortunately even though at last my music and business career was beginning to take off I was to experience more personal tragedies.

It was April when I got a call from my Mum telling me she was suffering from cancer and had to go to hospital for major surgery. I didn't even know she was ill, I went to Preston to stay with her for a few weeks and visit her in hospital. The operation was successful but she was in hospital quite a while to recuperate.

Sadly though, while my Mum was recovering in hospital my Uncle Charles suffered heart failure and died, I had to visit my Mum in hospital and tell her, it was terrible, she knew he had been taken to hospital after his heart attack but thought he had recovered and kept asking to see him. Telling my Mum about Uncle Charles was one of the hardest things I have ever done.

Apart from my Mum's time with my Dad or with me, virtually all her life was spent living in the same house as Charles and although they were actually cousins they were more like Brother and Sister and he was the nearest thing I had to a real Dad. He had a small amount of money and left most of it to me, he had planned to leave it to my Mum but she suggested he left it to me instead. It was the familiar journey again from Barry Avenue to the crematorium. Aunty Blodwyn once again declaring 'it was his final journey'.

The money Charles left me caused a major rift in my family, my uncle Dennis insisted on reading out the will during the wake and when he read out the percentages of how Charles' money would be distributed there was stony silence. I felt like saying I don't want the fucking money but I kept thinking Charles obviously wanted me to have it or he wouldn't have willed it to me.

A couple of days after the funeral I went back to London to get ready for a couple of University gigs. We did the two gigs in one night, the first in a University in Bristol and the second at around midnight in Oxford University.

Everything was going fine until our Roadie, Ian Westmorland somehow managed to badly burn his hand on our bazooka and went to hospital in Bristol.

After the show in Oxford we had to drive back to the hospital in Bristol to pick him up before the drive home. I got back at about 5am, totally knackered and pretty sick of hospitals.

What happened next was a complete surprise and I certainly didn't see it coming. Early that evening Joanna told me she was leaving, she packed all her stuff into plastic bags and rang her parents to come and get her.

Although I knew our break up was for the best for both of us it was still a shame, I got on well with her family and her brother was a really nice guy and toured with us doing special effects.

It's quite strange every time I seem to be going through a bad patch PNE seem to pull something out of the bag and cheer me up. After John Beck's arrival as manager they had got relegated but instead of, as previous seasons going into freefall, they had a decent season and ended up in the 4th division play offs. They were to play Torquay, first of all away then at home. They lost the first leg in Torquay 2-0. Never before had a team turned around a 2-goal deficit in the play offs, but once again I believed.

I travelled to Preston, stayed at my Mum's, picked up Basher and went to Deepdale for the game. Basher is epileptic and had had a fit whilst ice-skating, fell over and broke his leg. So he was in plaster and still a bit delirious. North End went 1-0 up, Torquay equalized with a ball put in by their forwards' hand. With away goals counting double it now seemed an impossible task. Torquay then had a player sent off for throwing a punch at Paul Rayner and Preston went 2-1 up just before half time.

Basher had an epileptic fit and missed the Torquay goal and insisted North End were winning 2-0. A two-goal lead however was soon restored and at the end of normal time the game was 3-1 to Preston. The game went into extra time and North End needed one more goal and had 30 minutes to get it.

I remember thinking they weren't going to do it but with three minutes left Paul Raynor rose to head home Preston's forth to take us to Wembley. The elation was unbelievable and only supporting a football team can give you this feeling.

The game also marked the last game to be played on Preston's infamous plastic pitch. On the final whistle I joined thousands of "Nobbers" and danced on the pitch like a lunatic completely forgetting Basher in his plaster cast having another fit in the stands. I ripped up a piece of the plastic pitch from around the centre circle and took it home where it is now framed and still adorns my wall.

A week later the North End fans outnumbered the Wycombe Wanderers fans four to one at Wembley but the team failed to live up to our expectations and we lost 4-2, condemning us to another season in football's basement.

I had decided to stop gigging for a while, give the band a new shape and plan a tour for the autumn. I wanted to create a new sound, sort of techno rock. Instead of a drummer I took on a percussionist called Rick Rockola and built a scrap yard percussion kit, very similar to what Stomp are doing today. I didn't need a bass player so temporally laid off Andy Higgins, I recruited a new guitarist Tony Quintini and new Keyboard player Kase.

We recorded the backing for the whole set and played live on top of the programmed music, it was completely different to our previous sound.

I also found an ally in an old girl friend, Janey Lee Grace who was now a Virgin Radio DJ and Sky News music correspondent she played the video for Destiny on Sky News.

We recorded and released a cover of Monster Mash to coincide with the tour and like Jivin', Monster Mash started getting radio airplays and the gigs were getting bigger and bigger both in venue size and theatrically.

The tour kicked off in London's legendary Marquee club and went around the UK and Ireland, generally the new idea worked but I treated it as an experiment and always intended turning it back into a rock band at some point.

Right from the reformation of the band in 1989 we used the name Haze and in true movie fashion added extra bits to the end. Haze II on one tour and Haze III on another until we settled on Haze Vs The X Factor, named after a Marvel comic.

We started to add a sub name to each tour, it would be Haze Vs the X Factor. 'The House of Wax' and then Haze Vs the X Factor 'The Circus of Horrors'

t was to prove the template to the monster that was about to be unleashed a year or so later.

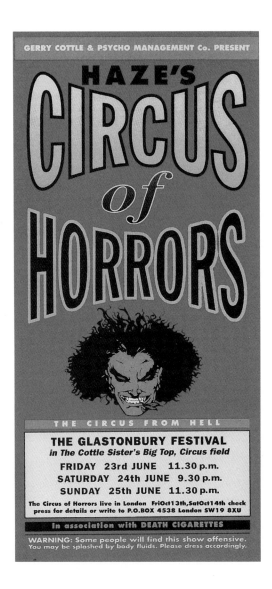

The first Circus of Horrors shows inside a big top. Flyer design by Paul Peculiar

CHAPTER ELEVEN
ANOTHER DEATH IN THE FAMILY
AND THE BIRTH OF A MONSTER

It was Christmas 1994 I'd travelled to Preston to see my Mum as normal. It was our first Christmas without Charles so it was a little different but Basher had come round on Christmas and Boxing Day and we'd had a good time not drinking much though as I drove him home and went to bed around 1.30am

At around 2am I was still awake and had a strange feeling, I had the radio on and listened to the news about a High Wire Walker had fallen and died at The Blackpool Tower Circus and I had a strange premonition.

Although no name was given I somehow thought I knew who it was, even though I did not know any High Wire Walkers and did not know who was appearing at the Tower that winter.

I just knew my phone was going to ring, when it did and I felt a shiver running down my spine. Answering it, I heard it was Billy Wild's voice, who I had not heard from in years.

He gave me the bad news that the person who had fallen was not a High Wire Walker but my Godson and friend Neville Campbell. At only 21 he had fallen during the second show in the Tower on Boxing Day from the appropriately named 'Wheel of Death'.

The explanation on the news was a smoke screen put out by the Police to protect the anonymity of the family who were away that night. Once they had been told, the media were in turn told the correct story.

Neville's father, Neville Snr. came on the phone and we spoke for a while but what can you say at times like these, he was so young, so talented and my friend, but most of all he was Neville's son.

He was taken at the pinnacle of his career, taken in such a public way, in front of a packed audience. He was born in a Circus, Christened in a Circus ring and died in Britain's most famous Circus building.

Neville explained that the family would travel down to Blackpool the next morning to identify the body and talk to the police.

I was just down the road in Preston so I offered to go along with the family the next day and help them with their grief, Neville agreed that I should come.

I hardly slept a wink that night and got up the next morning and travelled to Blackpool in the clapped out Ford Escort that was part of my redundancy package from Brooks. I arrived at a cold concrete hellhole of a Police station in Blackpool and asked to see the family, if ever a German concentration camp was built in England then this was it. I was taken to the room where the Campbell family were sitting, with them was Circus legend Gerry Cottle. I hugged all the family, the three brothers and their Mum and Dad, Pauline and Neville Snr and tried to console them.

The rest of the morning was total chaos, first of all we went to identify the body, the family went in and Gerry and I waited outside. They were understandably, completely distraught and we returned to the Police station. Unfortunately some of the Police Officers were unaware of the tragedy. The family were in the Police Station and therefore, the Police had a duty of care to look after this grieving family, instead they started to question who the boys were and asked them why they were walking around the Police station. The boys did not take kindly to this and one of them head butted a female Police Officer.

He was promptly taken to the cells, the other boys and their Mum, Pauline, were taken back to a private room while myself, Neville and Gerry were asked to hold a press conference for the awaiting massed Media. I spoke to the journalists first and asked them for respect and compassion, of course they agreed and they went and asked their questions with courtesy.

After leaving the Police station Gerry treated us all to fish and chips (well chips and gravy in my case) from a roadside chip van. It didn't seem quite right eating but I never could resist a Lancashire chip. We briefly went to the Tower to see the scene of the accident and the Wheel of Death, which was taken away and scrapped by Neville shortly afterwards.

Gerry and I had met a few times before, I wouldn't say we were friends but in a break from the confusion we spoke of what we were both doing. He was running The Cottle Sister Circus and I had a show, touring Universities and Rock Clubs called The Circus of Horrors.

We exchanged phone numbers, he took Pauline back home while I stayed in Blackpool with Neville and the rest of the family to successfully and thankfully get Karl released pending court appearance in the weeks to come. In the meantime I wrote to the Lancashire Chief of Police to ask for lenience. I don't know if it helped but Karl ended up with just a fine so guess it did.

Over the next few weeks I rang Gerry a number of times to discuss Neville's funeral but al to discuss my plans to turn The Circus of Horrors into a tented Circus with full blown Circus acts, Rock n' Roll and Horror.

At first Gerry was a little skeptical and at one point told me to go and talk to Martin Burton of Zippos Circus, although I like Martin I knew Gerry was the only Circus proprietor in the UK with enough insight, enough bollocks and would be mad enough to join me in this adventure.

I knew it would work, Archaos had caused a revolution and was the forerunner of the alternative Circus but was no longer touring. I knew there was a void in the market and knew The Circus of Horrors could fill that void, the tricky thing was to persuade Gerry of this. Gerry was still running Cottle Sisters Circus and the show came to The Wimbledon Theatre so I went along to see it and met Gerry there, he was beginning to come around to my way of thinking and asked me if we did The Circus of Horrors where we would begin, I suggested Glastonbury. He knew Arabella Churchill who booked the Circus field, which was normally polluted by Hippy Circuses posing and full of pretensions with very little skill. I was impressed by Gerry's sharp intervention and the fax he sent her at 9am the next morning.

The next day we had a fax back saying that Arabella was indeed interested in our new venture. Arabella was the granddaughter of Winston Churchill, she had appeared on the cover of 'Life' as a child and was supposedly rumored to be tipped as a future spouse of a certain British Prince. She firmly believed in the peace movement, and in the late 60's rebelled against her noble upbringing; she was staunchly against the Vietnam War. She left London for rural Somerset, where she helped lead the first full-scale incarnation of the Glastonbury Festival with Andrew Kerr and Michael Eavis in which T-Rex were the headline act.

She was keen to meet us and shortly afterwards we were booked to perform, Cottle Sisters Circus during the day and The Circus of Horrors around midnight for the three nights of the festival.

In our lead up to Glastonbury, I changed the band back to a more conventional rock band, Nick Rockola reverted to a traditional drum kit, Andy Higgins returned on Bass, Tony Quintini and Kase remained as guitarists and keyboard players. It was a really good band. To add to the theatrics I advertised for two Vampire girls and found two good-looking Goth girls from Kensington High Street Market.

We did about 10 gigs leading up to Glastonbury, all well attended and all really kicking, we seemed to have the formula right at last.

It was 25 years since the first Glastonbury Festival so for The Circus of Horrors to make it's debut at this historic anniversary, particularly as Marc Bolan had headlined it's very first year, was particularly satisfying for me.

Aside from the prestigious debut show that was pending, another thing in my favour was that Gerry's three daughter's all loved the idea of The Circus of Horrors and the thought of becoming vampires, I went along to the Cottle Sisters and told them which acts I thought we should use, then I would match and write the music that would fit the acts best.

Cottle Sister's were on Durnham Downs Bristol and myself, the band and the Vampire girls travelled to Bristol to rehearse.

We had just two days of rehearsals before Glastonbury and in the first show I think it showed. It was raw but it still rocked, we had about 400 people in, half of which walked out before the end.

1995 was very much the year of Britpop and the festival was headlined by Oasis and Pulp, but as always the festival was diverse both artistically and musically with The Cure and PJ Harvey both playing great sets. This year also turned out to be the first year the festival would host a dance tent where Massive Attack were to headline.

The second day for The Circus of Horrors got much tighter and the word of the 200 that stayed had spread and we had 800 inside, again about 200 walked out.

It was a rare Glastonbury when the sun shone throughout and the only downside for me was the Animal Rights Protesters outside the tent during The Cottle Sisters show. They carried banners of a performing elephant. Not that Cottle Sisters had any elephants just some horse that they rode. The animal rights protesters chose to ignore the Police on horseback that stood right next to them, it seemed to be OK to have Police riding horses but not to have horses being ridden in a Circus. They were also at a festival that was run by and on the land of Michael Eavis, a dairy farmer. It's a strange world.

By day three the vibe of The Circus of Horrors had spread like a virus and the 800 that had seen the show the previous two days had now swelled to over 1000, all rammed into the tent with 3000 locked outside. When the first few chords blasted out there was a near riot outside, this time no one left.

The Circus of Horrors had begun. The monster was born.

During the next few months we excitedly decided what to do next with the Circus of Horror. Psycho Management was also fast becoming a major player as an entertainment agen

The queue outside the Circus of Horrors tent at Glastonbury,
Photo credits, from Haze's personal collection

and was busier than ever.

My private life was good too, After Joanna I decided I didn't want a girlfriend for a while but my celibacy didn't last long. A frantic burst of promiscuity ensued first of all a girl called Rachel who was a Bolan look-alike and then another three in a bed romp, this time with the two Voluptuous Vampires who were now in the show. The ménage a trios was also a case of déja vu as again and unfortunately only two of the three participated.

then found myself a new more permanent girlfriend, I didn't have to travel too far to find her either as she lived in the same road as me. Her name was Filiz, she was just starting University and had wisdom well beyond her age. She looked great and we got on really well, she came with me to Glastonbury and shortly afterwards we had a brilliant holiday together in Turkey.

had many meetings with Gerry and the girls, they wanted to tent with The Circus of Horrors in a way that most Circuses do, I wanted to be a bit more exclusive but thought if the towns or cities were right then we would be OK.

round autumn, Iron Maiden decided to call their new album 'The X Factor', it was a name had used for my band for three years and we tried to sue them for 'passing off'. We had started talking to Mark Borkawski about doing the PR for The Circus of Horrors and he suggested that we serve an injunction against them. We thought they would either pay us off or we would get loads of publicity out of it. We got neither, we did however put the shits EMI and got a letter from their MD, basically calling our bluff and reminding us that if the case went against us we would have to pick up their legal costs.

e sensibly but reluctantly backed down. Instead we started to think about how we could prove the show and knew we had to make some changes, I felt I would struggle to artistically direct the show and perform in it. I had never directed anything of this scale, it was OK for a one hour show in Glastonbury but a full two hour spectacular would be beyond me at this time.

Gerry and I both agreed the best possible candidate was Pierrot Bidon, creator and Artistic Director of Archaos. Gerry travelled to France to see him, Pierrot loved the idea but wanted to hear the music, Gerry gave him our latest CD and luckily he loved that too and jumped on board.

Circus Archaos was the forerunner of the alternative or contemporary Circus, I firmly believe it paved they way for shows such as Cirque du Soleil and the Circus of Horrors. Pierrot was a real character, he had been jailed for being an anarchist in his French homeland, ran a horse driven Circus and had a troupe of performing chickens.

Pierrot had a theory that in bygone days if a horse drawn Circus used its horses to pull the show from town to town and then use the same horses to perform in the show, he could do the same with motorbikes.

He therefore decided to sell his horses and replace them with motorbikes, his forklift truck took the place of an elephant. He added a few chainsaws, some nudity, some French 'ne son pas donner a baise' attitude, some great acts and a huge chunk of Rock n' Roll and Archaos was rocking.

Archaos did amazingly well all over the world but particularly well in the UK and Scandinavia got loads of publicity and did to the Circus world what the Sex Pistols did to music and fashion.

Unfortunately, Archaos fell foul of the weather and a dodgy promoter in Dublin. Their tent blew down and was ruined, it was not insured. A new tent was hired but the promoter still failed to fulfill his duties to Archaos, leaving them with a massive debt and bankrupt. On the last night, Pierrot led all the artists into the ring and stunned the packed mainly corporate audience by declaring, they had not been paid and the only option left to them was to go on strike. This was pretty well the end of Archaos. One of Archaos' best cities was Brighton and now, with Pierrot as part of our team, we thought it would be a great place to take the show to next.

After our earlier discussions about the Iron Maiden saga we decided to bring in Mark Borkawski to handle the PR, Mark had worked with Gerry before and was the brains behind the great Archaos and Jim Rose Publicity stunts. Mark suggested we contact a local Brighton Arts Company Zap to help us find a site. We looked at a few but the most favourable was on the Marina, they set up a meeting with the Managing Director who was very keen until he saw our poster and suddenly his jaw dropped.

We were later to find out that he was a religious fundamentalist and told Robin from Zap that he could not go to Church on Sunday and sanction 'The Circus from Hell' to perform on his site. A little contradictory, the Cinema complex on the same site showed all the Horror movies and while we visited him it was showing re-runs of The Exorcist, but that's religious types for you. Thankfully the council were still keen on the show appearing in Brighton and offered us a site on the Racecourse and we decided it was the best venue on offer in Brighton.

The show was to change quite a lot over the next few months as we tried different artistes and acts and alter the look of the show. Until now we had piggybacked on The Cottle Sisters show but over the next few months we needed to decide if we were going to progress as The Circus of Horrors.

The first change had to be in the show itself. With Pierrot now on board there was sure to be many changes ahead.

Prior to Brighton we rehearsed and did a few preview shows in Addlestone Moor, Gerry's winterquarters and home.

We used most of the Artistes from the Glastonbury show, Jeff Jay decided to leave so Willie Ramsay did the Wheel of Death on his own. All the girls were still there and Sarah became McAbre and learnt a great sword and dagger act. Polly became Ragen and joined Salaam and Willie with an Arial strap act themed to the Exorcist. Ingo Dock did a cloud swing act and April became Pandemonium and the two of them did a Motorbike on the high wire act, we also had an amputee called Brian who's leg we chopped off each night after a mock hypnotism. Add to this Johnny Brenner who did a trapeze act with a Phantom of the Opera feel, a five strong troupe of Kenya Warriors who became the Pigmy Flesh Eaters and the Fakier Sinbad.

Sinbad's arrival came out of the blue, he hailed from mystical Morocco and just floated into Gerry's farm one day and asked for a job. Not as you might expect on a flying carpet but more mysteriously in a battered out Hillman Imp. The basic mystery was that the car actually went at all. Sinbad was to begin a great tradition of Fakirs in The Circus of Horrors.

The band had changed too, Kase decided not to come and thought the show wouldn't succeed and drummer Rick Rockola left to buy a chip shop, he was replaced by Mark Campioni who actually auditioned for the job two years earlier.

The show itself was a mismatch of virtually every horror genre there had ever been, even Frankenstein's Monster and Quasimodo made appearances.

The audience generally loved it but there weren't enough of them. The critics hated it and the bad crits probably contributed to the lack of audience.

Although it wasn't the critics' cup of tea the media in general did like it and in particular the non-stop photo opportunities that were coming thick and fast.

First of all we returned to Brighton Marina, they very place that had refused permission for us to perform. They didn't however refuse us permission to dock, so we arrived in Brighton Marina aboard a tall ship in a sort of recreation of Dracula's arrival in Whitby, although our crew arrived undead as opposed to dead and there wasn't a black dog in sight. This proved to be the fist of many headlines the show would encounter over the next 15 years.

Brighton however, despite the Archaos connection and the publicity stunts was not a success and although business got better towards the end of the run overall we lost money.

We moved the show to Crystal Palace and made a couple of changes, Kenny Darnel became Dead Elvis on Keyboards and we introduced two new illusions. First an Iron Maiden that Simon Drake had used to kill off Bruce Dickenson on their Raising Hell Video. We bought it from veteran illusionist George Kovari who also designed a giant hangmans illusion. An illusion that would be the backdrop and the finalé of the show for many years.

Johnny Brenner also added a new Balancing Act on top of a moving car, a mini that had had the Mad Max treatment, very Archaos.

We re-titled the show Gerry Cottle's Christmas Specdracular presents Doktor Haze's Circus of Horrors, it was a mixed message really and probably only confused people. We tone down the matinee shows so they were suitable for children. This was a harsh lesson to learn you simply can't tone down The Circus of Horrors otherwise it is not The Circus of Horror You can take out the nudity and the adult language but the attitude has to remain.

The media were good to us again and we held Vampire Auditions which got us loads national publicity and TV exposure, lots of people had now heard of The Circus of Horro but still not many people were coming.

Like Brighton, the crowds built up towards the end of the run. Proving we were gaining following but also like Brighton it was too little too late.

I personally believed we were expecting too much by spending so long in each town. It w decision time and we had to decide if we were to continue.

Zap had faith in the show and invited representatives from UK Arts Festivals to see the show. This resulted in an offer to take the show to a unique site in Manchester, right in the centre of town on The Old Smithfield. Another factor that encouraged us to carry on was the fact that we were offered an episode on a forthcoming TV show called Dani Dares and featured The Word presenter and serial football wag Dani Behr.

In many ways Manchester was doomed before it began, the area of the Old Smithfield was a dodgy part of town, we had not been there for five minutes when a pneumatic drill was stolen from one of our vans. We ended up having to employ security to patrol the site day and night, another expense we could ill afford. Our Bass player Andy Higgins even had his car stolen and used in a failed armed robbery.

Manchester was another Archaos stronghold and we changed the name of the show slightly to 2020 - The Circus of Horrors. 2020 was the year in which the show was set and in Manchester all the shows started at 20.20.

The show was very similar to the Crystal Palace shows, we opened on February 14th and called it a Valentines Day Massacre, for the first two days Dani Behr performed in the show and ticket sales were great. The omens originally looked good but someone certainly wasn't looking very kindly upon us, it was absolutely freezing cold and snowed most days.

I enjoyed having Dani in the show and apart from living in a caravan in the freezing weather and me sticking a sword in her fishnet clad leg during an illusion, I think she enjoyed it too.

Obviously Danni is as famous as a wag as she is a TV presenter and I couldn't help having a little fun at her expense. At one point in the show she was dressed as a gorgeous vampire dancing girl and we did a mock Bingo game. Everyone who entered the show got a passport with five numbers on it. We would draw out seven balls from a hat and by the seventh number, 66, everyone in the audience had won, of course the final number turned out to be 66 so despite the whole audience shouting 'house' we never got a winner.

On Danni's last night though I added two extra balls number seven and number nine, when I drew out number seven Johnny Brenner came out with a Ryan Giggs number seven Man United shirt on. When I drew number nine Quasimodo emerged wearing a number nine Newcastle shirt and bearing the name of her then current but secret boyfriend Les Ferdinand. 'Outraged' I pulled out a red card and sent them both off. Dani took it very well but chased me around the tent afterwards.

Manchester was supposed to be make or break and had we stuck to that The Circus of Horrors would have been dead and buried almost before it began. Thankfully that was not the case. We took all the equipment back to Gerry's farm in Surrey and started planning the future, we lined up a number of University shows, taking the whole big top and show to a number of summer balls. Zap also helped us to line up a significant tour of Arts festivals beginning in Bradford then moving onto Leeds, Stockton and the Edinburgh Festival.

I felt that one of the problems with Brighton, Crystal Palace and Manchester was the fact that we stayed three weeks in each location, for an unknown show to expect to run for three weeks in each town or city was more than a little optimistic.

The new tour, with the exception of Edinburgh was to be curtailed to 10 days in each town.

Unfortunately during this time my Mum's health took a downturn, she had come to stay with me at Christmas while the show was in Crystal Palace, I could see there was something wrong and like with Uncle Charles two years earlier I knew she wouldn't be with us for long.

The next few months were horrible, I would ring my Mum every day and you could hear in her voice that she was ill, she had been to her Doctors who assured her she was just run down. I was sure it was more than this and feared that the cancer had come back. I wrote to her Doctor and he tried to convince me too that she was only run down, I asked him directly 'has the cancer come back', he told me absolutely that it had not and unbelievably prescribed her vitamin tablets.

She had six monthly appointments with the hospital and her next one came in April. It confirmed my worse nightmare, the cancer had returned, this time there was no way back they gave her six weeks to live.

The Doctor, her GP, who assured me the cancer had not returned rang me and I asked him why he did not examine my mother properly earlier. His answer was 'Do you believe in God John', believe in God I could have fucking strangled him and in fact I should have.

I travelled to see my Mum and persuaded her to go to a hospice, we both lived a lie for the next few weeks. I knew she was dying but tried to persuade her that her doctor's original diagnosis was right and she was just run down and once she had gained her strength back she could go back home. She knew she was dying but used to tell me that she would go home once she was stronger.

I travelled to Preston as much as I could over the next few weeks and once again a lit solace came again from Preston North End. Two years after their play off failure they were back at the top of the newly named 3rd division (division four really). The previous year they had a massive cash injection, which resulted in a new stand being built, and new money available for players.

Manager John Beck had been sacked and replaced by his former assistant, Gary Peters. Gary took the team into the 1994/5 playoffs and recruited a young David Beckham on loan for five weeks.

They failed again that year but in 1995/6 season they were much stronger, with three games left, they went to play away at Brisbane Road the home of Leyton Orient and won 2-0 with two goals from Andy Saville, I was there to see a win that would confirm promotion.

Two weeks later they won the Third Division championship and on one of my visits to see Mum in Preston I saw them parade the trophy through the streets of Preston on an open top bus, a banner across the Harris Art Gallery proclaimed 'Preston North End - Our Champions', enough said.

Mum generally did seem to be getting a little better until she took a fall in the hospice and was too weak to get up, she was bed ridden for the last couple of weeks.

The Circus of Horrors was about to travel to Bradford but before that we had two of the University summer balls back to back in Guildford and Eastbourne. We did the first show in Guildford, pulled down the tent and I went home to Wimbledon.

I received a call the next morning at 9am from the hospice telling me my Mum was now seriously ill, the idiot Doctor came on and said she didn't have long and I should come down. We still had another show that night and I honestly did not know what to do. The Doctor told me she had about 24 hours, I don't know why but I decided to believe him. I was in a real dilemma, I tried to call Gerry but he wasn't there, I was at my wits end. I didn't want to let anyone down but I had to be by my Mum's side for her final hours.

I decided to take a chance and do the show that night, it was the day that England beat Scotland in the 1996 European Championship with that wonder Gascoigne goal, I watched in the pub and felt laden with guilt.

I did the show that night, it was great, inside though I was bleeding and the most poignant moment for me was singing 'The only Sure Thing in Life is Death'. I was really fighting back the tears at this point. Straight after the show I picked up Filiz and we drove through the night to Preston.

I got there in the early hours of the morning, my Mum was still alive but only just, it was horrible, she could hardly breathe although thankfully she did not know much about it, shortly after dawn broke the nurse woke her, she was on another planet but amazingly she did recognize me.

I stayed with her all day just wishing it was all over, I couldn't see my Mum suffer like this. There was nothing I could do and the nurse suggested I went home and get some sleep, promising she would call me if anything happened. I went to stay at Barry Avenue and went to bed. The inevitable phone call came at 5am. The hospice asked me to come down straight away.

I got dressed and drove there only to find I was a few minutes too late, she had gone but looked a million times better and I felt a huge relief. I went back to my Mum's house and had an hour or so more sleep. When I got up I went straight into town and made all the arrangements for the funeral and sorted her estate out, it seemed like I was on overdrive, I should have been mourning and here I was sorting things out, I just didn't know what else to do.

That evening the priest who was to take the funeral came around and I gave him a massive lecture about the hypocrisy of religion. If there was a God why did my Mum suffer like that what had she ever done. He almost walked out but he didn't and went onto perform his duties at the funeral well.

I travelled back to London, there was a week until the funeral and a week until the show pulled out for Bradford. On the eve of my Mum's funeral I went to Gerry's farm and picked up a caravan I had borrowed. I drove to Leeds unhitched it then drove across the Pennines to bury my Mum.

The next morning a number of my relations arrived. Auntie Blodwin made the usual statement about 'her last journey' that fucking statement again and that fucking journey to the crematorium. Thank God it was the last time I would hear it.

The funeral was fine although I really wish I had said a few words about my Mum but didn't have the courage.

I only had a small family but it was suddenly about to get a whole lot smaller, most of the family from Wales had come to the funeral but it was to be the last time I would hear from them.

I didn't realize but they were still seething about the fact that my uncle Charles had left r the bulk of his money. To this day I have not heard from them, I always send them a Christmas card but have not ever received one back.

My Auntie Vera and her son Julian still live in Preston, she still keeps in touch but she has been asked by the rest of the family not to tell me anything so apart from Christmas I find it very difficult to keep in touch with her too.

It's a real shame, every time I'm in Preston I want to go and see Auntie Vera but I don't want to cause her any unnecessary trouble.

The day my Mum died my whole family died too.

Mum
Photo credits, from Haze's
personal collection

Photo credits, from Haze's personal collection

CHAPTER TWELVE –
FROM BRADFORD TO BUENOS AIRES

The day after my Mum's funeral I returned to Bradford to start rehearsals in what was going to prove to be a very different show and was be a real turning point in the fortunes of The Circus of Horrors.

I had not expected Bradford to be the city that would prove to be the salvation of the Circus of Horrors, but it certainly was where the salvation began. Bradford has a large population and its diverse mixture of notable local residents included Donald Neilson, Peter Sutcliffe, Kiki Dee and The Bronte Sisters. We were on a site known as Infirmary Fields, it was on the edge of the city and the edge of the red light district.

Rehearsals were really hard and a pleasant break came when we resurrected the Vampire Auditions, again drawing loads of great media attention and resulted in us recruiting two girls from the city, one of which became our girl in the bottle for a while.

We had a really sexy show now with loads of great acts, still featuring things like Willie's Wheel of Death, Ingo's flying Cloud Swing and with April on the motorbike on the High Wire. McAbre's Sword and Dagger act and we finalized the brilliant exorcist themed strap act featuring Polly, Willie and Salaam. Some great trike riding on a huge three wheeled monstrosity made of bones and sword fighting from Kiss My Axe, a transsexual Fire Eater Jyn Daniels and the extreme Fakir John Kamikaze were all added to the show.

Kiss My Axe and John Kamikaze had joined after an ad in the Stage, asking for unusual acts and a one legged, lesbian dwarf. The ad was basically a dig at the politically correct do gooders, which would become the bane of our lives but also give us endless ammunition to feed to the media.

Previously I had seen Kiss My Axe when they were performing a showcase for an entertainment exhibition in Wembley Arena. Their sword fight on that night ended in tragedy. A sword broke during the fight and unbeknown to one of the fighters it went straight though the main artery of the other the guy's leg. He fell to the floor and his colleagues thought he was acting. After two minutes he hadn't moved, nor did he move when they kicked him. They turned him over and found a huge pool of blood. He was taken to hospital but was dead on arrival. We gave them a job.

At the time John Kamikaze was the most radical Fakir I had ever seen, he plunged giant hatpins through his face and neck, lifted bowing bowls through meat hooks in his nipples and swallowed a fluorescent tube.

The new show was proving a huge hit, the audiences had never seen anything like it and at the end of the shows they would stamp their feet on the seats. It sounded like thunder. We were beginning to gain a huge following, which would travel from venue to venue to see us.

It seemed to be simple to get publicity and things just kept falling in our laps. First of all a number of the tabloids photographed our new girl in the bottle under the title 'bottle blonde', we then had complaints from local Muslim groups for having two giant naked golden female statues standing either side of our box office.

The council asked us to remove them in case it insulted the Muslim community that lived in the area, we refused and went to the media, more column inches gained by political correctness gone mad.

I suppose we got away lightly though, Bradford is a city with a large Muslim community, some of which burned Salman Rushdie's book 'The Satanic Verses' in the late 1980's.

The endless publicity however almost backfired however when our next city, Leeds threatened to ban us. Again this was front-page news in The Yorkshire Evening Post. The Mayor of Leeds travelled to Bradford to see the show and loved it so the ban was lifted Triumphantly we moved into Leeds next.

While the show moved to Leeds I ventured over the Pennines to Preston to clear out m Mum's house, it was a job I had always dreaded but Filiz and Basher were there to help m I gave Basher some tables and his Mum the cooker and freezer. I loaded up my Land Rov with all the things that were sentimental to me and gave the keys to Help the Aged to cle out the beds, furniture etc and hopefully help some less fortunate people.

One thing I did keep was my Mum's diary for her final year, it still sits in my bedroo unopened.

I drove back to London with my Mum's things then back to Leeds ready for the show open there.

Business was even better than Bradford and we certainly were moving in the right directi The thunderous noise at the end of the show when the punters stamped their feet w getting louder and I knew we had created a Frankenstein's Monster of a show. I was a sensible enough to know though that without the support of Gerry and the creative genius of Pierrott it would have been very difficult to achieve our collective ambition.

It was then onto the festival city of Stockton on Tees! Before our journey North I had never even heard of Stockton but within ten days it would become a place I would never forget.

Stockton is famous for its associations with the Stockton and Darlington Railway on which ran the world's first steam hauled passenger train in 1825. The town has possibly the world's oldest railway station building, and also contains much Georgian architecture, one notable example being the world's oldest Georgian theatre constructed in 1766.

If you saw Stockton now you would never believe it had such an illustrious history, it contains street after street of council housed roads, a number of which containing families of chavs. Nevertheless the shows were amazing, just like a wedding, the chavs sat together on one side and the goths sat on the other. Both groups equally enjoying the show.

The other amazing thing about Stockton is the International Riverside Festival, which runs each year. It is Europe's largest free open-air festival. The festival has a five-day programme of outdoor Theatre, Street Entertainment, Circus, Music and Dance.

In1996 The Circus of Horrors took Stockton by storm. We launched with the now regular Vampire auditions and one popular auditionee turned out to be former Middlesborough and Eire centre forward Bernie Slaven. Nicknamed on the terraces 'The Wolf Man' he was a perfect candidate. He didn't get the job though, somehow that went to a girl with big tits.

Business in Stockton started slowly but within a couple of days we were ramming them in. Another piece of good fortune was the fact that I persuaded Dodgy to play in the tent one night, luckily it was the day they reached number four in the charts with 'Good Enough'.

The weekend saw us share the tent with Ardal O'Hanlon and Mark Thomas. In Mark's case we did a show at 5pm, he did a show of his satirical stand up at 7.30 then the Circus of Horrors did a 9pm show. I was stood outside the tent with Mark after his show and there was a huge queue snaking it's way from Trinity Church Ground right down the high street. We ended up turning away over 1000 people and had to add an extra show the next day to accommodate them.

Our legend in Stockton even surpassed our shows there, after we were accused of fornicating on the gravestones that were strangely situated around our big top. Well ask the Circus of Horrors to build up its tent on a graveyard and you can hardly expect anything else.

We then moved onto the Edinburgh Festival, it was to become our biggest challenge to date.

We needn't have worried though, we were once again the media darlin's and a huge success.

It was our first visit to Edinburgh and we didn't understand the protocol, we launched our dates by hiring a tank and parading down Princes street.

The Police had given us permission for the parade but warned Peter Norris our advance manager to keep us under control.

Keep us under control, Peter Norris had no chance. As the parade wound it's way down this famous Edinburgh street with the Castle to our left. The driver of the tank suddenly, somehow lost control with me sitting astride the barrel.

It went careering across the road and ground to a halt with the barrel of it's gun four inches from Virgin Megastores window, it's transporter was driven by Beau Denning which crashed into the back of the tank. The drivers of the two pieces of warfare then leapt out of the cabs and started fighting with each other. It was chaos people were running out of the shop, the buses ground to a halt and we caused a 2-hour traffic jam.

By some strange coincidence the media just happened to be gathered by the shop at the time and the whole incident was caught on camera. Gerry was traveling in the cab of the transporter and as soon as he saw the Police he dived behind the dashboard leaving poor Peter Norris to feel the wrath of the boys in blue.

Peter was frogmarched around the corner and warned that 'if he didn't get this shamble off the road in 10 minutes he would be arrested for causing an affray'.

The next day was the Edinburgh Cavalcade. We were driving around the town with a lorry and truck that had giant poster on each side and followed by the trike motorbike made of bones. We didn't even know what the Cavalcade was but we saw thousands of people on the streets so we decided to gate crash it.

We headed for the beginning of the parade and we were stopped by the stewards who asked us who we were, I spotted a friend of mine Hugh Lennon and his Hypno Dog and I said we are with him. They stupidly waved us into place behind Hugh and Rover. Once again proceeding down Princes Street, not careering into Virgin Megastore this time but nevertheless we were still the only picture used in the national press and we were not even supposed to be there. Anarchy ruled and we felt like we had replaced Archaos as the Sex Pistols of the Circus.

Edinburgh was brilliant and we were starting to get offers from all over the world. Originally we had planned to do the four arts festivals then take a break and see what came up but had been such a success we decided to take the show to London.

We opened on Clapham Common in London appropriately on Friday 13th September for a three and a half week run. It started a little slow but soon built up until every show was sold out again.

To help boost crowds we had a celebrity opening, but, in true Circus of Horrors fashion, it had to be bad taste, so obviously all the celebrities had to be dead. They were all there, John Lennon, Laurel and Hardy, Kirk Cobain, Brian Jones, Winston Churchill, Elvis, Jim Morrison, Marlena Dietrich, Marc Bolan and even Jesus Christ.

John Kamikaze had contracted blood poisoning shortly after we started in Edinburgh and had left the show. He swallowed an iron bar but failed to clean it properly. Originally trying to blame me for passing it to a girl to examine it. He claimed her perfume had contaminated the bar until I pointed out that this girl was in fact a guy with long hair, he really should have gone to Specsavers.

John's place was taken by The Mongolian Laughing Boy, AKA Tony Walls. Tony was the son of great Circus Fakir Barrie Walls but sadly Barrie had not shown Tony any tricks of the trade.

This is a picture of side shows and how they used to look.
It is at Epsom Downs in 1942.
The main guy stood at the front is Barrie Walls, AKA Baby Boy and Mongolian Laughing Boy's Dad.

Barrie, although now in semi-retirement was a huge inspiration to me, as a kid I would admire his and Jock McPherson's Fire Eating skills and try and emulate them. Not only did they do great tricks they would also do it with great showmanship. Barrie also did a brilliant Fakir act as Egyptian semi god El Hakim. He would thrust giant pins through his neck, face and shoulders, his pièce de résistance was when he swallowed a yard of wool, cut a hole in his stomach, placed his fingers inside his stomach and retrieved the wool. Amazing.

Although it was to prove to be Tony's debut as a Fakir he certainly wasn't his debut as a performer. Barrie showed me a picture of Tony at the age of four lying on a bed of nails, he progressed and became a Stilt Walker prior to his performing career going onto even greater heights. You can't go much higher than becoming a High Wire Walker, the problem was though, he was accident-prone. He learned to Wire Walk with Boswell Wilkes Circus in South Africa.

At one point he would ride a unicycle across the wire until the pedal fell off, the bike then fell into the net below. Tony managed to grab the wire but was not strong enough to hold on and he followed the bike into the safety net only for the safety net to collapse beneath leaving Tony wriggling like a trout in a fisherman's net but thankfully not hurt.

He returned to the UK with his Dad and joined Gerry Cottle's Circus which was doing a summer season at Eastbourne Congress Theatre. He had learned a Russian Swing act, a sort of springboard type giant swing that would project him from one side of the ring onto a matt that was on the other side. His first performance on the Russian Swing was also his last as he flew too far missed the matt smashed against a wall and broke his shoulder.

Not the ideal candidate for an act that involves pushing giant hat pins through your face and neck, lying on a bed of nails and having the largest person in the audience stand on you and having your arse nailed to a block

Human Mobile at Battersea,
photo credits, from Haze's personal collection

of wood.

The Mongolian Laughing Boys pedigree was also plagued in incidents.

His father Barrie, although a great performer and one of life's true eccentrics could also be a little accident-prone. On one occasion while he worked for Gerry Cottle he was driving a lorry and caravan to the Circus site and had to wait until he could park in a certain place.

To get onto the site you had to drive over a level crossing, Barrie parked across the level crossing, as he believed no trains were running on that day. His wife and Tony's Mum Barbara went into the caravan to make a nice cup of tea. As she sat there sipping her afternoon brew a train came flying down the track and ripped the caravan in two with her still sat, unscathed inside it. She didn't even spill a drop of her Tetley's.

Mongy made his debut appropriately on Friday 13th September, at first an intrepid Fakir but he soon got better.

Our three and a half week run in Clapham Common ended as a complete sell out and Time Out described the show as 'Bloody Good Fun'.

After our triumph at Stockton and Edinburgh we were booked to perform in the Tolwood Festival in Munich for all of December and decided to fill the gap after Clapham by performing on a piece of land next to Chelsea Bridge.

The site wasn't as visible as Clapham Common and business wasn't as good. We needed to pull another publicity cat out of the hat, so we did two. First of all we projected the Circus of Horrors logo onto one of the towers of Battersea Power Station.

A year later we were sued for our supposedly illegal projection but they sued the wrong company and ended up sueing a company that did not exist.

We then went on to attempt a Guinness World record for the largest human mobile, where we hung 15 people from a crane that was suspended 300 feet in the air over the River Thames. It was terrifying but created a world record and gained loads of extra publicity.

While we were at Chelsea Bridge, myself and the band, which now included the return of Base, joining Andy Higgins, Dog Dog Championi and Tony Quntini recorded our first Album, Destiny and Desire my Enchantment with Fire. The tracks included Ave Armageddon, Destiny, Sin City, House of Wax, The Web, Under Attack, Girl, Monster Mash, Love Never Dies, Just a Psycho, The Only Sure Thing and Fire with Fire.

The album was released on Madman records in the UK and Germany. In December we took the whole cargo of coffins and chain saws to Munich for a month long sortie in Bavaria.

It was our first venture abroad and not one without incident. There were a few changes in personnel too. Jeff Jay rejoined the show as Wolf Man and also did the Wheel of Death with Willie. Kiss my Axe left so we replaced them with two other sword fighters Chris Holiday and Moog and we replaced the Trike of Bones for a Mad Max mini.

We all caught the plane from Heathrow except for Kase who had eaten some of Uncle Ganga's space cake for breakfast and fainted with a strange grin on his face next to passport control.

That was only the first of our pre-show incidents. Three days before the show was due to start we had a press call, we were all about to travel aboard the tube on the Munich subways in full Motley. I had started wearing cosmetic red contact lenses, I never really got on with them but my dislike of them was about to get worse.

It was freezing cold in Munich and my contacts had frozen in their container. It didn't stop me and I put the frozen contacts into my eyes, not a wise move. I had to get emergency treatment in an eye hospital, I was put on antibiotics for a few weeks and my eyes had swollen and would not open. It was hit and miss if I would be ready for the first show Miraculously I made it although I had to perform in dark glasses for the first week.

Business in Munich was reasonable and we got mixed reviews, one mistake was performing the show in English, I learned a few words of German but generally we were misled into believing everyone in Bavaria could speak perfect English.

While we were in Munich a regular visitor to the show was Helmut Kirchmeier, he was a former Tax Inspector who had taken up body art and had a piercing and jewellery stall in the Christmas Market.

Helmut fell in love with the show and came almost every night. In return he offered to give a free piercing to everyone in the show, McAbre had her eyebrow pierced to the disgust of Willie. The person who took the most advantage of this was The Mongolian Laughing Boy he had everything pierced including his dick.

This was to trigger a whole sequence of dick related incidents that would haunt The Circus of Horrors and more particular the Mongolian Laughing Boy for the next few years.

We didn't have to wait long for the first one though. The first show after his Prince Albert piercing, Mongy was lying on the bed of nails when a giant of a guy went to stand on him I jokingly asked him to place one foot on his chest and one on his dick. Without even waiting for me to correct him the guy stood straight onto Mongy's chest and nether regions.

Within the space of three hours Mongy dick went from having no piercing to resembling a sieve.

We had a break from shows over Christmas, some of the artistes stayed in Munich and a few of us came home. I spent Christmas with Filiz. I had a nice time but it was the first Christmas I had not been with my Mum and I was really missing her.

After the Christmas break we returned to Munich for five more days of shows and finished on January 1st and returned home.

In January it was decision time, this time though, not if we were to carry on, that was a 'given' but instead we had so many options it was a case of which one we should take. Offers had come in from Holland for six weeks, music festivals in Scandinavia and Belgium, another British tenting tour or an Arena tour of South America. I had a meeting with Gerry and his family, I wanted to opt for the Holland, Roskilde, Belgium option but Gerry and the girls preferred the South American tour. Either way it was going to be a great experience and I went with the flow.

In May we weren't the only people contemplating leaving the UK as The Labour Party swept into power for the first time in 18 years with the orange ultra spinning Tony Blair at the helm.

The South American tour was to be promoted by Francis Mortimer who had previously toured the continent with Holiday on Ice. We bought eight containers to load our equipment in and in June left for our amazing adventure.

The first port of call was Uruguay and it's capital city Montevideo, we were in a huge run down arena called De Junio Palacio Penarol, in a huge run down City. The main street had all the usual suspects such, as McDonald's, KFC etc but off the main street the potholes in the road were like moon craters.

Every car you ever owned along with every car your father and grandfather ever owned were still being driven around the craters of Montevideo. I'm sure I saw my Dad's old Morris Minor, still with no lights and my old Simca dodging the potholes in Uruguay.

The Arena was far too big and the publicity was none existent, consequently business was poor. Back in the UK if business was looking dodgy we would conjure up a publicity stunt to drum up interest. In South America we would always be greeted with the same response 'anyana'.

The only stunt we did in Uruguay was the human mobile on a crane over a speeding motorway.

For our Latin America tour we added Wasp Boy as the shrunken waisted Sword Swallower, created a brilliant Arial Bungee act performed in the dark by our flying skeletons and coached by Cirque Du Solie trainer Basil Schoolts. We also introduced the excellent hair hanging act or Mercia VI.

The only musical change was swapping Toni Quintini for Tommy Todgertoucher on Guitar. We did not fall into the language trap of Munich and recorded a number of voice-overs in Spanish.

After a week in Uruguay we moved onto Argentina and Buenos Aries, we took the very short plane journey and on our arrival at the airport we were met by around 30 photographers and five TV crews, it was as though Madonna was arriving, there was more media than people and we were herded into ten huge black limos and driven to the venue.

Kristina Gacia with Maradona, photo credits, from Haze's personal collection

Suddenly the PR machine seemed to have clicked into gear and the future was looking bright.

In BA we performed for two weeks in Luna Park, a venue the size of Wembley Arena. The publicity we gained arriving in town wasn't enough and generally business was poor. In hindsight it was a crazy idea to think we could fill a 10,000 seater arena every day for two weeks. We did a couple of high profile TV show's and also did the Human mobile again, this time right next to the Obelisk, it was not enough.

Our next two Argentinean cities were Rosario and Cordoba, they were small cities and we should have been able to get to the people better but Frances Mortimer had fallen out with Gerry and lost interest, on top of this the publicity got worse.

Once again, to drum up support we attempted to do the Human mobile, this time though it was to almost end in disaster. The keyboard player, Kase, had decided to go on the lash the night before, none of us realized there was anything wrong when we strapped him onto one of the pole frames.

We were hoisted 300 foot in the air and then someone spotted Kase had fainted and was sliding down the pole he was strapped to.

We started to call the crane driver to get us down but he had walked away from the crane. Hugh our soundman did hear us though but thought we were shouting to turn the music up, so he did.

At this point one of Kase's feet slipped out of the foot stand and the strap around his waist was now around his neck. Had his other foot fallen out he would either have hung himself or he would have fallen to his death. This would also cause the counter balance to flip the mobile over and we would all have come crashing to the ground. Luckily a 10 year old boy on the floor noticed the problem and alerted the crane driver who quickly got us to the ground. Kase was taken to hospital but released shortly afterwards with a flea in his ear.

A pleasant relief from the poor business and Kase's almost fatal liaison with a crane came when we all decided to go and see Rosario Old Boys play Boca Juniors in a team that contained an ageing and bloated Diego Maradona. It was there that we really discovered the hostility towards the English, never forgiven for our part in the Falklands War. The baying crowd chose the opportunity to chant racist remarks and spit at us.

Perhaps this hostility was part of the reason for the poor business, we were billed as 'Direct from London' so it wouldn't have helped.

Next and final stop on our South American tour was to take us over the Andes to Chile.

Santiago is a sprawling pollution laden city at the foot of the Andes. To overcome the pollution they have odd and even numbers at the end of each vehicle number plate and you are only allowed to drive in the city on alternate days.

Every street corner in Chile had a coffee bar, these were amazingly popular with businessmen. Not so much for the coffee more so for a look at the voluptuous mini skirt clad girls that work in them. It was something to behold, any one who's been to Chile will know what I'm talking about.

We were to perform in Estadio Chile, again a huge venue, this time a 5,000 capacity. Business was better but again it was too big an ask to expect to sell 5,000 seats six days a week for three weeks.

Frances Mortimer had appointed a local promoter Carlos Plastini. Carlos ran the venue and looked like a stereotypical Chilean bandit, twisted mustache and all.

Gerry's patience was becoming stretched and an encounter between Polly's boyfriend Salaam and Carlos Plastini ended in the Police being called. Originally they were going to arrest Salaam but after Gerry's intervention they decided to arrest him instead.

Gerry did not fancy being banged up in a Chilean cell so hid in my hotel room while I went to the British Embassy to plead his innocence. They intervened and all seemed fine as long as Gerry kept a low profile and trust me, getting Gerry to keep a low profile is no mean feat

I liked Chile and somehow got a taste for coffee while I was there, a great highlight was a skiing expedition to the Andes, it was amazing but as you would expect in South America typically dangerous, and a Health and Safety free zone.

As most of us were novices we had a morning on the small slopes, we enjoyed it so much asked if we could go on the larger ones, Willie, Hugh and Ingo were seasoned skiers an coped well, the rest of us not so. At one point I went careering down this slope at wha seemed to be 100 miles per hour, I couldn't stop. I could see the rest of our guys ahead c me standing like a row of skittles just waiting for me to score a perfect strike before flyin over the cliff into oblivion.

I had only one other option to guide myself to the right and crash into a pile of snow. It wa like ski Sunday I went flying, my skis came off and flew into the air and hit a passing ski on his head. Amazingly I survived with only my pride damaged. Johnny Brenner was not s lucky, he decided to snow board, went down a slope too fast, couldn't turn and went straig through a wooden fence. It was like a cartoon, just the shape of Johnny in the fence wi him lying like a sack of spuds on the other side.

After Chile we were offered to extend the tour and go to either another Chilean city or to Peru, we had no confidence in Frances Mortimer and decided to cut our losses and return home. We had completed our contract and felt that if we left now we could return home with our heads held high.

The big mistake was we left Carlos to load the containers onto the boat to the UK while we all flew home. Myself, Andy Higgins and Hugh Sadlier agreed to break our journey and have a week in Rio De Janeiro. Pierrot lived there and booked us into the hotel in Copacabana that Great Train Robber Ronnie Biggs first stopped in when he fled to Brazil.

Our holiday was disrupted when we received a fax from the UK telling us that Carlos Plastini had abducted our containers containing all our equipment and refused to load them onto the ship home unless we paid a $50,000 ransom.

Over the next few days phone calls and faxes were exchanged between the UK, Chile and Brazil. I felt like some character in a James Bond film 'Our man in Rio'. It looked like I was going to have to fly back to Chile to try and negotiate the safe return of our property. In the nick of time Carlos agreed to accept $7,500, he took the money and loaded the containers for their journey home. A shame in some ways I was looking forward to a cup of coffee or two.

For the rest of the week we had a great time in Rio, checked out all the local sites 'Cristo Redentor' the Estádio do Maracanã, and Copacabana beach. I even managed to mug a mugger on Ipanema beach, gaining a very fine, although unwanted Spiderman Video that my potential muggers had mugged from some other unsuspecting soul.

The journey home contained some unexpected guests, Frances Mortimer and his wife Clara were on the plane with us. I considered doing a citizen's arrest on him for his part in the container ransom scandal but decided against it.

I enjoyed our South American adventure but I must say I felt a little homesick, nowadays with the emergence of the Internet I think you can feel closer to home, but back then keeping track on North End was proving difficult.

As with every adventure it had to come to an end. I was now back on home soil and reunited with Filiz and just in time for the new football season to kick off.

The Roundhouse, photo credits, Chris Parker

CHAPTER THIRTEEN
ROCKED THE ROUNDHOUSE

After returning home it was decision time once again. We all wanted to carry on despite the fact that the show had lost money in South America.

We didn't really want to go tenting so we thought we would look for a tasty London venue.

The UK was now under the control of New Labour with Tony Blair at the helm. We also, with Katrina and the Waves, won the Eurovision song contest so no more nil points at least for a while. We were only back a few weeks before the death of Diana Princess of Wales and North End were off to a flyer with no fewer than three Man United youngsters in their squad.

Our quest for a new venue started and Gerry suggested The Roundhouse in Camden, it was occasionally used for corporate events but generally it just stood there empty and looking sorry for it self in a prime location in Camden. The Roundhouse is a former engine shed (or roundhouse). It was built in 1846 and used to house or turn around trains until 1867. It underwent various uses including a gin warehouse before being abandoned just before the Second World War. It re-opened in the mid sixties.

It become a Mecca for rock n' roll under the banner of Middle Earth or The UFO club, mainly hosted and arranged by the then superstar DJ Jeff Dexter. The Rolling Stones, David Bowie, Jimi Hendrix, Led Zeppelin, T-Rex, and The Doors all performed there during that period.

In the late 70's it re-emerged as a Punk venue with all the Punk and New Wave bands playing here, including the American counterparts such as The Ramones and Blondie.

In 1983 the GLC had passed the building onto Camden Borough Council and it closed as a venue until it was purchased by the Norman Trust led by philanthropist, retired toy maker and true gentleman Torquil Norman, who, in 1998, set up the Roundhouse Trust to lead its redevelopment.

I contacted Torquil and agreed to meet him. Once the deal was agreed I took Gerry along, we all got on fantastically and we arranged for us to rent the venue for one month in October.

Our reputation had certainly preceded us from our previous London visits 12 months earlier. We took the same show that toured South America and the brilliant gothic structure of the Roundhouse was the perfect home for The Circus of Horrors.

Business for the first four weeks was generally good so we decided to extend our stay until Christmas. To launch this we broke a 40-year-old record set by Laurel and Hardy when two teams of 20-a-side threw 3200 custard pies at each other in three minutes. Jeremy Beadle officiated and generally got extensively 'pied'.

It got us great publicity and again business was good throughout December, although I did feel more than a little guilty breaking a record that was set by such legends.

Our time in The Roundhouse was not always a bed of roses and at one point we did find we were a couple of performers down after Johnny Brenner fell of his Roller Roller while it was being driven around the ring. The driver, who else but The Mongolian Laughing Boy. Johnny had fallen off before and normally bounced like Indian rubber, not this time though, he broke his shoulder and was dragged out of the ring with the audience thinking it was all part of the show. Within a day, his girlfriend Georgia announced she was pregnant, the first of many girls who became pregnant after becoming a pickled person by daring to enter our bottle.

Georgia was temporarily replaced by a beautiful former Aerialist and Lap Dancer Micia Real, she had no qualms about emerging from the bottle completely naked and we had no qualms allowing her to do so.

We were still getting great publicity and a whole Big Breakfast was filmed at the show one morning, we also did the first of many Don't Try This at Home's when Darren Day attempted 'The Wheel of Death'.

My private life was a little rocky, I was still going out with Filiz but I did stray on a couple of drug and drink fuelled occasions with Canadian Vampire.

As Christmas approached business took another upturn, so much so, we added

Xtended until December 21st!

THE CIRCUS OF HORRORS

Directed by
PIERROT BIDON
Creator of
ARCHAOS

LIVE MUSIC BY
HAZE
V THE X-FACTOR

New single
'the Monster Mash'
released 20 Oct.
on KADRAN Records

"The show of the Festival...
the year's sensational outrage"
EDINBURGH EVENING NEWS

"Bloody Good Fun !"
THE CUT

THE ROUNDHOUSE CAMDEN
CHALK FARM
Every Wed. Thurs. & Fri. at 8pm - Sat. 6pm & 9pm - Sun. 6pm
COSTUME NIGHTS every Wed. & Thurs. £50 PRIZE for the Best Horrors Costume
First 10 customers in Horrors costume admitted FREE
ARENA SIDE £30 - FRONT VIEW £15 - RESTRICTED VIEW £10
LICENSED BAR (from 1 hour before)   Not for Unaccompanied Children
CREDIT CARD HOTLINE 0171 267 0007 10am - 9pm Daily
ROUNDHOUSE BOX OFFICE 10am - 9pm Daily - PAY-AS-YOU-GO: Seats available from 60 mins before start of show
0171 413 1423 (Big Fee). And all branches of TOWER Records, HMV & the CAMDEN TICKET SHOP

"The Funniest Show on Earth"
Abendzeitung Munich

http://www.circusofhorrors.co.uk.
CARD HOTLINE 0171 267 0007 10am-9pm

another two months and after a Christmas break we opened to a sell out New Years Eve bash and ran until the end of February. All in all we were in the Roundhouse for a staggering uninterrupted 17 weeks, the longest a Circus had stayed in one venue in London for over 100 years.

The next stop was Holland when we took the whole show back into to an Arena, this time in Arnhem. Once again very successful and great fun too, we were followed over there by the Canadian Vampire and her friend, Alice. I didn't help matters by doing the dirty deed with her again. It seemed that I wanted to have my cake and eat it.

We returned home and it was time to make one of those decisions again. Gerry asked me to consider mothballing everything.

Not selling anything but loading it into the containers and leaving it there.

The choice seemed to be either to put everything into storage or try and do a tour of British and Irish Arts festivals. We were offered The Brighton Festival to start us off and offers came in from various other Festivals including Glastonbury, Galway, Stockton and Edinburgh. Gerry decided to toss a coin, heads we carry on tails we stop, it came up tails. Gerry thought fuck it (he was never much of a gambler anyway) and we went to Brighton.

The show changed quite a lot from the previous UK tour and we added a new troupe of Kenyan Acrobats, a Double Cloud Swing, Psycho Clown Jan Eric and from Hungary possibly the world's smallest man Pitchu. Illie and Jeff took a job at Chessington

World of Adventures so we lost the Wheel of Death act but nevertheless it was an excellent show and got rave reviews.

My relationship with Filiz reached its inevitable end and this prompted a promiscuous spell that got off to a flying start in Brighton.

It wasn't the only thing that went flying in Brighton after I fell off the box office steps and tore the ligaments in my left foot, I went up like a balloon. I had to take painkillers to put my boots on and more painkillers to take them off again. Luckily my dick was still functioning properly and certainly put it to good use during our time in the trendy south coast town.

In addition to The Circus of Horrors we toured in a few of the venues with the brilliant Circus Ethiopia, sadly though apart from Brighton, Circus Ethiopia did not do very well and eventually it affected our business too.

It was the so-called summer of 1998. Business was good in all the Arts Festivals but the weather was awful and we were under two foot of mud in Glastonbury. Glastonbury was a milestone in the Circus of Horrors history when the show first performed on the hallowed soil two years earlier. A couple of years past and it would become a milestone in Gerry's life. Gerry's penchant for cocaine had been well documented over the years but in a festival where many people take their first drug, Glastonbury thankfully turned out to be the festival where Gerry took his last.

Our festival season finished in Edinburgh and we then went on to tour in a tent in Glasgow and Leeds. Unfortunately the weather got the better of us and business was badly affected.

After Leeds we were due to go to Manchester and Nottingham but we had no alternative but to pull in four weeks early.

We had simply got too big too quick and we now needed 20 arctics to transport us around the country. Gerry put most of the equipment up for sale and this prompted numerous rumors that the show had gone bankrupt.

Was this to be the end of The Circus of Horrors?

Although our tenting experience was over for a while we got offered some great TV opportunities, first of all a cameo role on London's Burning then a slot on a special Royal Command Performance to celebrate Prince Charles' 50th birthday, performing along with Robbie William's singing 'Let Me Entertain You'.

The show was at The Lyceum in the Strand, the place had certainly changed a great deal

Strangely smiling Psycho Clowns, Beau Denning & Jan Eric with Joan Collins
Photo credits, from Haze's personal collection

from the days when I last set foot in there to perform the first of our 'Adventures of Shock Rock' shows.

It was now back to its seated and splendid best.

The Green Room was like a who's who of light entertainment, everyone from Vinny Jones to Joan Collins, Steven Fry to Caprice. No sign of egos either all there for a common cause to celebrate with a member of the Royal Family and increases our own profiles along the way.

Of course the exposure you receive from these shows is huge. You are seen by many more people in a shorter space of time than you possibly could be during live shows.

Both TV appearances were massive successes and I also continued performing on, and supplying acts for the prime-time Saturday night ITV show Don't Try This At Home. Now hosted by Davina McCall. Up to this point we had certainly had our fair share of TV exposure but it was generally, the 'and finally' or 'drop the dead donkey' sections of the news. We did of course feature on Dani Dares but this was late night Channel 4. Big Breakfast, A Royal Command, London's Burning etc were all better but Don't Try This At Home was undoubtedly prime time. I also got to see Davina's very splendid and hidden Devil's horns tattoo!

Despite the TV exposure I had no intention of giving up on The Circus of Horrors, Gerry and myself decided to give the beast one last chance and booked The Roundhouse again. We were due to open on New Years Eve but Stomp were in before us and asked if we would postpone our opening until mid January, Stomp thankfully rewarded us generously for this and it helped us get off to a flyer in The Roundhouse.

Prior to our latest and forthcoming return to the Roundhouse I flew over to Holland to see Robin Hagen. He was the promoter who had taken us to Arnhem six months earlier. He was interested in bringing the show back to the Netherlands. He had taken over the Rijnhal now, so we would go there but he also wanted to take us to a few other more conventional theatres' in other Dutch cities. Unfortunately he couldn't persuade any of the theatre managers to do it.

I left Arnhem for Amsterdam and had a few hours to kill before my flight home, I can certainly think of a few worse places to hang out and killing a few hours.

So, would I go to Anne Franks house or visit the seedier side of Dam, not a hard choice to make.

I walked around the red light district during the day and nothing particularly tickled my fancy so I went to the Erotic Museum and then to a coffee bar to sample some coffee and a couple of joints, the skunk was so strong just one chuff almost blew my head off, I decided to go for a walk.

By now dusk was setting in and the goods on offer in the shop windows were certainly looking tastier. In many cases lit in UV allowing the white underwear that they were wearing to glow invitingly.

I had never been with a prostitute and although tempted, I didn't think I had the nerve to do it, even in Amsterdam. That is until I walked around the corner and into this raven haired Aphrodite who politely said hello, she didn't need to say any more. I stopped and thought should I, dare I, my heart was pounding, would I pay for the forbidden fruit for the first time? Then I thought no and walked on.

I got about 200 yards away and thought again, I decided to toss a coin, heads I go back and break my duck with a lady of the night, tails I carry on walking. The coin went up into the air, came crashing to the ground and landed in a crack in the pavement exactly on its edge I couldn't have done that if I had tried.

I thought fuck it, picked up the coin and headed back only to find the Aphrodite was otherwise engaged and the curtains firmly shut.

I spent Christmas partly with Paul Peculiar and his then barmy girl fiend Shirley and partly with Filiz, although we had split up we were still friends and she was spending Christmas with her Mum in my road.

I also went to Preston and saw North End take on the then FA Cup holders Arsenal in the 3rd round of the cup at Deepdale, unbelievably we went 2–0 up only to succumb to the powerful Gunners who ended up winning 4-2.

Back in London it was time to return to The Roundhouse.

We started mid-January for a four week stand. We replaced Wasp Boy and Pitchu with Barrie Walls recreating the electric man act of the 1950's and an African Guy strangely called 88. I had discovered 88 while we were in Edinburgh, he was a really extreme contortionist and dislocater, despite standing over 6' tall he could fit his whole body through a tennis racket. We also added the female sword swallower 'Ami' Miss Behave.

In Barrie's case, he had worked with us during the last Roundhouse run but was only playing a character, a Mad Monk. This time I wanted something different, he wanted to re-enact El Hakim, I wanted something more outrageous, I won.

Haze with Baby Boy, AKA Barrie Walls, photo credits, Judy Totton

After my exploits in Amsterdam I thought it appropriate to watch a TV show about prostitutes and the needs of their clients, one particular fetish was to dress up as a baby, perfect. Barrie had a shaven head, he was five foot tall and five foot round and looked splendid in his nappy, the pins holding it together would be used to shove through his face and neck before we strapped him into a electric chair, pump 300,000 vaults through his body and light fluorescent tubes from his ears.

The intention was to also bring in Nicci Christian with her giant snakes and tarantulas. Although Nicci stayed, the act only lasted one day, we had two complaints from ill informed members of the public about the snakes and Gerry asked me to get Nicci to take her act out of the show.

Business was better than ever and we ended up staying until mid March which included a special Valentine Day Massacre Party and on March the 6th 1999 the world's first Millennium Party in the alternative Millennium Dome opened by the alternative Prime Minister and great friend Screaming Lord Sutch.

Sutchy had been a long-term friend of mine and of the show, and his rendition of Jack the Ripper with me and my band on the 6th March was going to turn out to be one of his last performances.

The show couldn't end its Roundhouse run without another mishap by The Mongolian Laughing Boy. We had strapped the 20' tall gold ladies to the outside of the building with collars around their necks. The collars went into the building and back out again. We put a forklift under their feet and gave Mongy the apparently easy job of undoing the collars. He stood on the top of the seats around 30' off the floor and undid the collar. But in true cartoon fashion held onto the collar that he had just undone. It seemed like slow motion as we watched him crashing to the floor, despite the heroics of Andy Carpetslippers trying to catch him he once again broke his arm.

Gerry had tried to sell the tent and equipment to no avail and despite the upturn in business Gerry to decided once again to mothball the Circus of Horrors. Instead of selling the equipment though he decided to team up with his former business partner Brian Austen and use the big top and equipment for a new tenting version of Cottle and Austen Circus. A lot of our acts joined this show too and for a while The Circus of Horrors looked dead and buried.

Although disappointed we still remained friends and I agreed to start a media company and look after the Press and PR for Cottle and Austen.

This all helped to keep me busy and I resumed my mantle within The Psycho Management Company providing bands, comedians and specialty acts for anyone who wanted to book them.

It also gave me the opportunity of doing lots of TV shows, including loads more episodes of 'Don't Try This At Home' I was even offered a small slot on the show as a presenter until they changed their mind and opted for an actor who they christened Doctor Don't instead of Doktor Haze.

After my split up with Filiz 14 month's earlier and my promiscuous period, I started going out with Nicci Christian. Strangely, despite the fact that I had been involved in Circus for most of my life I had never been out with a Circus girl, until now. Nicci was a feisty and glamorous Snake wrangler. She would often bring her menagerie of giant Snakes, Tarantulas and Scorpions to my house. It was not uncommon for her to let the snakes come to bed with us and one day when my friend Paul Peculiar called, I had to warn him to beware if he went to the toilet because there was a 20 foot python loose in there.

He paused on the stairs and thought, 'believe everything Haze says, believe nothing Haze says' and went to the bathroom.

The snake, Sharon, had wrapped itself round the toilet, We heard a huge scream and saw Paul running down the stairs with his trousers round his ankles, he headed out of the back door and had a piss in my garden.

I personally liked the snakes but drew a line the day Sharon tried to join me in the bath.

In May I received a strange call from a guy from Morocco, the man said I had been recommended by someone at the Roundhouse and asked if I could meet him to discuss putting together a Circus for a party in Morocco. I agreed to meet him in Camden and he explained that his friend in Morocco was a high profile person, money was not an obstacle and the party was for his friend's birthday. He asked me to travel to Morocco and meet them.

I asked whom his friend, my potential client was, he was clearly reluctant to tell me and said I wouldn't know him. Possibly foolishly, I agreed to go.

I received a call from the mystery man a week later who said he had booked me on a plane the following weekend. I again asked who the client was, again he said, oh just a rich guy, you wouldn't know him. So I was due to fly to Rabat in Morocco to meet some guy who possibly wanted me to put a show together for him in some exotic land, I had no idea where I was going or who I was seeing. I didn't want to miss out on a potential pay day and great adventure to boot but I needed to at least have some clue as to who I was going to see, I had an idea, and asked the mystery man where I was staying. Yet again he was reluctant to tell me, I insisted, explaining that people I the UK may need to get hold of me, so he told me it was The Golden Tulip Farah Hotel.

I rang the hotel and asked if they had a booking for me, they confirmed that I was booked into a suite, I asked who booked it and they said The Royal Family. It turned out I was off to Rabat to organize a show for the Prince Moulay Rachid of Morocco.

Once I arrived I was taken straight through security, assigned a chauffeur and taken to my hotel. No checking of passports, no waiting for baggage reclaim just hustled straight though into the awaiting limo. I was driven to the hotel and told to wait until the Prince could see me, this turned out to be three days later. The suite was the size of a house and I was told I could order anything I wanted.

In the meantime I turned into Lobster Boy by basking in the African sunshine by the pool on the roof of my hotel whilst reading Dracula. I was offered girls to entertain me but although tempted I declined, to scared too take advantage of this very kind offer and far too scared of Nicci if she had found out.

I did eventually see the Prince and we got on well. I was taken to The Palace and went through a number of ideas. He seemed more interested in the unusual acts particularly Mr Methane, can you imagine I had travelled to Morocco in a cloak and dagger operation that would put MI5 to shame just to show the Prince a video of a guy farting Land of Hope and Glory.

Unfortunately none of ideas came to fruition as his father, King Hassan II died in July and the whole party idea was cancelled. It did mean of course that I laughed about rumbling rectums with the man who was to become King of Morocco, King Mohammed VI.

Very Carry On.

After I returned home we were invited to perform at the Kerrang! Awards at Virgin Megastore in Oxford Street. I took along, Satanica AKA Nicci, Barrie and Tony Walls AKA Baby Boy and The Mongolian Laughing Boy.

Cradle of Filth were amongst the guests. I had met Danny Filth a few years earlier when I and the rest of Filth came to see The Circus of Horrors at The Roundhouse.

Mongy got carried away with his newfound Rock Star status, got drunk before the show and left his props three floors above where we were performing.

First he forgot the firework that we lit while it was inserted up his arse and then the fluorescent tubes that we used in the electric chair. The thing is I didn't know he had forgotten them and I started the show.

The show was going down a storm until we got to the Electric Chair act, Mongy sat in the chair and we got two people out of the audience to touch him and feel the electric current run through his body. The cynical world we live in provoked us to prove the electric current was actually running through his body.

We proved this by inserting fluorescent tubes in his ears and up his arse.

Here comes the problem, I asked for the tubes and everyone looked blank at me. That is except for the Mongolian Laughing Boy who whispered he had left them in the dressing room.

The baying crowd of rockers were getting restless while we waited so the only thing I could think of doing was continuously bash Mongy over the head with a pair of plastic pliers, it seemed to temporarily entertain the crowd and certainly relieved my aggression. His head ended up with more craters than the moon, quite ironic as there was a solar eclipse next day.

At the same time Danny Filth had decided to take a piss in the DVD section and was escorted to an office next to our dressing room. The tubes eventually came and we lit them from Mongy's now throbbing ears. We finished the show by Blowing and Eating Fire and managed to set off the fire alarms causing the fire brigade to come rampaging through the store.

We went back to the dressing rooms, taking the lift upstairs to the fourth floor, I was still rowing with Mongy and still hitting him over the heads with the pliers. He kept saying, hit me more I deserve it, so I did.

We went to our dressing room and heard an almighty crash, Danny Filth had thrown a huge mirror out of his room to the floor four stories down then did a runner. The Police were called and after hearing myself and Mongy's altercation they thought it was us and tried to arrest us. We persuaded them that we were just acting and the lumps on Mongy's head were special effects.

the space of five minutes we had caused two of the three emergency services to be called out, well two out of three ain't bad. Now that's Rock 'n' Fuckin Roll.

the Autumn we teamed up with Bizarre Magazine to present a new show called the arnival of the Bizarre and tour Universities. It was a really good Rock 'n' Roll Freak Show, would sing a few of the songs from The Circus of Horrors on playback and we had acts like

Haze with Lord Sutch, photo credits, from Haze's personal collection

Satanica with her Snakes Tarantulas and Scorpions, The Mongolian Laughing Boy, The Electric Chair, 'Ami' Miss Behave Sword Swallowing, Lucyfire's Fire Eating, Angle Grinding and Glass Walking and McAbre's Sword and Dagger balancing.

We also took DJ's Allan and Dave from The Torture Garden and former guitarist com keyboard player and sound operator Drew Blood. It really was British Freakshow Royalty.

The shows were huge successes and we were paid a fee in each venue so I didn't hav financial problems. The Circus of Horrors had now been mothballed for almost a yea Financially it didn't make any difference to me, I was making just as much money as I mad while I was touring the show.

Inwardly though I really missed it and I knew a great deal of my success was down to th fact that I was the creator and undead ringmaster from The Circus of Horrors, as mar people wanted to book me for that reason as they did for my personal abilities.

The sad news that year was the death of my friend Screaming Lord Sutch, he had be suffering from manic depression since his mother died a year earlier. Following a career an early-'60's Rock 'n' Roller it became customary for the UK media to refer to him as Screaming Lord Sutch, or more simply Lord Sutch. His early works included recording the classic, (although not a hit) Jack the Ripper, which was produced by the legendary Joe Meek.

Sutch's album Lord Sutch and Heavy Friends was unfairly named in a 1998 BBC poll as the worst album of all time, despite the fact that Jimmy Page, John Bonham, Ritchie Blackmore, Jeff Beck, Noel Redding and Nicky Hopkins performed on it and helped write it.

His political career also started in the 1960's, he stood in parliamentary elections originally as a representative of the National Teenage Party.

The first time he stood was in 1963, when he contested the by-election in Stratford-upon-Avon caused by the resignation of John Profumo. He gained 208 votes. His next was at the 1964 General Election when he stood in Harold Wilson's Huyton constituency. Here he received 518 votes. He founded the Official Monster Raving Loony Party in 1983 and fought the Bermondsey by-election and in his pseudo political career he contested over 40 elections.

I first met him in a London club in 1996, we got on very well and he handed me one of his £50 notes, the next time I saw him was when he came to see The Circus of Horrors in Chelsea and then he would become a regular visitor to our Roundhouse shows.

His stepdaughter Alix even became our girl in the bottle for a while.

I had no idea of his manic depression even though I would speak to him regularly.

Sutchy would often ask me to come along and sing a tune with him when he played charity gigs and proudly told me of his proposed gig in Las Vegas on Halloween 1999.

I also got him a feature in a book about the millennium, they asked him what he would do if he inherited 10 million pounds. He said he would buy The Roundhouse, put The Circus of Horrors in it permanently and build a crocodile filled moat around it.

Sadly he never made it to LA or to see the millennium book published after he committed suicide by hanging himself. Leaving a note, which simply read 'DEPRESSION'.

Despite the sad news of losing a friend and ally in Screaming Lord Sutch and of course the demise of The Circus of Horrors, 1999 had proved to be a fruitful year for me. I had a new girlfriend in Nicci, a new spin off show The Carnival of the Bizarre and I was rapidly getting a reputation for my media work on both sides of the camera.

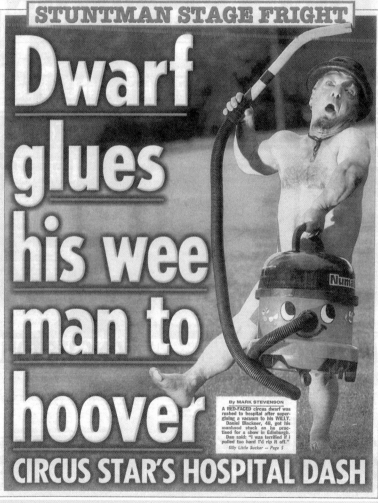

STUNTMAN STAGE FRIGHT

Dwarf glues his wee man to hoover

By MARK STEVENSON

A RED-FACED circus dwarf was rushed to hospital after super-gluing a vacuum to his WILLY.

Daniel Blackner, 48, got his manhood stuck as he practised for a show in Edinburgh.

Dan said: "I was terrified if I pulled too hard I'd rip it off."

Silly Little Sucker – Page 5

CIRCUS STAR'S HOSPITAL DASH

CHAPTER FOURTEEN
THE SPIN DOKTOR

Never let the truth get in the way of a good story.

The art of the publicist goes back as long as time began, many people think the Bible was written to 'repel the masses' to make them think that if they didn't believe in God Almighty and that his son Jesus Christ died on the cross, then you will rot in Hell.

Look at the propaganda used in wars, all publicity in one way or another, all publicity used to make us think in different ways. Churchill's 'We'll fight them on the Beaches' speech was a perfect rousing piece of politics and perfect spin in a day when none of us had even heard of it.

It was suggested that the legend of Greyfriars Bobby was in fact a Victorian era publicity stunt by local Edinburgh businessmen to drum up trade for that particular part of town. If it was, it certainly worked.

In more modern times the word spin came to prominence the day Tony Blair swept into power in 1997, with his director of communications Alistair Campbell featuring prominently in his campaign and during most of his time in office. Many people became sick of 'spin' as his years as Prime Minister became tainted by the Iraq War. Both Gordon Brown and David Cameron vowed to end spin and add substance but both still courted Rupert Murdock and News International. In Cameron's case possibly to dangerous proportions after he appointed Andy Coulson, the man allegedly involved in the phone hacking scandal whilst he was editor of The News of the World.

My personal involvement in spin came from an entertainment perspective, a way to increase profile and consequently sell more seats. It was never an ego thing but a business decision and one that can be great fun too.

Of course I have lots of influences and mentors in the art of spin, Marc Bolan was brilliant at it with tales of living with a Wizard in Paris, it was probably a dirty weekend with a magician in France but Marc chose to elaborate on it and it was used on numerous occasions in his publicity spin. Spin can often be associated with great showman and you don't get much greater than PT Barnum, a true genius.

Look at the Fiji (Feejee) Mermaid, it looked like the body of a monkey stitched onto the tail of a fish to me but it was still exhibited for a week in Broadway and later in Barnum's American Museum and it is still spoken of today. Two of Barnum's other great discoveries were in different ends of the spectrum, General Tom Thumb stood a mere three feet, three and a half inches tall and who under the employment of Barnum toured the world and appeared twice before Queen Victoria.

From the smallest to the tallest. Jumbo the giant Elephant stood an amazing thirteen feet one inch and weighed 928 stone when London Zoo sold him to Barnum. His very name 'Jumbo' became a word used to explain something extremely large but it was actually likely to be a variation of a Swahili word Jambo, which means hello.

In the days well before telephone, let alone the internet, it was amazing that Barnum's stories were circulating the world.

My other influences came closer to home, Gerry Cottle was a master of publicity and of course so was his one time publicist Mark Borowski. Mark dreamed up great Circus related stories for Gerry, Archaos and for Jim Rose. Aside from this Mark also represented a diverse mixture of performers and companies such as Michael Jackson, Graham Norton, Van Morrison, Joan Rivers, Sir Cliff Richard, Bolshoi Ballet, Cirque du Soleil, The Three Tenors, Eddie Izzard, Led Zeppelin, Virgin Megastore, Horlicks, American Express, Oxfam, Amnesty, Selfridges, Vodafone, Harrods, Cadbury, Mamma Mia and of course The Circus of Horrors.

In one of my first meetings with Mark I told him I was going to start my own media company at some point, he just rolled his eyes as if to say 'yeah I bet you will'. Ironically once I had started independently from The Circus of Horrors, Mark actually hired me to work on some of his Guinness related stunts.

I suppose I dipped my toe into the quirky world of publicity when I was twelve and put posters up for Fossett Bros. Circus, quickly moving to placing ads and securing editorial in the local papers in the Towns and Cities we were visiting. I soon started getting more adventurous when with Circus Apollo, I organized my first TV stunt. I was 17 and I persuaded Blue Peter to put Bionic Bertha our full sized mechanical Elephant onto the show.

The next TV appearance was on ATV Today when I spun a story to take the artistes from Circus Apollo to perform in the gardens of a children's hospital on the pretense that 'if the kids can't get to the Circus, the Circus will come to the kids', the presenter was Chris Tarrant in his pre Tiswas days and long before "Who Wants To Be A Millionaire' was conceived.

My first column inches in the Nationals came in 1978, Neville Campbell had asked me to organize the Christening of his numerous offspring in the Circus Apollo big top, The Daily Mirror covered it with a photo of all the artistes along with the screaming babies and the vicar who performed the ceremony.

My biggest story came later that year, I was in Stoke on Trent with Circus Hoffman. It was a freezing cold winter and there was a thick covering of snow on the ground. I had a bright idea to get one of the elephants to push Allan McPherson's car out of the snow. We had a big media turn out and the elephant did a brilliant job. The pictures got in virtually every national paper the next day.

I did try another one a few days later when we called out the AA to repair a motorbike that the bears rode, it was a brilliant picture with the AA man leaning over repairing the bike with a full sized Himalayan Bear sat in the side car looking at him. The headline read AA to Boo Boo. This time surprisingly it only got the local papers, but that's it with the media, you win some, you lose some.

That pretty well turned out to be the end of my Circus career and consequently the end of my media activities for the time being, of course I did the 1979 election campaign with posters declaring "Vote Flash Harry" we didn't get any printed media for that story though.

I always believed, through spin I could hype a band to number one in the charts and waited for the right time to attempt this with "Flash Harry" or its later incarnation 'Haze', that 'right time' never came however and I'm still waiting. It was really in the 1990's that I started to excel, obviously we still did the poster campaigns but started to get more and more media features, once we started touring we would get the local paper's and radio, I also started to get more stories and reviews in the music press particularly Kerrang!

We did a few TV shows too, generally miming to one of our songs, it was building up nicely and bubbling along when The Circus of Horrors started.

The first commercial COH shows were in Brighton and Mark Borkowski was hired to handle our PR, he did a great job and I certainly learned a lot.

Our first stunt under Mark was to arrive on a haunted ghost ship into Brighton Harbour, both ITV and BBC covered it on the local news, as did the Brighton Argus and a few nationals. When we moved to Crystal Palace, London Tonight were there with their then 'have a go' presenter Vince Rogers. He had become something of a 1990's version of John Noakes, we strapped him onto a motorbike and drove him into the roof of the big top on an inclined high wire.

It made great tele, so too did the Vampire auditions which got us The Evening Standard for the first time.

Media activity doesn't always instantly transform into greater sales though, we found with the COH we were slowly building up a brand and once enough people saw us in the media they would start to come.

The shows next stop was Manchester, we had quite a few advance previews but the press call could have fallen flat as it was unfortunately held on the day that Take That split up. We were saved though by Dani Behr. Dani was with us filming an episode for her forthcoming series Dani Dares, she agreed to do the press call with us but threw a strop when she heard The Sun were coming.

The Sun had apparently written something uncomplimentary about Dani's private life so she decided to boycott the press call until the Sun had gone.

Of course this simply pissed the other media off and they also went and slagged Dani off furthermore the Sun did get their story when a picture of her in her Vampire make up appeared in the paper with the headlines Dani's strop - a Behr faced cheek.

Dani's reluctance to talk to the press actually got us more press.

After Manchester the show's next stop was Bradford and the re-emergence of the Vampire Auditions, it was agreed that I would take over the media duties for Bradford, Leeds and Stockton and Mark Borkawski would return for the Edinburgh Festival.

Of course we got the local TVs, radios and printed media but when we did a story about our new girl in the bottle we got a few nationals again under the headline of 'Bottle Blonde'. Mark was none too pleased and felt if we got the nationals now we wouldn't get them in Edinburgh. I disagreed and thought back to my plan to hype a record to number one and waiting until 'the time was right'. Sometimes you can wait and miss your chance, I wasn't going to do that again.

Rumours were abound that Leeds Council would ban us from the City. I went to the media again, the story got the front page in the Yorkshire Post and two days later got Front Page again once the ban was lifted.

The press call in Stockton followed the template of Crystal Palace and Bradford with the Vampire auditions. The addition of local hero and Teesside football icon Bernie Slaven aka the Wolfman as an auditionee helped us again with the local TV Radio and papers, it also helped him promoting his book.

In Edinburgh and London Mark again took control, working generally on the outrageous stories. One of the councillors in Edinburgh was always opposed to anything a little different coming to the Festival.

We had received a letter from 'do gooder' from Wales who had supposedly seen the show, she thought it was very bad taste and blasphemous; we suggested she wrote to the Edinburgh Councillor. Once the councillor received this letter the Councillor went to the press saying we shouldn't be allowed at the Festival and generally did our job for us.

The reviews were getting better and Malcolm Hay from Time Out gave us a brilliant crit with the headline 'Bloody Good Fun'. This came out on the day we opened in London and also coincided with our Dead Celebrity Night, Vince Rogers covered it for London Tonight and also turned up when we created our first World Record by suspending 15 people on a Human Mobile 300' above the Thames. Vince joined us and was this time strapped to a pole and hoisted up with the rest of us. Although shitting himself he managed to interview me from our lofty structure.

We got quite a lot of media coverage in Germany and South America, including quite a few TV appearances, the only real stunt though was the Human Mobile by The Bavarian statue in Munich. Over a motorway in Uruguay, next to the Obelisk in Buenos Aries and almost fatally in Cordoba.

When we returned to London and The Roundhouse, Mark again helped us. After reading The Guinness Book of Records he suggested we attempted to break Laurel and Hardy's 70-year-old record that was set for the film 'The Battle of the Century'.

We agreed with Guinness that to break the record we could have two teams of 20 aside who had to throw a minimum of 3200 mustard pies at each other in less than three minutes. We hired a cement mixer to mix the mustard and got a master baker to bake us 3200 pie bases.

'Outrageous' circus of horrors to play in city

BY CHRIS MAGUIRE

A CONTROVERSIAL circus horror show slated in Bradford for being too being violent is coming to Leeds.

The *Circus of Horrors* simulates performers having their necks slashed and features the "human impaler", who sticks 250 pins in his body, and will be staged at Quarry Hill in July.

The show forms part of the "Rhythm in the City" Musical Festival and has been partly funded by Leeds City Council.

In Bradford political, religious and educational chiefs raised concerns over the same show which is being held in the city's Infirmary Fields as part of the Bradford Festival.

Deputy head at Bradford's Grammar School, David Crowther, said the show glorified violence adding "We live in a violent enough world without having this rammed down our throat."

But Bernard Atha, chairman of Leeds

Council defends grant for 'human impaler' show

City Council's cultural services committee, said: "As a matter of principle I am a very strong opponent of censorship.

"What is offensive to one person is not offensive to another. Certain standards have to be maintained and I am sure they will be."

Fantasy

He said a council grant was awarded to the West Yorkshire Playhouse, which is staging the "Rhythm in the City" Music Festival.

Organisers for *The Circus of Horrors* defended the show but admitted it was not suitable for children under the age of 16.

John Haze, who is the show's ringmaster, said: "It is outrageous but it is not sensationalising violence. Personally I find John Major a lot more disturbing."

"I would describe it as a fantasy show. It is like a horror show which has come to life.

"People are not interested in the ordinary idea of a circus any more. They expect something different and that is what we are supplying.

"If I had kids I would be happy for them to come along."

● Tickets for the show, which starts an 11-day run at Quarry Hill on July 11, cost between £8-12.

ROSS'S VIEW

CIRCUS OF HORRORS

Jo's fling with Beadle

By JENNY EDEN

Showbiz Reporter

STUNNER Jo Guest and joker Jeremy Beadle got themselves totally pie-eyed and sticky to set a new world record.

The beauty and the beast flung themselves into a charity flan-flinging frenzy to help throw an amazing 3,300 pies in three minutes.

They joined 18 others at London's Circus of Horrors to break the record of 3,000 thrown by comedy duo Laurel and Hardy in 1927.

Blonde beauty Jo was happy to say "Be my Guest" while practical joker Jeremy was quick to admit that by the end of three minutes as a target, Beadle was about plastered.

BE MY GUEST: It's a very sticky moment for Star favourite Jo

BEADLE: I've been stained

Jo Guest and Gerry Beadle with the COH at the World record custard pie fight at The Roundhouse.

The then page three model Jo Guest was a special guest (excuse the pun) pie thrower and stood opposite me. She became more of a target than thrower really. Jeremy Beadle refereed the event, stood right in the middle with guess who, Vince Rogers, who again covered the event for London Tonight and duly, got covered in custard. We managed to throw all the pies at each other in a staggering 2.5 minutes breaking the world record. We got great media coverage but we were still cleaning up the custard a month later.

We did a whole Big Breakfast from the show the next day and took the girl in the bottle into their studios a few days later. We also started the first of many Don't' Try this a Homes where Willie and Jeff taught the then presenter Darren Day to walk the Wheel of Death.

The show finished in March and we went over to Holland again using the Human Mobile our main source of publicity, for the next venues, Brighton and Glastonbury we again did the mobile and in the latter it proved to be a great way of escaping the mud.

Galway was easy, our naked Nun in the bottle provoked controversy and loads of column inches when she emerged from the 18'' jar wearing nothing but a Nuns veil.

In Stockton we introduced a Jaws look-alike the 7' 3'' tall Gary Tiplady to meet 3'5'' Pitchu, it made a great picture and got in the Times and The Sport!

Onto Edinburgh again, a five star review in The Scotsman got us off to a great start but we also did for the last time the Human Mobile. This time it was filmed by a TV show 'Record Breakers', we broke our own record by suspending a terrifying 21 people 300 feet off the ground.

In Leeds we did a great story about Pitchu and what is was like living your life if you are 3'5'' tall. He was pictured doing things we just took for granted like checking the oil in his car, posting a letter. The story got six of the nationals. We then started a flurry of TV exposure. It started with a cameo role on London's Burning followed by a Royal Command Performance to celebrate Prince Charles' 50th birthday, we performed A Circus of Horrors with Robbie Williams.

I then recorded a Don't Try This At Home which came out while we were in the Roundhouse. We had at last turned The Circus of Horrors into a brand but probably didn't realize it. Foolishly we closed the show down after The Roundhouse and didn't capitalize on all the publicity we had generated.

I, of course, carried on with my TV appearances and for the next year or so I either appeared on or I supplied many acts for Don't Try This At Home, on a personal basis I taught someone to fire eat on the show, I pumped 300,000 vaults through The Mongolian Laughing Boy's body and I drove my Land Rover Discovery over the top of a Strong Man who was lying on the ground.

Aside from the TV appearances Gerry and Brian asked me to take over the media for Cottle and Austen Circus, doing all the local stuff but also spinning national stories. One of the first of these was in Brighton where we placed an advert in the local Job centre for a Knife Throwers assistant. We had around 10 auditionees and lots of column inches in the national media, the winner was Yanna Rodinov who became the shows 'Target Girl'.

When the show moved to Wales we agreed with the media office at Swansea City Football Club to send our Kenyan acrobats to the ground to do a good luck dance in the centre circle. The Swans were having a difficult time in Division One and we persuaded them that it would bring good luck. That is until their then manager John Hollins rang my office and stopped the stunt going ahead. The show moved to Plymouth who were also struggling in the league so we used the same story again, this time the club accepted our good luck dance.

The stunt took place and was used on the local media and on Soccer AM. Ironically Plymouth's next game was against Swansea, of course Plymouth won and survived in the league that season whereas Swansea got relegated and John Hollins was sacked.

A year later and Gerry and Brian asked me in addition to controlling the media for Cottle and Austen but also to do it for the other shows they ran. The Moscow State Circus and The Chinese State Circus. This continued with me being asked to do the publicity for National Circus Day which was on April 7th. The intention was to incorporate all the English Circuses, traditional or contemporary. I agreed with Hamleys Toy Shop in Regent Street to use it as a venue and to hold the reception there. I also arranged to use Piccadilly Circus as a performance area.

The whole event became under threat when the Animal Rights Protesters got wind of it and threatened to throw paint on Hamleys window. They also made personal threats against me. To avoid confrontation we agreed to not use Norman Barret's budgies in Hamleys, sadly that meant Zippo's Circus boycotted the event. It was nevertheless a great stunt with lots of acts at Hamleys, then a parade down Regent Street where LBC had announced we were going to catapult someone over Eros. I had to give my assurance to the people running Piccadilly Circus that this wouldn't happen but we did it anyway with a springboard troupe from Robert Bros Circus. We also squeezed in a Guinness World Record when two girls from The Chinese State Circus balanced head to head whilst spinning plates for over a minute.

Unfortunately National Circus day happened to be the day Baghdad fell to the West and all papers and news stories were full of images of Saddam Hussein's statue being pulled to the ground and in turn pushing us deeper into news.

Nevertheless, in Cheltenham, The Moscow State Circus also broke a world record with an acrobat performing the longest jump from one trampoline to another.

Cottle and Austen were also too far away to attend so they too created a world record, in the case, the most amount of knifes thrown around a human. Yanna the target and her now boyfriend Jayde throwing the knifes. This Morning read about the record and asked if we could recreate it on their programme on Friday.

This Morning goes out at around 10am but when you appear on the show you have to arrive 7am. Jayde and Yanna did two shows in Warrington the night before and travelled down with Jan Erik, they were pretty knackered.

Jayde attempted to re-create the record and had 90 knifes lined up on a table beside him, Fern Britton counted down from 10 seconds, then some of the knives started falling out and hit Yanna on the head. Fern went up to Yanna and said Oh my God there's blood, Philip Schofield said, she does have a cut but do we know how many that was! Then he said 'round of applause marvellous', round of applause for hitting your fucking girl friend on the head with a knife? The first aiders were on hand and duly bandaged up poor Yanna's head like a Mummy. The paparazzi were quick off the mark and were waiting to greet Yanna as she left. The story knocked the Iraq stories off the front pages and gave me my first cover stories in the nationals.

Over the years I helped to create or break a whole host of world records and started doing them for PR companies aside from my Circus related stories. Bowkawski enrolled me to front a series of records based around the most amount of people we could squeeze into a Smart Car. The original record was set in Germany and was 13, we simply press ganged members of the public who were walking down the street and asked them if they wanted to be involved in a new World Record. We broke it in Nottingham and got 14 in, we broke it again in Brighton with 15 inside, emulated that in Leeds and got 15 in again. Next stop Trafalgar Square in London, it was the 8th September and the eve of England vs Germany. On this occasion we had two teams and two cars, one team from England and one from Germany, thankfully England won by getting 15 inside where as the Germans only got 14. I had hired Andy Higgins to bring his PA along, originally to play background music but I had advised him to play Vindaloo and Three Lions should England win. It was brilliant to here the England anthems ringing around Trafalgar Square.

Various media and TV companies including some from Germany interviewed me. They asked me what I thought the score would be tomorrow, I flippantly said England five Germany one, the next day they must have thought they had interviewed Mystic Meg.

We hadn't quite finished the Smart Car saga yet and we gave it one last stand, well three actually. I also used the opportunity to publicize The Chinese State Circus. We amazingly mashed the record by ramming an unbelievable 18 girls from the show into the car, the organizers were so pleased we did the same stunt three days running.

did two more records for Bowkaswski, the most amount of shots drank in unison, it was an easy record really we just lined up 200 shots 200 people, as soon as one finished they slammed the glass down and the next followed on domino fashion. The next was in Selfridges when we got 77 Elvis impersonators to sing Viva Las Vegas simultaneously. The Elvi were everywhere and we did the record spread along three escalators, with the stunt re-created on Blue Peter the next day.

nother PR Company, Free Range, which is run by a friend of mine Julia Knight, asked me to arrange a number of records for them. The first a pretty tame 'most people inside a giant bbble', the next, anything but tame, the Worlds Largest Trebuchet in Warwick Castle.

This stunt was particularly terrifying, as I had to measure the length of the throw whist trying to dodge out of the way of this giant rock that came hurtling towards me. We returned to Warwick that winter to record 142 skating Santa's performing a conga for two minutes, the final record for Julia though was my favourite and we did it at in Thorpe Park where we had 78 naked roller coaster riders, breaking another World Record.

We mustn't forget the other records created or broken by The Circus of Horrors, Hannibal Helmurto pulled a four ton truck 100 meters along Princes St., Edinburgh with just two meat hooks in his back and the numerous performances on Guinness TV world wide. Garry Stretch of course holds the record for the most amount of clothes peg on the face and the stretchiest skin, plus Blackheart the Barbarian broke the record for the worlds strongest tongue, Ami Miss Behave for Swallowing five swords simultaneously, The Kenyan Warriors for the most amount of flaming hoops jumped through in one minute. Helmut also broke his own record of meat hook truck pulling in Italy and Anastasia hung upside down with an Ariel hoop and Steph Mercury performing a trapeze act solely from Anastasia's hair.

Moving on from Guinness World Records there have been loads of other great stunts spun by my media company, starting with The Chinese State Circus, obviously there were many photo ops but one of the more interesting ones were when I spun a story about rubble!

Trapeze artistes ordered to wear helmets

Hard-headed: A Moscow State Circus trapeze performer   in her safety hat

FOR generations, circus performers have thrilled audiences with their astonishing feats on the trapeze and high wire.

But, while they can defy death at dizzying heights, the daredevils cannot defy the down-to-earth Provision And Use Of Work Equipment Regulations, as amended by Brussels.

Under the edict, stars of the Moscow State Circus have now been told to wear hard hats during performances in case they are injured. Even jugglers must don

Daily Mail Reporter

protective helmets to guard against dropping something on their heads. The news came yesterday from a consortium of seven insurance firms which provides cover for the circus, currently touring Britain.

Circus spokesman Paul Archer said: 'This is bureaucracy gone mad. They have basically said that jugglers should wear helmets in case an object falls and hits them.

'They also say the trapeze performers and the high-wire walkers should wear hard hats too. I don't know if this will spell the end of

circuses, but it is certainly going to lose some of the magic.

'People come to circuses to be shocked and watch danger and risk. Even if we decorate the hard hats with sequins, nothing would ever be the same again.'

Mr Archer said performers have been practising with hard hats worn by construction workers who put up the tents.

But he said they could prove to be more dangerous than protective. 'If they come loose and impair the vision, it would be a problem.' He added: 'We regularly get these sorts of communications and they all seem to stem from Brussels. If

we ignore the advice, then it may just be that some elements of the insurance are compromised in the event of an accident.

'These sort of guidelines would only be followed in Britain – just look at other European countries where people ride around on motorbikes without helmets.'

The Moscow State Circus was formed in 1917.

Since the fall of the Soviet Union it has been run as a successful business that delights hundreds of thousands across the world each year. Emma Grange, a spokesman for the Association of British

Insurers, said the issue of circus safety had 'no set guidelines'.

She added: 'Because of the nature of the job and the associated risks involved, employers might set their own guidelines to limit the cost of insurance. If you limit risk, you limit premium. It is quite a bespoke kind of insurance.'

David Clark, the circus's health and safety manager, said: 'The regulations would be fair enough if it just applied to our performers putting the tent up and down.

'But it means that anyone working above the height of 2.1 metres (7ft 6in) needs to wear a hard hat.'

In the show the Shaolin Monks would break bricks on one another's heads with sledgehammers and I had a great idea as to how to recycle the bricks. First of all I rang my friend Bruce Carter in Lytham St Anne's and asked if he would like some genuine Shaolin crazy paving for his garden, he jumped at the chance. We turned up on his front door with two Shaolin Warriors in full costume, 10 bricks a sledge hammer, oh and two film crews. We duly smashed the brick on the Shaolin's head with a sledgehammer in Bruce's garden and gave him the bricks. The stunt went so well we repeated it in Swansea, this time supplying the bricks to another old friend Animal Jones.

I even got a story in The Sun under the title 'How many China men does it take to change a light bulb', the answer was four as they stood on each others shoulder until they were four man high to change the bulb that was trickily positioned in a stair well.

Onto the Moscow State Circus, I had found out that the husband and wife crossbow team were having personal difficulties and I asked the show's manager, Paul Archer, if they were getting divorced. Paul said 'I don't think so', I said 'well can they'. Paul asked them how serious their problems were and indeed they were considering divorce, bingo.

The act consisted of the husband and wife taking turns at firing a crossbow at each other, of course each time narrowly missing. The act culminated in the wife triggering seven cross bows, the 1st flew across the ring hitting a target which itself fired another crossbow to hit another target and so on. The last target fired a crossbow which unbelievably hit an apple precariously balanced on the head of her husband, a real William Tell moment but more to the point a great stunt 'Hell hath no fury like a woman scorned'.

The media loved it and it went everywhere, all the nationals, all the TVs.

The next stunt for The Moscow was playing on our ever-increasing infatuation with Health and Safety after a visiting H and S adviser complained that everyone in the show should wear sensible shoes whilst climbing ladders. Our Clown wore size 15's whilst climbing an unsupported ladder as part of his act, hardly sensible but great ammunition for a story.

I hadn't finished with the Health and Safety quagmire yet and our next stunt turned out to be a really beauty. It all came out from a flippant remark from a Euro H and S expert. He asked us how we cope with the working at height regulations with regard to our Flying Trapeze act. I said to him 'oh come on you'll expect them to wear hard hats next and he laughingly said 'Yes I'm sure we will'. Wham Bam Thank You Man.

I spun a story 'Flying Trapeze act told to wear hard hats', It was massive, my biggest story so far, we were getting interviews from all over the world, it hit almost every national paper, loads of TVs and Radios and Richard Littlejohn dedicated his weekly column in the Mail to the story with a cartoon of the barmy H and S goings on.

We had run lots of stories with Cottle and Austen and the knife throwing incident kept coming back, first Yanna became a knife thrower's assistant after answering an ad in the Job Center. She then started to go out with her knife-throwing partner Jayde. He then threw the knife that hit Yanna on the head live on national TV and finally they married each other. I got them on 'This Morning' again and Philip Schofield and Fern Britton presented them with a wedding cake that had a knife stuck in it.

Aside from This Morning I got them a well-paid magazine deal to help with the cost of the wedding and loads of column inches in all the national papers.

My favourite Cottle and Austen stunt came when they were struggling to get someone to become 'A Human Cannon Ball'. Brian Austen had by this time purchased Gerry's shares in the company that ran The Chinese State, The Moscow State and Cottle and Austen Circuses Brian decided to add The Human Cannon ball act to the Cottle and Austen show and had asked Hand Balancer Igor Zagorata to take the role of the Human Rocket. Igor agreed and went into training for the forthcoming season. Igor never really got on with the act and kept hurting his

I've been fired!

And you won't get anyone else of my calibre, says the human cannonball sacked over fear of flying

Dangerous: The cannonball act

By Dan Parkinson

WHEN it comes to being blasted through the air at 60mph, Todd Christian is utterly fearless.

It is a death-defying feat he has successfully completed more than 100 times.

Unfortunately, the more conventional form of air travel terrifies him.

As a result, the 26-year-old human cannonball has lost his job at the big top.

His employers, the Cottle & Austen Circus, fired him after he refused to fly to South America for special training to help him cope with the pressure on the G-force he experiences when launched into the air.

The decision has stunned Mr Christian, who is convinced that he is still the best cannonball in the business.

His terror of flying came to light after he twisted his knee as he landed on the safety net during a performance last month. His bosses discovered he had a long history of injuries to his legs and arms and decided he needed to strengthen his body.

They wanted to send him for specialist training at the Guiana Space Centre in French Guiana, which lies to the north of Brazil.

The satellite launch facility, owned by the European Space Agency, lets astronauts become accustomed to the pressure on their bodies that they face in space.

But Mr Christian said the journey was out of the question.

'I know it sounds silly because I'm a human cannonball, but I don't like long flights and if I'm on

a plane for a long time I start to panic,' he said yesterday. 'The thought of being in a plane flying over oceans for 12 hours just fills me with dread. I just can't do it.

'So I refused to fly to Brasil and they sacked me on the spot.'

Mr Christian, who is now living in Kent, said his lawyer was examining whether to launch a legal claim for unfair dismissal.

The performer, who comes from

a circus family and has also worked as a lion trainer and trapeze artist, joined Cottle & Austen in February.

He has been offered a new role as a clown with the circus - currently based in St James Park, Paisley, as part of its Scottish tour - but says he wants his old job back.

Marnie Dock, who is the circus's expert cannon trainer and who became the world's first female

cannonball at the age of 16, insisted that Mr Christian had to be sacked for his own safety.

The cannon consists of a 13ft long tube with a platform inside which is pushed forward by air pressure, sending the performer 50ft into the air.

They need strong leg and back muscles to cope with the pressure they are put under.

Mrs Dock said: 'We are very

strict about the people we take on because it can be a very dangerous stunt.

'Without the proper training it would be too dangerous for him to continue his career as a human cannonball.'

The role has now been taken over by Brazilian Diego Zeman - known as Diego the Human Rocket - who has trained in the Guiana centre.

d.parkinson@dailymail.co.uk

Forced out: A disgruntled Todd Christian (left) with the man who has replaced him in the cannon, Diego the Human Rocket leg when he landed in the net.

I went over to see the show and Igor told me he was going to give up and I said to him 'Human Cannon Ball gets Fired', suddenly those bingo chimes started ringing again and I decided to spin the story. The only problem was Igor wouldn't play ball and we had to draft in Nicci's brother Todd to become the Human Cannonball and duly get fired.

Todd though was now having the jitters and I told him I could arrange for astronaut training in the States to get used to the G Force. Todd refused to go on the grounds that he was frightened of flying. We now have a Human Cannonball who got fired and was afraid of flying. The final piece in the jigsaw came when we rang ACAS, the Advisory, Conciliation and Arbitration Service. We told them that Todd was going to get sacked from his job, he asked how long he had been there, we said one month and they said 'He hasn't got a leg to stand on'.

I had one Hell of a story. I put it out the next day and it was huge, all 11 UK national papers covered the story as did The New York Times and loads of TV. In years to come I even found a question in a Christmas cracker which asked 'Why did the Human Cannonball get fired?' The answer 'He got fired'. Perfect.

By the mid 2000's I had taken on a new client, Carters Steam Fair, A beautiful enchanted fun fair with some of the rides dating back over 100 years and everything restored to its former glory. It is easy to get local stories for them and also easy to get photo shoots. They had struggled to get any national stories.

The first one I ran was while the Fair was in Pinckney's Green, they had appeared on the Green virtually every year but this time they were only allowed to come if they didn't use steam. Now its not too easy to have a Steam Fair without Steam so I spun a story about it 'Not Full Steam Ahead as Steam Fair told the can't use Steam'. The story got a few column inches but mainly just with the local press.

I needed to put my thinking cap on and decided to look at London's congestion zone, I thought I'd drop them an email with what I thought as a very legitimate question. *'A vehicle transporter drives inside the congestion zone and then unloads 20 cars inside the area. The cars will then be driven around inside the congestion zone all day but they will remain within an area of 20' x 40'. Do the transporter and all the cars have to pay the congestion charge'?*

The answer came back, 'yes they will'. Perfect, Transport for London had now given me an email to confirm that Dodgem Cars would have to pay the congestion charge. I spun the story and got loads of coverage.

It was the Dodgems again that got us the next story. It came about after Anna Carter spotted a group of teenagers holding their ears when they heard her son Seth playing Cliff Richard records. She told me and I thought what a great story. Cliff had already taken a pounding after Radio 1 refused to play his records, Radio 2 followed suit, so now even the beige brigade couldn't stand listening to Cliff. The hoodies were bound to hate it. I spun a story saying the fair had been having trouble with groups of hoodies hanging around the fair but had found the ultimate deterrent – to play Cliffs greatest hits. The story was massive, all the nationals covered it and it was on both ITV and BBC local news.

The next story helped me combine both Carters and The Circus of Horrors. Joby, another of Anna's sons had asked me if I would put together a Victorian Freak Show and perform it in a booth he had built on the Steam Fair. Of course I agreed and to avoid any confusion we decided to call it Doktor Haze Freak Show. Joby then had a site meeting with the council and gleefully told her they were bringing a new attraction 'The Freak Show'.

The woman's face dropped, it was Brighton Marina all over again. "You can't have a show called 'A Freak Show' on our land" she told him, "why not" asked Joby, "because it is demeaning to call people freaks". Joby told me and I could just see a great story here, you can't beat being banned unless you are banned then the ban is lifted. That's exactly what happened to us. We were allowed to perform as long as we changed the name to The Original Incredibles. We got big features in The Independent and the Mail but lots of other coverage too including an appearance on Richard and Judy.

The Carter's story I loved the most came when Joby asked us to do the publicity for his upcoming fairground and memorabilia sale. I said what are you selling and he said Paul McCartney's head amongst other things. Great can you get me a picture of it, I said. He told me 'I can do better than that I'm going to see Peter Blake tomorrow, I'll take it with me and get a photo of Peter with it'. Peter Blake was the guy who designed the iconic cover for The Beatles Sgt. Pepper's album.

Joby had the picture taken then took the train and headed home to Reading, once he got off he realized he had left the head on the carriage. He reported it to the station manager and the rang me. This triggered a whole load of "Where's Paul McCartney's head" stories. All the papers covered the story the next day as did various TVs and radio stations. We offered a £200 reward and got a load more column inches.

We then had a call from the Sun telling us a tramp had found the head and had turned up Abbey Road studios with it tucked beneath his arms. Luckily it was a day when a big name band were recording at Abbey Road and consequently there were already a load of paparazzi outside, they gladly snapped away at the vagabond and again the pictures went everywhere the next day. The strange thing was the Tramp looked remarkably like The Mongolian Laughing Boy with a wig on!

The next thing was to reunite the head of Paul McCartney with Joby in return for the £2000 reward, again two TV stations and various national newspapers filmed this. It also had a large feature on 'Have I got news for you'.

Of course my other career as a Spin Doktor wouldn't be complete without a look at the stories spun about The Circus of Horrors. There were loads of TV appearances some stunt led and some not. We had auditions for the pickled person to see who had the most bottle to be rammed into a jar 18 inches x two feet. We searched for freaks on our special Freak Factor all of which got us great TV and media exposure. There was also Emilia's appearance on Big Brothers celebratory hijack shortly after she worked for us.

More rules and regulations helped us with our next story when a stage manager wrote me an email banning our performers from smoking on stage. It wasn't an original story, Keith Richards had been fined £50 for smoking on stage in Scotland. What made our story more prominent though was the fact that our performers who smoked on stage also fired an arrow from a long bow with her feet while contorting, or walked a ladder of swords in bare feet.

It made a brilliant story 'You can fire a bow and arrow with your feet but you can't smoke a cigarette in public'.

Helmet also told me he was training to become a Hypnotist, I asked him how he practiced and he said on volunteers. I asked "have you ever tried it looking in the mirror"? He did and lo and behold he hypnotized himself, the story 'Hypnotist Hypnotizes himself' went everywhere.

The big story so far though was undoubtedly the day Danny got his wee man stuck inside a Hoover but we've already covered that. The story keeps resurrecting itself though, usually at the expense of poor Danny being banned for his non-pc association with a domestic appliance.

An even bigger story was yet to come though so in the meantime this chapter has to close with a final quote from possibly the greatest publicist of all time . . .

Every crowd has a silver lining". Indeed Phineas, it does.

McAbra, in Iron Maiden, photo credits, from Haze's personal collection

CHAPTER FIFTEEN
THE RETURN OF THE MONSTER

1999 had proved to be a strange year, The Euro was established but thankfully did not become the currency of the UK. The Brit awards decided to combine 'The hottest acts of the moment', B*Witched, Steps, Tina Cousins, Cleopatra and Billie joined forces to create 'Thank ABBA For The Music', which goes on to prove what a god awful state the music industry was in. The Millennium Dome and the London Eye were created in readiness for the new century.

The Circus of Horrors had been mothballed in March but I still did loads of shows, mainly with the bastard son of The Circus of Horrors, the Carnival of the Bizarre, but also lots of TV, from loads of Don't Try This At Homes to more low profile shows on Bravo.

In addition to these and my new found career as a Spin Doktor I was making as much money as I ever had, the thing was I was still missing my baby. Things were about to change though.

In December I was introduced to a promoter called Paul Bernard. He had previously promoted The Rocky Horrors Show amongst others and he was keen to take The Circus of Horrors on a theatre tour.

I spoke to Gerry about the idea and as we were to be paid a fee by Paul Bernard we did not have a financial worry. We always wanted to turn The Circus of Horrors into a theatre show and thought this was our chance.

Paul went about booking a theatre tour and we contacted the Arts Council of England who agreed to give us a grant of £50,000 to turn The Circus of Horrors from a show in the round into a Theatre production and a show that would fit into a two dimensional proscenium arch venues.

The main reason for the Arts Council funding us was to try and attract a new audience to our ailing theatres, in the main they had become something for old people, the dreaded beige brigade.

The West End was slightly different but one thing was for sure, cool people didn't go to 'The Theatre' and sooner or later their aging clientele would snuff it and unless the theatre bookers did something about it the theatre would snuff it too.

Thankful they did and The Circus of Horrors tour was beginning to take shape.

One of the few negative comments we used to receive about our previous shows was that it did not have a story. This time round we decided to do something about it. The new show was set in 1900, the end of Queen Victoria's reign and the year of The Freak Show.

I wrote a new story and lots of new songs including what was to be the title of the new show "Welcome to the Freak Show".

The story told of a young girl, Ragen, it started with her in a giant bed awoken by the barker beckoning the crowd into the Carnival Mid Way. She was not sure if she was awake or was dreaming or was having her worse nightmare.

Her journey saw her run away and join the Circus, fall in love with the Jesuit Priest, then, rejected by him she sought solace by taking opium and tripping in a grave yard among acrobatic and bungying skeletons until she was sacrificed by the evil Doktor.

In the second half she was reborn as an undead Vampire in 2020 and joined the rest of the now Cyber Circus and was hell bent on revenge of her Victor.

Sounds great, unfortunately it went straight over the audience's head, they had come to see daredevil and bizarre Circus acts but found them submerged within a Musical. All be it more of a Musikill, but never the less it had certainly lost it's edge and we were in danger of losing our audience.

I still maintain though, the concept would make a brilliant film, a sort of Alice in Horrorland

Artistically a few mistakes were made, Circus artistes can be great performers but it does not make them great actors and I include myself in this. We also did not realize that some acts that worked great in the round would not work so well in a two dimensional setting.

Potentially we had some really good acts, Willie's Cloud Swing went down a storm as did the exorcism act, we introduced a brilliant Glass Eater from Guyana called Moro. He would break and eat around six wine bottles, unfortunately most people did not believe it was real glass.

Wasp Boy returned to the show, his skill as a Sword Swallower could not be questioned but he was a poor showman, this shone out in our new setting as it did with his girlfriend and assistant Kristy.

McAbre also performed her Sword and Dagger act and Nicci, aka Satanica a Hair Hanging act. We also recruited a brilliant double contortion act from Mongolia and two female singers

Carrie Harvey, who became our bearded lady and the gypsy queen Silvana Salone.

In addition to the new set, new show and new artistes we also brought two new large-scale illusions from Holiday on Ice, a levitation illusion and a giant sword box, both expertly redesigned by Andy Dingley our new special effects man. It was all there, it just didn't gel.

Mind you the show almost ended as soon as it began. Towards the end of the show on the first night I was inside a Heath Robinson style sawing in half illusion when the half that contained my head went careering down the stage towards the orchestra pit. To make it worse I was singing 'I will survive' at the time. Not only had we misjudged the fact that we were now in 2D but also forgot about the rake on the stage.

Dingy Dangler and Gezmond were supposed to put a brake on the illusion but had smoked so much dope before the show they forgot what planet they were on, let alone the brakes. Luckily Willie caught me in nick of time.

In addition to the mistakes we made with the production, the promotion was appalling. Paul Bernard was another Frances Mortimer and was completely useless promoter. He promised national publicity but it never came, basically he had offered to promote the show but he had no money or resources to do this. The simple fact is, no matter how good a show is if it's not promoted no one will come.

The deal we had with Paul was that he would pay us a weekly fee, we got this most of the time but he ended up owing us £20,000.

We tried to sue him for this and after a few court appearances we looked like we would win the case. Unfortunately he had no money and no assets to pay us and unfortunately we had to write off the £20K he owed us.

That winter we returned to the Roundhouse, looking for a salvation but ended up almost losing our shirt, instead of extending our time there we cut it short. I was at my lowest ebb, I had waited 20 months for The Circus of Horrors to return and when it did it fell completely flat.

I seriously thought about putting a gun to my head and committing suicide at the end of the last show.

Obviously I changed my mind and luckily as one door closed another one opened, in fact several doors opened. Out of the blue we were offered a record deal to record 'The Welcome to the Freak Show Album' on Silva Screen Records and then booked to take the show to The Fuji Rock Festival in Japan.

Once I had got my head straight I also wanted to try the theatre option again, I knew we could promote it better ourselves and also knew that we could learn from our mistakes and create a theatre version of the show. I still believed there was great potential there and so did a number of Theatre Managers so I set about booking a theatre tour myself.

Preston North End also once again did their best to boost my spirits by reaching the Championship play off finals, they were within a whisker of being promoted to The Premiership, the nearest they had come to reaching the promised land since I began supporting them.

They reached the final in spectacular style too, losing the first game against Birmingham City 1-0 at St. Andrews, they took them back to Deepdale and won 2-1, it went to penalties and we did it. The ecstasy and the pride was unbelievable, once again I dodged past the police with a dip of the shoulder, shimmy and burst onto the pitch in a way Tom Finney would have been proud of.

Left to Right: Bruce, Danny's children Sam and Dawn, Haze, Basher's son Aaron, Danny, Basher Front Row Bruce's wife Dawn and their son Ben. Outside the Millennium Stadium, Cardiff to watch PNE in the Championship play off final. Photo credit Bruce

e ecstatic pride continued as my self, Basher Briggs and his son Aaron, along with Bruce, awn and their son, Ben together with Danny and his family, drove with hordes of PNE fans n their way to the Millennium Stadium in Cardiff. This was two tribes on their way to war. nfortunately we lost the final against our Lancashire rivals Bolton.

; normal North End picked me up then dropped me down just as quick.

ere were more reasons to be cheerful in the summer of 2001 though. The record deal me about after a friend of mine, publicist Judy Totton recommended us to Reynald De lva who owned the label.

dy had a lot of clout and in an addition to handling the PR for the Circus of Horrors her evious clients included, Kiss, David Bowie and Status Quo.

e album was recorded in the new Fortress Studios in London and included, Prelude, elcome to the Freak Show, Thought you were in Heaven, Double Trouble, Secrets part one nd two, The Gemini, Look What You've Done, Death of A Wasp, Hey Boy - Hey Boney, The nly Sure Thing, The Destiny and Desire Zygote, The Samurai, Tubular Bells, The Monster ash, Just So Psycho, Judgement Day, Fire with Fire and Epilogue.

managed to persuade Silva Screen to allow us to include cameo performances from a umber of current and former rock stars. First up was Dave Hill of Slade.

oved Slade but in the 70's I hated myself for loving them. Forgetting that Dave Hill was w a Jehovah Witness, I recited the tale of my Christian time where I prayed to God for rgiveness for wanking and prayed to Marc Bolan for forgiveness for buying Slade records. e looked at me both shocked and confused.

espite this it was a real pleasure having Dave Hill, a Rock 'n' Roll icon and 70's superstar aying on MY album, he played on two tracks. Welcome to the Freak Show and Double ouble, and grooved around the control room as if he was on Top of the Pops in 1972.

'e did a deal with Dani Filth of Cradle of Filth to play on one track in exchange for me erforming in one of his shows that was going to become a DVD. Myself, Nicci, her brother dd and Mongy all also appeared on Cradle of Filth's Burial Ground Video.

still needed two more guests, I tried to get hold of Dave Vanian of the Damned to sing on vo of the songs. I had met Dave on a couple of occasions, he had come to The Circus of rrors in the Roundhouse and we had a drink together afterwards. I then bumped into him : 'Dracula the Ballet' at Saddlers Well's.

Like Dave Hill, getting Dave Vanian on board would have been a real coup for me. I first saw The Damned supporting T-Rex back in 1977 and had been a fan from then on. Unfortunately I couldn't get hold of him as he was touring The States with The Damned, supporting The Offspring at the time of our recording.

Mark Champion had a great idea that we ask The King. The King was basically a brilliant leather clad Elvis impersonator, the difference was he did not sing Elvis songs. He had hit album called Gravelands, all the songs on it were originally recorded by singers who were now dead, and it included a brilliant version of Bolan's 20th Century Boy.

Luckily The King was well up for it and sang on Secrets part one and two.

This was the first time The King had sung on anyone's song that is still alive, I suppose though being Undead made this statistic slightly different.

We were almost there, we had one more track to record and it was a song that segued, Arthur Brown's "Fire" and my song "Fire with Fire", there was no one more appropriate to ask to perform this duet with me than the god of hellfire himself Arthur Brown.

I knew Arthur quite well, we had mutual friends in Felix Dexter and Simon Drake. Arthur would come and see us regularly at The Roundhouse and loved the show. I was sure he would jump at the chance.

I rang him and as I expected he was really keen, he asked me to contact his manager who amazingly turned us down. I couldn't believe it and rang Arthur again. He was sympathetic but decided to stand by his manager, even Judy Totton tried to persuade him.

I had resigned myself to the fact that my duet with Arthur was dead and buried then suddenly the phone rang. I was in the studio, just finishing the backing tracks, it was Arthur asking if it was too late to come along and enquiring as to how much he would receive for the session. I offered him £500 and he got the next train from Brighton to London, it was brilliant to see him and amazing to duet with him, he did a fantastic job and the song sounded great.

I asked him to read the prelude and epilogue to the album too which he did in a true Vincent Price style. I had one final idea that I wanted Arthur to do.

The original song started with Arthur saying "I am the God of Hell Fire" I wanted my version to start with me saying "I am the God of Hell Fire" and Arthur to say "NO YOU'RE NOT, I am the God of Hell Fire", the problem was I didn't have the nerve to ask him. How could you ask the God of Hell Fire if I could nick his most famous line?

Mark Champion thought it was too good an idea to overlook and said he would ask him, I ran out to the loo to hide, only to come back to be told 'yeah he'll do it', It was a excellent final track for the album with the ultimate tongue in cheek opening.

The album was due out in October and I had booked a six-week theatre tour to coincide with its release.

I still had all my marketing responsibilities and spun away between recording tracks, performing the shows with Cradle of Filth and doing their video. I also had to organize the shows in Japan. In addition to all these we had two trips to Hamburg and Stuttgart for TV shows. The first with Wasp Boy and Polly Cottle, the then girl in the bottle, then with Baby Boy. It's a shame I wasn't collecting Air Miles.

The biggest excursion though was the trip to Japan and the Fuji Rock Festival. The Fuji Rock Festival was named as such because the first event, in 1997, was held on the foothills of Mount Fuji. It moved to Naeba, nowhere near Mount Fuji in 1999 but despite that the name remains the same.

Fuji is the largest outdoor music event in Japan with more than 100,000 people attending the festival each year. In 2001 it featured Eminem, The Manic Street Preachers, Neil Young and Crazy Horse, New Order, Oasis, System of a Down, The Stereophonics and of course The Circus of Horrors.

It turned out to be was a huge success, we dropped the story line because of the language barrier and just emphasized on the theme.

I learned a few words in Japanese and comically used them during Wasp Boys act, particularly the word for nipples.

The promoters built us a great set with a huge PA and lighting rig. To avoid taking too much equipment we asked for the promoter to provide a giant ramp for the roller skating Johnny Brenner to catapult himself from. This also housed Kase the keyboard player and another 12' high drum raiser for Mark Championi.

We also asked for a car that we could cut up, adapt and turn into a Mad Max mobile It would be part of the set and at the same time contain Johnny's balancing table. The turned up with a welder, two giant angle grinders, and a brand new car!

Fuck me, we expected an old banger and protested at first until the promoters convinced u it was OK to wreck this gleaming Toyota, so we did.

We had to perform two one-hour shows each days for three days, we trimmed down th cast, we took Johnny Brenner to do his Car Top Balancing act, Willie and Polly did the Exorci act, Willie also did the Cloud Swing and Knife Throwing. Nicci did her Hair Hanging, an Willie's wife McAbre did her Sword and Dagger balancing. Gezond Junior flaming Diab and Angle Grinding, Nicci's brother, Chain Saw Juggling Todd and Uncle Ganga as an annoying cameraman who had his leg amputated with a chain saw, completed the ensemble. The freak factor came from Wasp Boy.

Of course we needed some gratuitous nudity so Frances Richardson emerged topless from the bottle. She was strapped upside down on the knife board and did an aerial rope act while McAbra walked upside down on the trussing above the stage. We also took our own lighting director Bobinstien Mander.

Live music was important for this venture and The X Factor of Andy Higgins, Drew Blood, Mark Championi and Kase all as always played brilliantly. The show went down a storm, we were in our own area called 'The Palace of Wonder' and we had a capacity of over 10,000 watching each of the shows.

Regular visitors to The Palace of Wonder were Eminem's band D12, they seemed to love our show but I think the gangster rappers probably loved our bitches more.

It was a real taste of Rock n' Roll debauchery and some of the guys took it quite literally. After one night of alcohol-fueled fun, Gezmond, Bobinstien and Johnny stole a forklift and drove it up to the top of the adjacent mountain and walked back to the hotel completely naked. Bobinstien was also proud to let us know he had popped his cherry with a Japanese girl on the forks of the forklift.

The Rock 'n' Roll vibe didn't quite stretch as far Eminem though, before our show we received a message asking if he could borrow one of our chainsaws. He used to start his show by walking onto the stage in a Jason mask wielding the said chainsaw.

Of course we agreed and added our livery to the chainsaw with numerous COH logos and then went about our performance, leaving the chainsaw on a table for The Slim Shady to collect. When we came off, the chainsaw was still sat on the table. I asked why no one had collected it but know one seemed to know.

I strolled across to the main stage to watch Eminem's show, he walked out adorned in his Jason mask but not wielding a chainsaw, instead a Hedge Trimmer! Fucking Hell he looked more like he was going to trim privet rather then becoming the new Leatherface.

We returned home but our travelling had barely begun, in mid September we started the first of our six weekend trips to a theme park in Stuttgart, we would perform a 20 minute version of the show three times a day three days a week.

We took over, Willie who did his Cloud Swing and Frances who together did the exorcist act, Nicci's Hair Hanging, Drew on keyboards and we alternated the freaky elements between Wasp Boy, Baby Boy and Garry Stretch.

We did intend to use Mongolian Laughing Boy on these shows but he had one of his funny turns.

The night before we left I rang Mongy and reminded him that our flights were at 9am the next morning and we had to be at Heathrow at 6.30am. I got up at 4am to leave for the airport, I rang Mongy and he said he was on his way. We got to the airport, no sign of him. I rang again and he assured me he was on his way. The rest of us checked in, still no sign of Mongy. I rang again, 'where the fuck are you, you little Twat' I said, 'just coming under the underpass' he said.

Still no sign, I rang again 'Where the Fucking Hell are you are you' 'Just coming up to the departures he said, I can see you'. Still no sign. I rang again, no answer.

I then rang his girlfriend, she answered. "Where's Mongy" I said "He's still in bed" she said. "I'll kill the Fucking little bastard" I said and went to Stuttgart without him, vowing never to use the useless prick again.

The Mongy incident aside, the German shows went really well. Our globe trotting was still continuing and in addition to commuting between Germany and the UK we added in quite a number of Carnival of the Bizarre shows in Universities and also did a corporate show in The South of France.

To top all this travelling off the first theatre show turned out to be in Ireland.

Looking back on it I can't even think how I managed to do all these shows all over the world and still fit in time to help Mark Bowkawski with his various Smart Car world records.

I still recognized though that The Circus of Horrors was for me where all this had begun and I looked forward to getting back on the road again, this time no Paul Barnard to fuc' everything up, this time the show would be self promoted.

First stop for the new Circus of Horrors was Derry, this show saw Garry Stretch make hi debut in the show.

We still used the Welcome to the Freakshow theme, dropped a few of the laboriou narratives, turned the music up and gave the show a Rock n' Roll edge again. I had come t realize that although our venues were predominately theatres we were not a 'Theatre Show but an alternative rock n' roll Circus that happened to be performed in theatres.

For the next few weeks we took the show to 10 British Theatres performing for anything between one and six days in each venue.

Business was not great but it had certainly taken an upturn from the year earlier, we were beginning to understand how Theatres worked and which acts and which format worked best.

The line up was similar to that of the previous year. But instead of chopping Brian's leg off in a hypnotism scene we chopped it off for disturbing the audience by selling programmes once the show has started. You should have seen the usherettes do a runner once they saw Brian being handballed onto the stage.

Once the main part of the tour ended in early December I travelled over to Addlestone to meet Gerry and Brian, strange as it sounds after such a busy and successful year they tried to persuade me to give up The Circus of Horrors and work full time as PR for all three of the EEC show's. Gerry told me he thought the days of The Circus of Horrors receiving five star reviews at the Edinburgh Festival were gone.

There was no way I was going to do that. I loved The Circus of Horrors and I felt that it opened the door to other opportunities, not only for me but for The EEC. In the year to come this philosophy was going to prove me right.

I returned home that night feeling pretty fed up and took about 50 mushrooms that had been given to me. I had forgotten my vow to never take mind-expanding drugs if you're not in the right state of mind. I had a shit trip, made even worse by watching Eastenders followed by Walking with Dinosaurs, Fucking Hell Pat Butcher is one scary bitch when you're on a trip.

I spent Christmas with Nicci in her caravan in Sittingbourne, she lived in a nice American trailer but living in a caravan in midwinter was never going to be for me and I looked forward getting on the road again.

2002 started where 2001 had left off with another trip abroad, this time a trip to Holland to play in arenas in Arnhem and Amsterdam with our good friend Robin Hagen. The shows were relatively successful but I tend to think if we were in 1000 capacity venues in a few Dutch cities as opposed to two huge venues it would have proved more fruitful.

Andy Higgins, Gezmond and Bobinstien decided to have a night out on the town in Amsterdam and went to the Bananenbar (Dutch for Banana Bar, of course). For a fixed admission charge you gain entrance to the Bananenbar for one hour, and all drinks are free.

You are handed a glass for either beer or spirits, which will then be kept filled by the performers, all the lads chose Jack Daniels and Andy is so tight he had to get his money's worth and drank the JD like he was drinking water. He was so pissed he failed to see Bobinstien enjoying a Banana or Gezmond getting one of the girls to sign their autograph without using her hands.

They returned to the Hotel via a Chinese takeaway and fell asleep, that is until Bobinstien discovered Andy being so violently sick the bean sprouts were coming out of his nose. and dripping onto Gezmond who was lying next to him.

After Holland we did a small theatre tour during January and February. A successful pattern was beginning to take shape. We got another great break during this time when we were offered to perform on Ant and Dec's Saturday Night Take Away. It was a part of the show called 'what's behind the curtain', the lads were stood in front of this large circular curtain and genuinely didn't know what was behind it. Once it lifted they were asked to watch the proceedings then after the commercial break join in.

The show was still getting around 18 million viewers so it would prove great PR for us. It was a strange one, we had to rehearse without Ant and Dec to maintain the surprise.

The curtain was lifted and there we were, Hair Hanging, Acrobatics, Birds in Bottles, Balancing Swords on heads and Fire Blowing, - Then its Ant and Dec's chance to have a go.

The show is filmed live so they literally have the time on the commercial break to get ready, I can honestly say they were shitting themselves.

Dec asked me to go easy on them and I assured them to just listen carefully and they would be fine. I was compering this feature and as it was live I had a great chance to ad lib.

First they saw our Voodoo Warriors limbo under fire, then they had a go. They were then strapped face down to two tables had their shirts ripped off and we strangely put lobsters on them (it was supposed to be tarantulas and scorpions but we

Gerry Cottle with McAbre,
photo credits, from Haze's personal collection

could not find out if they suffered from anaphylactic shock). If they thought it a little bizarre and tame to use lobsters they could not be aware of what was coming next. Nicci and her brother Curly emerged with her 20 foot long python and laid it across them.

They didn't have time to breathe when they were picked up made to stand back to back before Bibi and Bitchu juggled knifes in front of their faces.

They survived but went berserk at the show's producers, it made great tele though. In fact when Ant and Dec were asked to do a pilot for the show for FOX in the States they asked us to be the special feature.

In the spring of 1993 the Media side of Psycho Management took another step forward, I was now doing all three of the EEC show's Moscow State Circus, Chinese State Circus and Cottle and Austen Circus.

To assist me in the office I brought in Gezmond Junior, Gerry Cottle's son. He was really the first full time PR assistant. The previous years I had Joe Murphy who was a great guy and potentially a real asset, unfortunately ill health made his time with us short lived. I then inherited Paul 'Spider' Web from Paddy's Surrey office as assistant and lodger. It all proved too much for Paul though. When I look back at my workload the previous year I needed a dynamic PA. Paul found it too stressful. and he ended up doing a runner.

Gezmond was certainly chucked in at the PR deep end. On his first day we heard Nicky Campbell talking about "the smallest dog in the world". I told Gez to call five live and tell them that at Cottle and Austen we had Pitchu the smallest man in the world.

He got on air but Nicky Campbell gave him a roasting about exploitation of dwarfs. Of course this is a load of bollocks, Pitchu was simply working in his chosen profession and earning a pretty penny doing so.

I started booking another theatre tour for The Circus of Horrors and in the spring I received a call from Frank Wilson. He was a good friend and booked all the acts for The Stockton Riverside Festival, he asked me if I would be interested in bringing the show back to Stockton. We decided if we were going to take the show to Stockton we might as well go onto The Edinburgh Festival as well.

This would mean returning to the big top. It was ironic, only two years earlier we had geared to change the show into a Theatre production and now we were on the verge of taking the show back into a big top and returning to Stockton and Edinburgh again.

Jesuit, on silks, photo credits, Seventhwave Imagery

CHAPTER SIXTEEN
BACK IN THE BIG TOP

2001, the world was in turmoil, Al-Qaeda pulled of the most monstrous act of Terrorism I had ever known after hijacking and flying two passenger-carrying planes into the Twin Towers of the World Trade Centre. George W. Bush, who incidentally looked older than his father, was somehow the president of the USA. He quite rightly declared war on terror and ordered the invasion of Afghanistan. Music was still generally in the doldrums and I had virtually stopped buying albums. Gerry and Brian had tried to persuade me to give up the COH. Despite this I decided to take the show not only back on the road but also back in a big top.

Frank Wilson and I had agreed to return to the Arts Festival in one of our old stomping grounds, Stockton-on-Tees. As we were doing Stockton, the logical thing was to take the show onto Edinburgh for our 3rd Festival and after that onto Bristol. As we were performing in a tent again we needed to add more daredevil acts that would befit the surroundings.

The tent we were in was not big enough for a Wheel of Death or a Motor Bike on the High Wire so we opted for the brilliant act of The Skating Aratas, we revived the Flying Bungee Skeleton act and Willie's Cloud Swing looked brilliant in a small tent, we also had Nicci's Hair Hanging act. It was a cracking show and did brilliant business as always in Stockton.

We also added a male contortionist called Rubber Ritchie re-christened Rubber Johnny.

By the time we moved onto Edinburgh a few people were feeling the strain. Some have forgotten how hard tenting could be and other newcomers such as Rubber Johnny found it 'back breaking' and left. We weren't quite as busy as previous Edinburgh visits so I did a series of stunts. The Skating Aratas, a four handed rotating Roller-Skating act by mother Carmen, with her offspring, Victor, Billy and Emilia performed on a roundabout at the end of Leith Walk with traffic speeding all around them. We had a Double Sword made that lowered Space Cowboy from the top of the tent by his feet and he and Wasp Boy swallowed different ends of the same sword before cutting it in half when it was inside both of them with an angle grinder. We also defied all the odds and got that five star review again.

I had booked another theatre tour, it was larger than the last one, now taking in 30 theatres and we were due to start just after Halloween. It was strange only eight months after Brian and Gerry suggesting The Circus of Horrors had had its day, they were now encouraging me to take the show tenting to Bristol for a month.

It was me this time that had doubts, again I felt four weeks in one venue was too long and I was proved to be right. We had hired a tent from Brian for all three venues and the costs were simply too high. The show went down well though, it was similar to the Stockton and Bristol shows but without The Skating Aratas and Wasp Boy, his place taken by Blackheart the Barbarian.

Before we went to Bristol I was booked to do what would undoubtedly be the most bizarre corporate gig on earth. It was organized by a company called Moteration and it was for Renault, it was supposed to be a team building exercise for their executives.

It was held in a haunted mansion in Telford. The place was totally run down and supposedly had been exorcized on seven different occasions. As though this wasn't enough, the director employed by Moteration dreamed up a hellhole of an event.

The delegates where taken from room to room and asked to perform some pretty nasty feats. If they refused or failed they were taken down to the see the jailer who happened to be me. If they conformed they were given or had to retrieve a key, the person with the most keys at the end won.

The rooms consisted of a key inside a vat of green pea soup, an actor was drinking the soup and pretending to vomit into back into the vat where the key was hidden. The thing is the actor was so repulsed by the whole thing, he really was being sick into the vat that the delegates had to put their hands into.

Nicci was in another room dressed in a PVC bikini and black fishnet tights, she sat the guy down, and took off their shirts. They had to answer a question if they got it right they won a key if they got it wrong they had a tarantula or scorpion put on them. A naked Monk was in the next room and the delegates had to retrieve the key from a meat hook that was attached to his dick.

If, or more to the point, when, they failed any one of these tasks they were brought down to me in the dank dungeon. They were bound and gagged by my henchman played by Andy Dingley, I blew fire into the air and they were made to kneel down in a pitch black room that was full of rotting dog shit that had been saved apparently for three months by the director.

It was pretty repulsive even by my standards and I was so worried that they would either try and fight with me or throw fermenting dog shit at me. I asked for a spade so that I could protect myself with and used it to hammer on the walls to terrify these poor normally suited and booted souls even more.

After about an hour of total humiliation almost all the delegates did a runner, the director tried to persuade himself and us that it had been a huge success and got us into a circle to sing "swing low sweet chariot", what a prick. The event was a disaster and the director correctly got the sack, we still got paid generously though.

After our Haunted House experience and the shows in Bristol we began a new theatre tour, again, Welcome to the Freak Show. This meant resorting back to the 2D version of the show and choosing acts that fitted this setting better. Originally the show was more influenced by the likes of Archaos than Jim Rose but the public's fascination of the Bizarre and the restraints put on us by performing in Theatres made me realize that the Freakier End needed to come more to the fore.

Wasp Boy had been our regular freak for a while and returned for the theatre tour. We now also featured his electric act and the amazing stretchy skin of Garry Stretch. There was a doubt though if they could work together after they had a blazing row about a gig they had done together. They got over their differences but never spoke to one another.

The theatre tour would take us through November and then again in January and February.

Business was generally OK without breaking any box office records although costs were high. However any profits were completely wiped out when within two weeks of one another two of the venues, Newcastle and Blackheath, went bankrupt and gave me cheques that bounced totalling over £27,000. I eventually got a small amount of the Newcastle money back and all the money from Blackheath although that took me six months and only after I stuck out for the full amount.

The Circus of Horrors had certainly broken the mould as far as theatres were concerned. In the past 30 or 40 years Circuses hadn't worked in theatres, we had proved that they could work and aside from venues going broke they certainly could be profitable.

Consequently in 2003 I not only booked theatre tours for The Circus of Horrors but also booked them for The Moscow and Chinese State Circuses. Gerry and Brian almost had cold feet though, worried by the historic fact of Circuses in Theatres didn't work and told me to try and cancel the Moscow and Chinese State Circus theatre tour's. Luckily I persuaded them otherwise and both the tours proved to be hugely successful.

By now Gerry and Brian realized that I was The Circus of Horrors 'till I die and they accepted that I had to continue to perform but I could combine that with the PR for all three EEC show's. What they did insist on was that I worked two days a week in Gerry's farm in Addlestone Moor.

My secondment to Addlestone was to turn out to be short lived as a huge shock was in store in the spring when Gerry offered to sell his shares in the EEC to Brian, sell Addlestone Moor and buy Wookey Hole Caves.

I nevertheless managed to spin my hard hat story before Gerry threw the towel in.

The whole deal took some time to be completed and in the meantime myself, Willie and four silk performers trucked off to Hong Kong to do a stunt where we would suspend a cross shaped truss from a crane 400 foot in the air. The corner of each cross would have a set of silks and in the centre Willie would do a Bungee Trapeze act.

I was stood by the crane with a walkie talkie, we measured the bungee cord and worked out how far Willie would fall before bouncing back up and once the crane reached a safe height I would cue him from the floor and he would dive seemingly into oblivion. Fucking Hell it was scary, he is a braver man than me, he had to have total trust in my judgement and I had to have total faith in my ability to judge distance. I did this by standing in the same place and working out the distance between the elevating structure and the adjacent buildings.

In the autumn, The Circus of Horrors pulled out of Gerry's farm in Addlestone Moor and our one battered artic truck turned out to be the last Circus to leave Gerry's Farm.

Addlestone Moor had become synonymous as far as Circus winter quarters were concerned. It had housed huge herds of elephant's and was home to lions, tigers and a whole host of exotic animals.

Gerry had created many great shows on that piece of land and in many ways it was quite sad that the last show to pull out of Addlestone Moor was us. Gerry shortly afterward moved into Wookey Hole Caves in Somerset, a beautiful part of the world with an attraction based around this piece of natural beauty.

Brian had bought all Gerry's shares in the EEC and become the largest Circus operator outside the Americas. He asked Gerry if a number of people that he considered to be Gerry's friend would stay with the EEC, these people included me so I suppose I was sold along with the EEC.

After that fateful farewell to Addlestone Moor the Circus of Horrors next tour begun a

was it a revelation. The tour went from previously 30 venues to 58 venues and ran from
end of October to early December in the UK and Ireland. Then again from mid January
il the end of February.

Circus of Horrors had well and truly turned the corner and was now a recognized as a
jor feature in British theatre and business was good almost everywhere.

show itself wasn't hugely changed from the previous year but we just got it now, we
w what worked and what the public expected to see.

g term drummer Mark Champion filed down his fangs and jumped ship, he was replaced
Steve McGrill and Polly and Jeff were succeeded by former Hula Hoop queen Yana and
h of Nicci's brothers, Todd and Curley, along with her nephew Ginger. The tour was
elling but fruitful and it was great to see so many people turning up to see the show.

erally the spirit within the camp was good too and aside from a night in the Golden
le in Stockton when Curly dragged Andy Higgins out of his bed with a belt around his
k.

penultimate night of the tour was eventful after a night of drink and drugs in a hotel.
somehow did two shows the next day and thankfully the adrenaline got us through even
did call Croydon, Hackney only to be corrected by the audience.

en we returned back home it was back to the PR and my office at the back of my house,
v shared by another of Brian's acquisitions from the EEC, Peter Norris.

er originally came from the edge of the New Forest in Dorset and like Gerry ran away
m home and joined the Circus.

st of his professional career had been spent with either Gerry Cottle's Circus, Austen
thers Circus or the often-amalgamated Cottle and Austen's Circus. These amalgamations
included things like Garry Glitters Rock 'n' Roll Circus, Gerry's travelling Theme park
adu and, of course, The Circus of Horrors.

ne of us believed Gerry could settle down in Somerset but I am glad to say he has and
de a great expanding business in Wookey Hole Caves without losing any of its charm.

h three shows now to publicize and three theatre tours to book I was extremely busy
I tend to thrive under pressure so it didn't faze me too much.

personal life tended to comprise of me driving to Sittingbourne most weekends to stay
h Nicci in her caravan and returning home on a Monday and working and spinning like

a demon all week long. Still finding time to see my mate's Psycho Skull, Paul Peculiar a
Basher Briggs and of course PNE as often as possible.

This wasn't enough for Nicci though and she needed something more permanent. While
were performing at Hackney Empire she told me she was sick of being a weekend girlfrie
and wanted more. A year or so earlier on the 29th February she had asked me to marry
but I just didn't think it was right.

I couldn't see how it was practical, I lived in a house in London, she lived in a caravan
Sittingbourne, there was no way I was going to live in a caravan again and there was
way she was going to live in a house, so it was pretty much stalemate.

For the time being at least Nicci seemed to accept the situation.

She did, though pretty well demand that I bought her a dog and not only a dog but a fuck
£800 Pug called Pergitrude. Fucking hell I could have bought two season tickets to see No
End for that and I wouldn't have to clean dog shit off the floor either, or even worse c
shit off my prized PNE shirt.

Shortly after the tour ended I got a strange fever, originally flu like but quickly tuning i
pneumonia. It was terrible, I'd never been ill before, I lost about a stone in weight, felt aw
and experienced hallucinations greater (or worse depending at which way you look at
than any mushroom inflicted trip. I was for a while though seriously ill, the infection affec
my lungs, kidney and liver and it took me weeks to get back to normal.

The illness, in addition to the hallucinations also made me have a number of premoniti
and I knew what was going to happen before it did. I could virtually pick up the phone a
say hello whoever, I always knew who was at the other end of the phone before they spc

One thing I couldn't predict though was North End's fortunes. Thankfully I had recovered
time to see another PNE revolution. North End had changed their manager a few times, fr
David Moyes to Craig Brown and then to Billy Davies. In his first season in charge Billy to
us to the play off final for the second time but again the elation of following PNE sc
turned to depression as we lost the final to West Ham.

We were still doing various corporate and Uni gigs with The Carnival of the Bizarre, but t
needed spicing up a bit and I also needed someone to entertain me. I had brought '
Mongolian Laughing Boy back into the fray for the Renault gig. Of course in his time
being ostracised he had pretty well done nothing, occasional Taxi driving or working stack
shelves in Tesco, where he claimed to have a homosexual experience in the pet food isle

Haze at the Play Offs with Basher Briggs and his son Aaron, photo credits, from Haze's personal collection

m sure he isn't gay, it was just a bit a attention seeking, although a pet food isle was a range place to 'come out'. At least George Michael chose a more conventional public toilet leap out of the closet and inspire a Sun headline 'zip me up before you go go', in Mongy's se in must have been more 'zip me up before you go cat'.

ad a call from Bonzi TV, they wanted someone to push pins through their face, have a ckled onion inside their mouth and see how many pins would have to be extracted before e pickled onion fell out. A sort of human Ker Plunk. They also wanted someone to run over oed of upturned electric plugs. There was only one person I could think would be daft ough to do it, The Mongolian Laughing Boy. He jumped at the chance and did a great job th saliva, blood and vinegar dripping from his toothless mouth whilst hopping on the turned plugs.

ortly afterwards I was asked to do The Reading and Leeds Festival and I used Stretch, sp Boy, Nicci, Uncle Ganga and Mongy.

Mongy arrived at my house and instead of his trademark shaved bonce he had a full head of hair and beard, he looked more like Fred West than the Mongolian Laughing Boy and I told him to shave it off. He was making such a shit job I helped him and as I shaved away the hair I also shaved away huge lumps of his scalp. I always fancied myself as Sweeny Todd. He turned up with me in Reading and everyone thought he had had Leopard Skin tattoo on his head. A week later at our next gig he decided to insert a firework up his bum, he lit it and it burned away with no problem, that is until he took it out and was dancing round with the firework in his hand, he then held it upside down and it went bang blowing a hole in his palm, Mongy's return certainly didn't last long.

He wasn't the only COH performer to have an accident that Autumn, Uncle Ganga had decided to leave the show and took a job selling pretty well anything. It seemed as though he sold the wrong thing to the wrong person and irony of all ironies he was attacked with a chainsaw. For year's I had been chopping off his limbs with a chain saw and within months of him leaving he was attacked with one.

The autumn saw us take the show to Thorpe Park to do what was about to become an annual visit for their Fright Nights for two weeks over Halloween. We would perform seven 20 minute shows each night, it was pretty hard but worked really well.

After Thorpe Park we moved straight back into theatres and begun another successful theatre tour, now expanded to an astounding 78 venues. We kept a similar theme for the show but changed a lot of the artistes,

Wasp Boy had decided to leave, what he didn't know was I wasn't going to use him again and had already contracted Blackheart the Barbarian and Captain Dan, so he jumped before I had chance to push him. Garry Stretch remained a crowd favourite as of course so did Willie, it was clear though that my theory to include more freaks was working.

The band changed too Andrew Higgins, Drew Blood and Steve McGrill remained and we brought in another brilliant player from Swansea, Jeremiah Armstrong on keyboards, who for some reason preferred to be known as Kev.

My relationship with Nicci was deteriorating rapidly and although we still stayed in the same room it was often in different beds. It was not long before she started seeing someone else, an Uncle Fester lookalike although she never owned up to this. In the gap between tours during December my weekend visits to Sittingbourne had ended. Nicci did come see me on my birthday but went home afterwards. She invited me to her caravan Christmas but made it clear I couldn't stay so I declined the offer and spent Christmas my own. I woke up on Christmas morning and felt so lonely, I walked down stairs and looked at the Christmas tree with presents below it, I sat there and opened them on my own, thought fuck it, switched on my computer and played Football Manager where my PNE slaughtered Blackpool 5-1. Bliss

I got calls from Gerry and Paul Peculiar who when they realized I was on my own immediately asked me to go over and see them. Of course I declined these offers too, not so much being a martyr but more not wanting sympathy.

The second part of the tour finished in a pretty uneventful manner and for the first time I was glad it was over. I couldn't take the tension of the Nicci situation anymore and needed time to get my head back together.

Normally at the end of tours I'm pretty down, almost like a drug addict going cold turkey but not this time. I had had a 7-year relationship with Nicci, ironically the same as Kim.

As my personal life had taken a massive change so too would the Circus of Horrors and the next tour was going to be the last one with the 'Freak Show' theme. The next show was called The Evilution which bridged the gap between the old show and the new one that was still a year away.

Willie was the last of the original line up apart from Andy Higgins and myself. He decided to throw the towel in, and so for the fist time since the show's conception it wouldn't feature 'he cloud swing act'. I also decided not to use Blackheart again, instead looking at a new, as yet untried 'Freak'.

While the show was at the Hackney Empire we had an unrecognizable but nevertheless friendly audience member, a guy called Helmut Kirshmeier. A message came from the stage door that he would like to see Danny and myself. I had no idea who it was but I have only ever met one 'Helmut' in my life and Danny assured me that I knew him.

It turned out to be Helmut from Munich but Fuck Me did he look different. Helmut was a frequent visitor to the show while we were in Bavaria, where he ran a piercing stall in the Christmas market. He was a former Tax Inspector and he looked pretty normal, maybe a couple of piercings but that's all.

Now he was covered from head to foot in tattoos, had elongated ears, scarification on his face and a forked tongue. After leaving Germany he had travelled with Danny in The Kamikaze Freak show, run by our old freak John Kamikaze. Like most people they both fell out with John and left, he now lived in London. I had found my perfect new freak.

After the tour finished I met Helmut in Camden and asked him if he was interested in joining us for the new tour, he jumped at the chance.

During the spring and summer months I was kept busy spinning my media stories, booking the various theatre tours, planning the new COH show and doing all sorts of gigs from University Balls, to Butlins and even quite posh corporate events. One of these was in The Conservative Club in Knightsbridge, they booked Mongy and myself, we thought we'd keep it clean and he did his human pincushion act, we finished and went off. The organizer, a 'young Conservative' asked us if we could do anything else and offered us some more money, I had an idea. I said don't give us more money but let us keep any donations the other young cons wish to donate, he agreed. Mongy then jumped on a long table with about 20 male Tories sat around, took off his filthy underpants, shoved a meat hook through a piercing in his extremely small willie and hung an ice bucket from it. He then walked up and down the table and I encouraged everyone to put any loose change in the bucket, the more money they put in the longer his dick grew, it was like a skinny, long worm quickly escaping from his foreskin. We ended up 30 quid to the good and Mongy had lost his virginity to an Ice bucket.

The next show was The Metal Hammer Golden Gods Awards and it gave me the chance to reunite Helmut with Danny, Mongy and Stretch completing the bill. Helmut brought his beautiful girlfriend Asia with him.

The award ceremony ended and we were asked to perform at the after show party then do a walk about and have our picture taken with various rock celebrities.

Mongolian Laughing Boy decided to do this completely naked with the ice bucket hanging from a meat hook that was hung from his dick.

This was all fine until he was walking up the stairs, caught the bucket on one of the steps stood up and ripped the end of his penis off. By the time I found him he was sat having a fag with his dick in a bucket of ice that was quickly turning claret. Asia's first ever encounter with Mongy was collecting the ice for the bucket. It was also the first time Helmut had seen him since he pierced Mongy's dick in Munich. Now ten years later he had ripped the piercing out along with the rest of the top end of his dick. He refused to go to hospital and his cock is still to this day forever forked.

The theatre tours were coming thick and fast, again starting at Thorpe Park before turning into the full-blown Evilution show. On the eve of the show's rehearsals in Croydon I saw Nicci for what was to turn out to be the last time.

Todd was still touring with us and was now living with our singer Claire, they had asked Nicci for a lift to the hotel where everyone was staying. I went over to say hello to everyone. Nicci started nagging me until I reminded her that she wasn't my girlfriend any more.

She then asked if we could have a chat, we went outside and told me she wasn't happy and really missed me and said she'd like to go out with me again. I was gob smacked, we hadn't exactly parted as the best of friends. I asked if we could wait until the first part of the tour was over and we would talk, she agreed. In December I did ring her but I had decided I didn't want to go back but to be honest she never mentioned again either.

The Evilution was quickly proving to be the perfect choice of names for the new show as some of the established artistes were leaving and being replaced. In some cases by new blood but in others as a return to former glories.

Nicci had obviously left but so too did Willie, he did though help us put the new show together and did the first four venues with us. His place was to be taken by The Veslovkis, Genna, Angela and Ksuska, along with Angela's brother Denis. We also brought in another aerialist called Leo who worked with Yanna who had taken over as Regan.

In some cases, there were also changes to personnel that were certainly not planned. First of all The Veslovskis were two days late arriving because of problems with their visas. Helmut who was making his debut as a Sword Swallower had brought with him Asia who we rechristened Anastasia IV, she walked a Ladder of Swords.

Helmut's debut as a sword swallower didn't last long, one and a half days in fact. He had trouble swallowing the sword and pressed a little harder than he should and forced it through his esophagus. He carried on but said he felt a little unwell, the next morning it had got worse and his neck had swollen to the size of his head, he was taken to hospital and kept in for three weeks to allow his throat to repair itself.

In the meantime Asia stayed with us even though I received a couple of emails from her sister claiming she had been kidnapped. All the changes forced us to alternate the other performers between The Veslovskis, Hula-Hoop, Roller Skating and Whip Cracking acts, Denis's German Wheel, The Voodoo Warriors, Johnny Brenner's Balancing act and the contortionists Karina and Iona, plus Stretch and Danny.

Guitarist Drew had also left and was replaced by Per Astropt and Jimmy Riddle. Thankfully none of this chopping and changing spoiled the balance of the show, which was still a great success and went onto perform in 82 venues.

The intention was to give the Evilution, a continuation of The Welcome to the Freak Show a last hurrah before we temporarily buried it and created a new show. That theory almost worked until we got offered the chance of taking The Circus of Horrors to the Stockton Riverside Festival and The Edinburgh Festivals, once again in a big top plus in the comedy festivals in Derry and Dublin. We called this show appropriately 'The End of Evilution'.

For these shows we were joined again by the Skating Aratas who by now were two, Victor and Emilia. They performed their astounding Roller-Skating act. They had already won the TV show "I Wish I could be Famous". In the next year they were the only brother and sister to become house mates in Big Brothers Celebrity Highjack. In our show Emila also played a brilliant Ragen with a great Silk act with our new Jesuit Denis Remnev.

Predictably we stormed Stockton but Edinburgh was a struggle and the show we presented didn't have enough big acts to fill the vast big top, relying more on the freakier end. Although it was the so called Freak Acts that helped us pull a media rabbit out of the hat.

First of all when Hannibal Helmurto broke his own world record by pulling a four ton truck with meat hooks in his back 100 meters along Princes Street and then of course Danny's infamous liaison with a Hoover.

Before the end of our Edinburgh run, I had come to the conclusion that you must never trust a clown with your car, or in fact with a motorbike and certainly not a bucket of water. Tweedy had joined us for our summer run and I gave him the task of driving my car from Stockton to Edinburgh, he arrived almost 12 hours late after accidentally setting his satnav to Edmonton. His next foray with a motorized vehicle came when he tried to drive Danny' motorbike out of the ring and accidentally got the throttle stuck. It dragged him into the band stand and just kept running scattering the band in every direction. His final "don' trust a Clown" scenario came when he was due to throw a bucket of water over a stooge in the audience. The idea was, a girl sat in the ringside seats, despite being warned, continue to smoke a cigarette. The only way to stop her was to throw a bucket of water over her. Tweedy had been throwing the water a little too tamely and I whispered I his ear "throw with more gusto". He some how thought I said something else and proceded to throw the water over a member of the audience who had paid £20 for his ticket. When I asked him what the hell he was doing he said 'I thought you said "Throw it over Guss". I don't know who the fuck Guss was but it certainly wasn't this poor guy in the audience.

Derry and Dublin were both great and Danny's notoriety had spread when again we got fro page news as a priest called for the show to be banned from Northern Ireland. The same happened when he was due to perform in Cambridge. Booked as Captain Dan the Dem

Dwarf a professor thought it was wrong to allow a dwarf to perform because there was another Dwarf studying in the University! So much for the intelligence of great seats of learning.

Prior to the tour I also decided to record and release a three track CD, the principal track 'From Hell' was coupled with 'Beauty and the Beast' and our own version of Marc Bolan's Jeepster. It was 30 years since Marc's untimely death, we had performed at a special show at Café De Paris with Boy George to celebrate what would have been Marcs 60th birthday. It seemed a fitting time to record a version of what was the first record I ever bought. The From Hell CD was released to co-inside with the new tour.

The tour also saw the debut of the new show 'The Asylum'. The Idea came when people kept asking where do we get all these amazing performers from. In truth, in the main they find me but I thought I would elaborate and exaggerate this for the new show, I mean, come on, where better to recruit performers for The Circus of Horrors from, than an Asylum. Gerry however preferred the idea of doing a Moulin Rouge type show. I wanted to do "The Asylum"so we compromised and made it an Asylum in France, this may not seem much of a compromise but I worked out a elaborate and cultural way of doing this thanks to Google.

I Googled 'Asylum France' and it kept coming up with Vincent Van Gogh, so I thought right I'll write a story where I buy a Stately home in the late 1800's. It would become a prequel to the "Welcome to the Freak Show". The new show would be set in this former stately home and now mad house, St. Remy's.

In the story, I buy the stately home that had been lived in by Vincent Van Gogh, not realizing I had bought the institution where Van Gogh famously committed himself after cutting off a section of his ear. The story continued, I was looking for a venue to put on my new show 'Blood Thirsty and Burlesque' in an attempt to beat Moulin Rouge who were then an Operetta but planning to become a Dance Hall of Decadence. Once inside this 'Stately Home' I found it inhabited by cruelly treated inmates. My role was to cleanse the venue, turn the inmates into my performers and kill the evil wardens.

The Lunatics have taken over the Asylum.

The second half sees me complete my plan and put on my fabulous show 'Blood Thirsty and Burlesque'. It all of course ends in chaos.

Pierrot Bidon agreed to return to help me direct the new show so I flew over to see him. I explained the new story and he said 'oh good, I'll take you there', I asked 'where', he said 'St. Remys, its here in Aryls the town I live in'. Not only had I found great subject matter, I had also found the very institution where my story was to be set. It all helped to give us great imagery for the new show.

It did mean having two sets, a first half set where all the lighting was sepia and all the costumes were white, except for mine, the second half was really colourful and exuberant. It worked a treat.

The show was to prove a massive hit as were the new songs we recorded. "From Hell", "Beauty and the Beast", and "Jeepster". I had started having more luck with the finer sex too, after Nicci I was in a similar situation as to when Kim left. Guess it was just a long time being with one person and you forget how to flirt.

Thankfully as The Asylum was becoming successful so too was my private life.

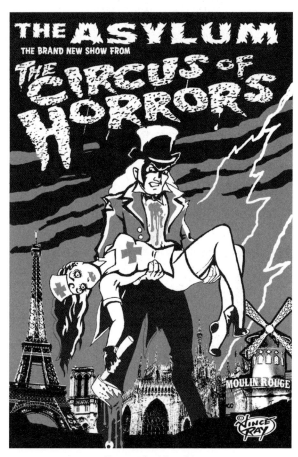

Photo credits, Vince Ray

Hannibul Helmurto, photo credits, Sarah Photogirl

CHAPTER SEVENTEEN
DWARFS BANNED IN HASTINGS

The autumn of 2007 was proving to be eventful in many ways, we had finished our dates in Stockton, Edinburgh, Derry and Dublin. We were on the verge of our Asylum tour and we had recorded the three tracks for the From Hell CD.

We had also been approached to perform at a celebration in memory of Marc Bolan on what would have been his 60th birthday. It was held in Café De Paris, London, it certainly wasn't like any other Marc Bolan event. I took along Dan, Iona the contortionist, Garry Stretch, Anastasia and Helmut, we all performed with Boy George and a mixture of unknown bands, some playing Bolan songs and some their own. There were poets, Sebastian Horsley read from his brilliant book 'Dandy in the Underworld' Marc's friend and DJ Felix Dexter spinning the songs he and Marc listened to in the 1960's and our bunch of Freaks. There were far too many egos on view and I couldn't believe the lack of T-Rex tunes, I rectified that as much as I could by performing to the big hits, Get it On, Children of the Revolution, Ride a White Swan etc.

Just over two weeks prior to the event I went to an art gallery where they had a Bolan exhibition, there were some great iconic images of Marc and I strolled around admiring in awe. There were lots of fellow Bolan fans there. While I was chatting I spotted Marc' girlfriend Gloria Jones walking in behind me. It was a hot day and shortly afterwards I went and stood outside. I noticed Gloria watching me and a few minutes later she came outside walked straight up to me, held her hand out and said 'hello, I'm Gloria', I said 'yes I know who you are', of course I should have said 'Gloria who'. She was with her new husband, Chris Mitchell and we spoke for ages. I got on really well with her and she kept telling me there was something spiritual about me. I told her that I never met Bolan, she said 'Marc would have loved you', Fucking Hell! Marc Bolan's girlfriend had just told me my hero would have loved me!

The fallout from Danny's Hoover incident was still thankfully hanging over us and gaining us masses of publicity, whether it came from pompous Deans in Cambridge Uni or God Fearing Do Gooders in Ireland, it was all great publicity. We were then invited onto Radio to appear on Scott Mills Breakfast Show.

I had met Scott on a couple of University gigs where we were performing and he was DJing. At one point he sat on a box in our dressing room having a chat, until he found out the box he was sat on was full of snakes, you've never seen anyone move as fast.

Scott was standing in for Chris Moyle's and the Breakfast Show had millions of listeners. We had a chat about Danny's accident then Dan gave them a demonstration of Penis Hoover pulling, it was brilliant, Scott and I were commentating and he just kept saying 'Unbelievable". That was a lot more than his other studio guest Yvette Fielding said, she just screamed, pure Howard Stern. All this publicity just before the tour kicked off was prefect.

Prior to the tour starting we again went to Thorpe Park, this time we performed in one of the theatres in the park which was a huge improvement to the cages we worked in the year before. We moved straight from Thorpe Park to Wookey Hole, Gerry had built a really cute little theatre there and allowed us to rehearse in the venue before we opened at the end of the week.

Pierrot flew over and helped me to direct the new show which now included another Anastasia who we re-christened Nastasia to avoid any confusion.

The show was completely different to anything we had ever done, opening with Beauty and the Beast to accompany Denis's brilliant new Arial act on chains and out of a tank of water.

The show started with a sell out and pretty well followed the same pattern as the tour progressed.

We had our usual winter break and Danny took a job as one of Snow White's Seven Dwarfs in Basingstoke and stayed with me over the festive season. Danny and myself went over to Paul Peculiar's for Christmas Day. Paul was now living with his girlfriend Zoë in Walton on Thames. We had a great time, Danny had a little too much to drink and started lap dancing in front of Zoë, Paul was none too pleased and tried to throw a bucket of water over Dan but with pure slapstick timing Danny ducked and the water went straight over his head and completely soaked Zoë. To make matters worse she was sat on a new sofa that they bought a day earlier from DFS. We quickly made our excuses and left, leaving Paul with a mop, bucket and a raging girlfriend.

The second part of the tour started in early January and I met this beautiful creature. Her name was Stephanie and she had contacted me four months earlier via Myspace.

Steph apparently asked if I knew somewhere that she could learn Ariel silks, I didn't answer the question but gave her my number, if you'd seen her picture you'd understand why.

On Boxing Day she texted me, of course I replied and we agreed to meet prior to our show in Wimbourne.

She arrived in the pub near the theatre and I went to meet her, I couldn't believe my eyes she was truly stunning, I remember just staring at her beauty. She came to the show and I saw her briefly afterwards before we moved on. I obviously invited her back to our hotel but she sensibly declined the offer.

The tour continued up to the end of March and it proved to be the best selling show to date. All the publicity had spurred us on and the tour proved to be the most successful ever despite the credit crunch that seemed to be gripping Britain we were enjoying a 20% increase in business with a third of the venues completely selling out.

It was pretty well back to normal when I returned home, still spinning the stories for The Chinese and Moscow State Circuses, booking the next tour and doing various Carnival of the Bizarre gigs. There was still a few TV appearances and I was asked to put together a piece for Saturday Night TV where the Wire Walker from The Moscow State Circus taught model Nell McAndrew to walk the high wire.

One of my first dates with Steph proved to be pretty eventful and she must have thought I was completely mad. I had wanted a Jukebox for years and Gerry told me about a Juke Box sale in Brighton, it was god-awful weather but I asked Steph to come with me.

When I got there all I could see was refurbished Wurlitzer's looking great but playing CD's this was definitely not what I wanted. I felt a little depressed until I turned round and saw this vision. It was a 1970 Mexican Wurlitzer that played vinyl, it was a work of art, it only played 50 records but there are only 25 T-Rex singles so 50 was fine, I asked the guy how much it was and he said £4,000.

I looked around and saw a American Shell petrol pump, I said if I buy the Petrol Pump too will you give me a deal, he agreed and suddenly I now owned not only a juke box but petrol pump as well. Pleased with my day's shopping I continued to walk around the exhibition and I saw a Creature of the Black Lagoon Pin Ball machine and bought that too. There were loads of record stalls and I attempted to buy my whole T-Rex collection again so as to not ruin my original copies in the Jukebox

Steph must have thought I had a compulsive buying disorder and I must admit I was beginning to think that too. At least my spending spree was over, that was until I start looking at old movie posters. Steph was surprised how expensive the posters were at around £250 each. I remember thinking 'Oh fucking Hell please don't let there be any Marc Bol posters'. Lo and behold the next one I looked at was a T-Rex Born to Boogie poster, I had always wanted one, it was £300 but I just had to buy it. I then said get me out of here quick, leaving the sale £8,000 poorer. To celebrate we then enjoyed a more modest bag of chips in the pouring rain on Brighton beach.

We didn't have many shows during the summer months so I decided to use the time recording a new album, my first CD Destiny and Desire had been deleted and second hand copies were selling for £22 on Amazon, I had very few copies of Welcome to the Freakshow either so I thought the time was right to release a Double Album called 'An Evil Anthology', it contained tracks from the first two albums, tracks that were only available on singles and previously unreleased songs plus seven brand new songs from the Asylum show.

Maxi Priest, Waterboys and Robin Trower producer Livingston Brown had done a great job with the From Hell CD so I thought he would be perfect to co produce and play the keyboards on the new Album. I used Andy Higgins and Greg James on Bass and Drums but bought back Drew Blood to play the guitar parts and on one song 'Outa Site'. I reunited three quarters of Flash Harry when Animal and Chris Cleen made guest appearances.

The album was released on Wolf at the Door Records in time for the next tour, which was an expansion on the Asylum theme and called The Apocalypse in the Asylum.

Prior to the new tour we decided to try our Freakshow that had caused a stir at Carters Steam Fair in Reading, this time we took a much larger version of the show to The Great Dorset Steam Fair.

Of course it wasn't my first time at GDSF, I performed at the event some 30 years ago with Circus Apollo when it was known as Stourpaine. On that occasion having a romantic interlude with a snake charmer. Great Dorset Steam Fair in 2008 was a much larger affair regularly attracting around 120,000 visitors with another 30,000 people living on the site. Amazingly this made the fair the third largest population centre in Dorset, only Bournemouth and Poole have more.

Roby had made a brilliant performing front and booth, which was straight out of a Victorian side show. We were positioned on the midway right next to The Wall of Death. It was a great site to see the two Barkers, myself on the Freakshow and David Wikes on the Wall of Death going head to head and shouting ourselves horse in an attempt to attract more people.

The Great Dorset Steam Fair was certainly gruelling but also a great success. After which I had a short holiday in Paris with Steph and recharged my batteries prior to our final visit to Thorpe Park.

We did our two weeks in Thorpe and then moved onto Wookey Hole to rehearse the new show. Pierrot rejoined us in Wookey to help direct the extravaganza, sadly it turned out to be our last performances in Thorpe Park, it also turned out to be the last time I would work with Pierrot.

For the Apocalypse in the Asylum show we added Twisted Kiros with his extreme dislocation act where he squeezed his whole body through a tennis racket. We also brought in another contortionist, Alina from Russia.

The show worked very well and like its predecessor it proved to be a great success running from October to March, the only sad thing was that, prior to the tour ending Garry Stretch decided to throw the towel in, he simply found it too hard. Thankfully Garry still works with us but not on the full blown tours.

Aside from Garry leaving the major talking point on this tour was Captain Dan's need to visit Specsavers and his ban from Hastings.

After his normal Snow White sabbatical he was due to rejoin the show in Aldershot but had a Tweedy moment and read his destination as Alderholt and ended up in a small village in Dorset.

He just made it to the show with five minutes to spare. The greatest incident though was in Hastings and involved some of my favourite people – Traffic Wardens.

I just don't get it, why would anyone want to be a Traffic Warden, I don't know if it's an authoritarian thing or the uniform or just a job for jobsworths.

Anyway the show was in Hastings and there is a time limit on the parking meters. I somehow had a premonition, not about a world changing moment but about a fucking traffic warden and I asked Jeff Jay where he had parked. He said 'on a meter' but he hadn't put any money in, I said 'don't blame me if you get a ticket'. We went outside and lo and behold there was a traffic warden joyfully putting a parking ticket on Jeff's car. He was then talking to Dan, came along and asked him about our other vehicles he told me I would have to move mine to the other side of the road but said Garry Stretch's car was fine. We turned away and headed for the Theatre, I glanced back only to see him putting a ticket on Garry's car. We all rushed back and asked him what he was doing. He said the Dwarf told him it was not one of our cars. I then said 'you can't just call him a Dwarf' and he said 'I know I shouldn't have called him a Dwarf, Dwarfs are illegal in Hastings', what the fuck! This guy's uniform must have really gone to his head and suddenly thought he was Adolph Hitler.

His superiors soon arrived, ordered the warden to go away and ripped Jeff and Stretchy's tickets up – result!

The tour ended in Doncaster and like its predecessor The Asylum is was still doing good business despite the recession the country was experiencing.

The summer months were forming a predictable pattern, I still ran the media office for The Moscow State, Chinese State Circus and Carters Steam Fair, even adding Continental Circus Berlin for eight weeks in July and August. I would see Steph as often as possible and had a great holiday in the States.

It was time to come up with another new show and we decided to call it The Day of the Dead, about the Mexican celebrations of the same name. I started writing some new songs and I had had a few conversations with Pierrot about it, he was really excited, I was due to fly out and discuss the concept with him. On the eve of the day I was due to travel to see him I received a call, it was Pierrot who told me he had to go to hospital and I wouldn't be able to go.

I asked him what was wrong, he told me he had a fuckin alien growing inside him. This was Pierrot's way of telling me he had cancer. He asked me not to tell anyone.

A month later, Pierrot called again and told me he had changed his mind and he was 'coming out', and asked me to tell his friends Gerry Cottle and Mark Bokawski. Pierrot was having an operation that summer, sadly not only did this mean I couldn't travel over to see him but also that he wouldn't be fit enough to help me direct the Day of the Dead show.

After five years of opening in Thorpe Park they decided to go in a different direction so instead we opened in Blackpool, Pleasure Beach in this really cool venue known as The Globe. I used to love going to the Pleasure Beach as a kid, a truly magical place, I would never believe that years later I would be performing there.

The Pleasure Beach is run by a friend of mine, Amanda Thompson. She had used the venue for a couple of shows she produced, Eclipse and Forbidden and created a great set for these shows, what's more it was a set that we were allowed to use. This basically meant we would produce two shows, The Last Night in the Asylum in Blackpool before moving to Wookey to revamp the show into The Day of the Dead. One downside was the fact that both myself and Asia managed to get Swine Flu. I felt pretty shit but still managed to do the show and even perform on the hallowed turf of Deepdale on Halloween prior to North End's game against Crystal Palace.

It had to be said The Day of the Dead show was not up to our normal standards and took a while to get going, once we had run it in it did get a lot better though, it didn't help that the new show started shortly after the banking crisis which sent the UK into recession and we too were now suffering from the financial state of the nation.

Just before Christmas I received a call from Pierrot, he sounded rough but he proclaimed 'The alien is dead but the Clown is alive' I was really pleased and honestly thought he was getting better.

I spent Christmas with Steph and her family in Dorset and in the new year the second part of the tour commenced, by now it was better but we were about to receive some bad news.

Pierrot's cancer sadly came back and in March I received the awful news that he had died. We were in Torquay and dedicated the show to him, the audience went wild and we certainly gave him a great send off. On that day I decided to dedicate the next tour to him.

I didn't go to the funeral as we were still on tour but I am told it was like a scene from a Quentin Tarantino film, with all these strange looking people dressed in black suits and wearing sunglasses.

We had been running for 15 years now so we decided to call the show The Four Chapters from Hell, it would be split into four sections, Starting with the Asylum, then Day of the Dead, onto Welcome to the Freakshow and finishing in 2020, Sin City, the place it all began and very Archaos.

Before the tour though there were a lot more shows to jam in, predominantly our appearance at The Waken open-air festival in Germany. Waken is the largest open air metal festival in the world and we were all really excited at the prospect of performing there.

The promoters came over to see the show in Bridlington, of all places, the show was a little quiet but thankfully they loved it and in our meeting they said 'The Circus o Horrors would rock Waken this was music to my ears bu not as much as what the were about to tell me. I aske who else were on the bill, the

Alice Cooper, Arthur Brown and Doktor Haze
A trio of terror (Alice's words, not mine). Photo credits, Judy Totton

told me Iron Maiden, Motley Crue and Alice Fuckin' Cooper, I nearly creamed myself and had they said Rob Zombie was playing there I probably would have.

2010 was to prove to be one of those years of change both on and off the field, to coin a phrase. On May 6th David Cameron guided The Conservative party to win the general election, it was a close call though and to form a government he had to form an alliance with The Liberal Democrats, this coalition was aptly abbreviated to the Con-Dems. Whether we would be condemned was debatable but it had to be better than the boring Gordon Brown led Labour party that had left us a nation in debt, and one hell of a debt at that.

Despite the state of the nation I had a business to run and although I had to be a lot more careful the intention was to continue doing what we do best and ride out the recession entertaining people along the way.

The first major show that year was a fifth visit to The Stockton Riverside Festival, this time though we were due to perform inside a Spiegiltent. Spiegeltent is Dutch for "Mirror Tent", from spiegel+tent, it is a large traveling tent, constructed in wood and canvas and decorated with mirrors and stained glass.

It would prove to be a perfect setting for a specially devised show called Freaks and Feathers. This show consisted of our Royal Family of Freaks, Stretchy, Dan, Helmut and Asia plus a Burlesque Stripping Pianist called Chris Columbine, Contortionist Iona, Hula Hoop girl Alona and, making her COH debut, Steph, who now performed a great Silk and Arial Hoop act. Aside from the freaks and myself the only male performer was Denis Remnev who performed his Arial Chains and German wheel acts.

The show went down a storm and of course played to great business as always in Stockton.

The next adventure needed a much rockier feel, when we took on the might of Waken. We brought back the band, which were now, DA Angelo on guitar, Steve McGrill on drums, Levon Truck on keyboards and Drew on bass. Back too came Uncle Gaga who this time as unwanted camera man had his leg chains sawed off. All the Freaks, Alona and Denis were there too plus of course the obligatory topless girl in the bottle, this time performed by Daniel Martine.

The only mishap came when I tried to chainsaw off Brian's good leg, It had been a long time since we had done this stunt and I simply picked up the wrong leg. Luckily I realized just in time.

After the festival there was a poll where people picked their best of the fest, Iron Maiden came first, we came second. The Circus of Horrors really did rock Waken.

The third and final festival that summer saw a return to our now annual appearance at The Great Dorset Steam Fair and I somehow managed to squeeze in a brilliant holiday in Las Vegas with Steph before the Four Chapters Tour commenced.

We started in Blackpool Pleasure Beach again and this time we got it spot on, a real epic of a show, the punters realized that and again business took an upturn. The first part of the show ended in London 02 before a trip with Steph to Belgium and back in time for a short run of Freaks and Feathers dates in Norwich.

I spent Christmas again at Steph's but I knew 2011 like 2010 was going to be another year of change.

For the past 10 years I had run the media office for Brian Austen's company to publicize The Chinese State and Moscow State Circuses as well as booking theatre tours for the two shows.

2010 though had proved difficult for Circuses in general and business had taken a dip. The Chinese State Circus was particularly hit and Brian decided as far as he was concerned it's success had come to a natural end.

I had booked theatre tours for both the Chinese and Moscow State Circuses. I handed the Chinese theatre tour that I had booked over to the Gandy Organization in return for the normal commission.

Brian decided that after the forthcoming theatre tour The Moscow State Circus would also close down unless he could find a buyer.

That buyer came from pretty close to home, Paul Archer who was the general manager of the show threw his hat in the ring, as did Anthony Anderson who had run the team that handled the poster distribution. I too decided to join them and the three of us would become Directors of the company and buy the whole huge touring Circus City.

I had gone from performing in a tiny tent under the headlights of a Land Rover to becoming a Director of The Moscow State Circus, the most famous Circus on earth. Not that I would allow any of this to affect my true love The Circus of Horrors. 2011 was about to prove to be a significant year in the history of the COH too.

Another bright moment during our Asylum period was the day that Helmut and Asia decided to get married. furthermore they asked me to be best man. Wow Basher Briggs & Pat Peculiar had both blown me out from their respective best man duties but Helmut and Asia had chosen me. I was duly honoured and shitting myself. They were married in one of the caves at Wookey Hole so I guess that made me best cave man, quite appropriate.

Kristina, photo credits, Sarah Photogirl

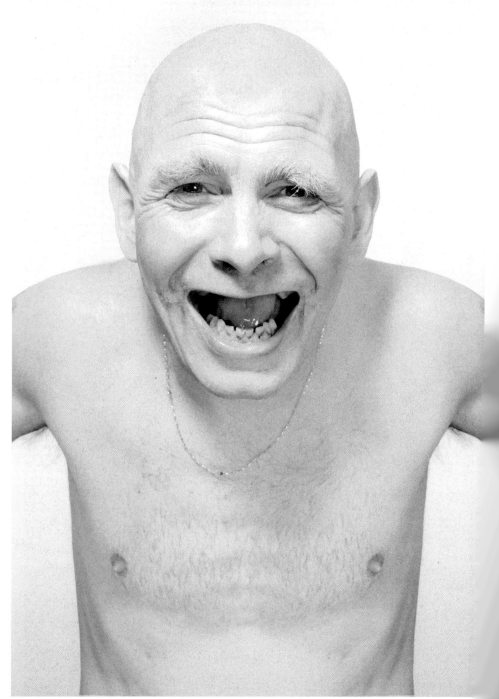

The Mongolian Laughing Boy. I wouldn't say he was dodgy but when he went to court on a driving offence he asked the magistrate if the points could be added to his Television Licence. Photo Credit Sarah Photogirl

Ksusha, photo credits, Sarah Photogirl

CHAPTER EIGHTEEN
HELL FREEZES OVER

Music had been in the doldrums for quite some time now, there was simply nothing new any more, I always liked the theatrical side of music, of course there were a few exceptions but I think people like Lady Gaga are just imitations of Madonna. If I thought the 80's were bad the 2000's were dire and there didn't seem to be any way out of the mire. The rocky indie stuff was there to a certain degree but where were the songs, where were the great melodies?

The main problem was the never-ending parade of boy and girl bands, I even had an issue with them calling themselves a band. In my eyes a band is a group of musicians fronted by a singer, T-Rex were a band, The Rolling Stones are a band, Oasis are a band, The Spice Girls and Take That were not bands, they were a group of singers, all be it very successful groups of singers.

The problem was once the Spice Girls and Take That had success, everyone tried to emulate them and any originality went straight out of the window.

Saturday night TV was also struggling and ironically it was various programs trying to find the next best thing that got people watching prime time again. At the same time these programmes have become what I believe to be the death knell in the music industry, this and free downloads of course.

The first of these, Pop Idol preceded the X Factor, I really didn't like them, I didn't like to see hopeless wanabees given false hope and paraded in front of the judges prior to the inevitable humiliation. I also didn't like the fact that Simon Cowell had chosen to call his companies The X Factor and Sycho. Far too close for comfort to my band and my agency but that's another story.

My main gripe though was, the programmes snuffed out all individuality, I mean can you imagine if Marc Bolan, Mick Jagger, John Lennon, Bob Dylan etc. were being auditioned they would be laughed off, yet these are true talents, the songs they wrote were immense and they all had real distinction in their sound and voices.

The variety side of Saturday night TV was represented in another show, Britain's Got Talent.

Around seven years ago I was on Holiday in The States and I received a call from a television executive telling me about a new show they were commissioning.

I had worked with them before on Don't Try This At Home and Ant and Dec's Saturday Night Take Away. They explained it would be a huge new talent show broadcast on Saturday night prime time and would feature everything from performing dogs to singers, with just about everything else in between.

I said I would be interested if the price was right, she promptly told me there would be no fee but there would be a large cash prize for the winner. I was a little taken aback, like most people if I do any work I expect to get paid for it.

Nevertheless I did say I would talk to her again in the future, I put the phone down and didn't hear from her again.

I believe the show turned out to be Britain's Got Talent.

Four years later, then every year around late summer/autumn I would receive an e-mail from one or another researcher from the show asking if any of our acts would be interested in auditioning. After seeing the first two series my answer was always the same, 'Hell would have to freeze over first'.

The winter of 2010 was a little different, I had already received the 'stock' e-mail and gave my stock answer. In December though, I received an e-mail, titled 'media enquiry' upon opening it I found it simply asked who was the media contact for The Circus of Horrors. It did not specify any particular TV show but it was from Talkback Thames. I replied that I was the media contact and gave my number.

The next day I received a phone call from the same researcher who had e-mailed me, this time explaining that she was from Britain's Got Talent and asking if we would be interested in auditioning. I thought 'Oh God', of course I refused but she was persistent and asked me why. I explained, there were three reasons:-

You don't get paid.
You could get humiliated.
You do not say where you are from, they may say John from Preston but are they really going to say Doktor Haze from The Circus of Horrors?

The next day the same researcher rang again, and said, we can't see any reason why you cannot do it as 'Doktor Haze and The Circus of Horrors', suddenly my ears pricked up. I thought to myself, yes you could still get humiliated, no you don't get paid, but 10 million people would see two minutes of The Circus of Horrors.

Suddenly the idea seemed a lot better idea.

I spoke to the rest of the cast and they all agreed that it was worth the risk and we agreed to do it. One proviso I insisted on was that I played my own music and they wouldn't edit the music out and replace it with something else.

We were on tour while the auditions were taking place and the only time we could fit it in was when BGT were in Birmingham Alexandra Theatre, a venue I knew well as we perform there every year.

We were in Stoke the night before and Hereford on the night of the audition so the only way we could do it was if we went on first at 2pm, then got away quickly to get to Hereford in readiness of the show that night.

We put together a really exciting piece with loads going on, jamming everything into a two minute 20 second segment. It was still touch and go as to whether we would perform though after seeing the release form, but after various assurances from the shows producers, we agreed to do it.

I was still conscious that we were a professional act, and the fact that people would think we shouldn't be there, the only way I could see around this was to tell it as it was. In the interviews with Ant and Dec I referred to the time I appeared on their 'Saturday Night Take Away Show', I also spoke of the Royal Command performance we appeared on.

It was our time to take to the stage, I even planned what order we would walk on Mr. Methane was on the show a year earlier and told me as soon as he walked on the crowd were jeering, it was like a bear pit.

So I had a plan, if Helmut and myself walked on first we could feel the wrath of the audience if we choreographed our entrance though we could turn that round and still look natural.

First to walk on was Tony Garcia a good-looking lad with a look of Elvis with crow make up followed by Asia and then one of the Kenyan Warriors.

It worked a treat and the audiences were really cheering before we did anything.

I spoke to the judges and the audience from the stage, explaining why we were there a the fact that I simply thought it was a great promotional tool, I explained we normally play Theatres the size of the Birmingham Alex and maybe perform to 1,000 people each night. I continued . . . doing Britain's Got Talent would allow us to be seen by 10 million people in one go, Michael McIntyre even applauded what he described as my 'business acumen'.

All my references to previous media exposure and the size of venues we normally play were edited out of the final cut but at least I knew my conscience was clear and I hadn't tried to hide anything.

We went on and did two minutes 20 seconds of Hell fire rock 'n' roll Circus to the strains of 'Welcome to the Freak Show'. As soon as the song finished everyone stated to get up, it was like a tidal wave starting at the back and flowing right up to the judges, it ended up with what seemed like a five minute standing ovation.

We'd survived the dreaded buzzers but now was time for the potential humiliation with the comments from the judges. David Hasselhoff, led the way with comments such as 'Fantastic, That's what I call entertainment' and said 'I want to party with you guys', Amanda Holden followed on and said 'It was gruesomely good' and claimed we were 'like Rocky Horror on acid'.

Michael McIntire was more sarcastic, but being a comic he seems to think he has to make a joke out of everything, he did say he enjoyed it though.

So off we went feeling pretty triumphant, and set off for Hereford where the rest of the crew had prepared everything in readiness for that night's show, it was sold out too – so a pretty good evening.

During the following few weeks, e-mails were passing back and forth, the next round, the nd round was when they revealed who went into the semi finals. It fell however on days hat we couldn't make due to touring commitments. Our new Researcher assured us that ven if we couldn't make it, it wouldn't affect our chances of getting into the semi finals if he judges deemed us worthy.

he dates of the reveal however got changed on two occasions due to the sad news that manda Holden had lost her baby.

new date was set for April. This was after our tour had ended and although half the troupe ere away six of us could actually make it.

ried to put the Britain's Got Talent scenario to the back of my mind and continue with the ur. Business had certainly picked up from the previous year and we looked back on track again. The show was great and we were getting loads of positive feed back, we had added the long bow contortion act from Kristina Garcia and gained lots of publicity with the 'no smoking' story.

The tour ended in Wookey Hole and everyone went their separate ways.

I travelled to Cheltenham to help Paul and his wife Irina put the new Moscow State Circus show, Baboshkins Sekret together. It was a real buzz driving onto Cheltenham Racecourse and seeing this monster of a show in all its glory knowing that I now owned a third of it. It was an even bigger buzz when I entered the tent and saw some of the wondrous acts that Paul and Irina had managed to book for what was to be our maiden voyage with this historic show. The main act to catch my eye was the brilliant high wire act of the inappropriately named Stalkers. It was fantastic to see five people walking the high wire and when one of the performers did the splits from two of her fellow performers head's on this tiny metal thread 30 feet in the air it was simply jaw dropping.

I went straight from Cheltenham to Bournemouth to pick up Steph, she was going to Italy to perform on a Guinness World Record show with Asia and prior to this we spent a couple of days in Torquay, the sun was shining and we had a great time.

We went from Torquay to London and she boarded the plane with Asia and Helmut the next day. It was a real gruelling time with all our TV exposure, while I was in Cheltenham Denis Remnev and Asia recorded two episodes of BBC's Slammer and both used my music.

Over in Italy, Asia created a new Guinness World Record by hanging upside down from a crane 20 meters in the air and Steph performing a Ariel hoop act suspended only from Asia' Hair, pretty amazing stuff.

While everyone else was abroad I was left to hold the ship, deal with all things BGT, spi stories. We now added Anthony's Extreme Stunt Show to our media portfolio alongside Th Moscow State Circus and Carters Steam Fair. I still also had one eye on the future and booke the Theatre tours for the COH and MSC.

The next round, the reveal round for BGT was looming, we met in a hotel at midday ar were told to get changed into the costumes we wore in the semi finals, no dressing room everyone cramming into any empty bog to get ready.

Myself, Denis, Juma and Dan met at the hotel and Asia and Helmut joined us later. We we then herded like cattle across to Hammersmith Apollo and back numerous times, along wi around 1,000 other semi final wannabes

I discovered there were a few people also in the same round as us that I knew, the magicians David and Karen, Strong Man John Evans, a aerialist called Lucy who performed with a troupe called Enchainment. There was also a young lad called Pooper Hoffman who although only 11 years old, did a brilliant act where he rode a motor cycle in Globe of Death. I actually worked for his Grandad's Circus back in 1978.

Our audition back in January was only a fleeting visit so I didn't see any of the other acts and although we were recording the reveal programme the first show in the series hadn't been aired. So apart from the guys I knew I could only go by appearances to guess the calibre of the other acts.

On the Sunday we were all taken back to Hammersmith and split into three groups A, B and C, we were in C and Pooper was in A. To my surprise he was in the group which unceremoniously were told they would not progress into the semi finals. I couldn't believe it and genuinely thought he could win. It shocked me to see the likes of Pooper going. I could only go by appearances but I doubted their talent could be greater than Poopers. There was a Terminator impersonator, a bell ringing husband and wife appropriately called Gay and Allan and a Brittany Spears look alike called Lorna Bliss.

All the survivors were paraded in front of the judges again, the 10,000 who originally applied or auditioned was now down to 60 and had to be further reduced to 40 acts for the semi finals.

Again the queue spiralled around Hammersmith Apollo, they chose to leave us until last, ahead of us was The Terminator who astounded me by getting the green light to progress into the semis. So too did Enchantment. It was now our turn.

Amanda was the one chosen to address us, asking if we were nervous, fuckin' right we were.

She spoke very quietly and reminded us of the responsibility of the judges, quoting that they had to find something new, something that would fit on a prime time TV show and to a younger audience and that would be appropriate for a Royal Command Performance.

We all believed she was referring directly to us, it was like one of those clever evangelists speaking to the whole congregation, everyone thinking she was referring directly to them. It took me back to my days as a born again Christian although if I were blushing now it certainly wouldn't show beneath my white make up.

We needn't have worried, it was all part of the drama and she told us the judges were 'unanimous' and we were 'fit for a queen'.

So jubilation again, it was a huge relief and we all were genuinely elated to have reached the semi finals. Our status at BGT seemed to increase too, on the first day of the reveal programme we thought we were on a school outing when the packed lunch we were given arrived and consisted of a sandwich, apple and a small bottle of orange. This had now increased to an almighty jacket potato, and a can of coke, we'd hit the big time!

There were a few issues on the contract but these were rectified quite quickly so we started getting ready for the semi-final. On the eve of the screening of the new series of Britain's Got Talent, the media decided to publish the fact that we had already appeared on TV and in particular on Ant and Dec's Saturday Night Takeaway. Nothing new there we had openly told everyone about this during our audition and off camera I even reminisced about it with Dec.

To be honest, I believed it was our right to appear on the programme and the producers had every right to ask us. We still had to audition and we could still have been kicked out at the audition stage the same as everyone else. Mr. Methane a year earlier had also 'been invited' but was kicked out by the judges in the theatre audition. So the fact that you were asked to audition doesn't give you any God given right that you will progress.

Think of it like the FA cup, the beauty is that an amateur team can knock out a professional team, like Whitely Bay being paired against Man Utd. The possibility of the underdog winning, which I suppose, inevitably is what happened to us.

What was strange though was images that were used in the media coverage, two great pictures of us, taken at the audition show. At first I wondered where they had got the pictures from. I looked closely at the pictures and in the bottom corner and saw copyright ITV. It could only be the BGT press office that had given the images to the media? Either way, I didn't care, my purpose of entering the show was beginning to pay off and our profile was growing by the day.

On the 10th May we took a sort of 'Freaks and Feathers' version of the show to The Brighton Festival to perform in the Ladyboys of Bangkok tent. The show was different to last year as I wanted to give it a more of a BGT feel, this was partly because we had to film some extra for the programme while we were in Brighton.

We decided to audition for a new bottle girl and the story was covered by ITV's daybreak. We performed all week in Brighton but on the Saturday performed in a small theatre Andover.

We had a call the day before informing us that our audition would be on BGT on the

Saturday. Prior to every episode they trailed some of our act as 'coming soon', our time had come and on Saturday 14th May we were on. The anchor introducing Show Four actually said 'Its Britain's Got Talent with The Circus of Horrors', I don't think they did that for any other act. We had tweeted all day and got a good vibe going. We would actually miss the show though as it was broadcast while we were on stage in Andover.

I could tell it had been well received by the 250 'well done' messages received on Facebook. I saw it at the Hotel later. I was really pleased with the edit. We stormed it and overnight were installed as between third to sixth favourites by the bookies. Foolishly I thought we had a great chance of reaching the final and even began to believe we could win it.

The next day the BGT cameras filmed us in Brighton, walking around the streets in all our Motley. Everyone wanted their picture taken with us, it was a great feeling and we started to feel just a little bit famous as opposed to our previous stance of infamous.

The next day the Daily Mirror did a double page feature entitled 'Britain's Gore Talent' generally featuring the more gory sides of the show, with comments such as 'Like a scene from a horror film', yes that's generally the idea.

The power of BGT was beginning to show and ticket sales in Brighton certainly increased, we were now getting of a new audience.

We returned home and back to something more like normality, visiting Steph and The Moscow State Circus as often as possible, still spinning and finalizing the theatre tours.

We were trying to conform to the BGT requirements by referring all media enquiries to them, although I think we could have got a lot more column inches had we done it ourselves. We did though get loads of local media in all the towns and cities that our performers came from. Over the next few weeks however something strange was about to happen, our odds which had been as good as 6-1 had decreased to anything between 16-1 to 25-1 and in some cases 40-1, I couldn't understand why.

The other thing I found strange was the viral campaign, in particular the You Tube hits. Some acts were getting as many as 1.5 million hits where we had around 200,000. Still a lot but a massive difference, it's as though virally people weren't seeing as much of us?

You can understand the crazy acts such as Will Blair a 'financial' Dolphin Man would get a lot of You Tube hits, simply people laughing at him and telling their friends how bad he was.

The question was, how did Les Gibson get over 1.5 million hits, don't get me wrong, I like his and got to know him on the set, he is a pretty good impressionist. He doesn't though, fall into the 'Crazy acts' or the 'crying kid singer category', so where did the 1.5 million people come from?

It was great to see all our fans and friends rally round and pledge their votes to us, plus the support from Bizarre magazine and the alternative community, the question was, would there be enough of them?

We tried to get a sort of Rage against the Machine or Lordi vibe going, the alternative taking on the establishment, but it never really got off the ground.

Judgement Day was almost upon us, we went to the studios on the Saturday prior to the live show to rehearse. It was shit, the set looked great but the winches they provided were set too high so our Ariel acts of Asia and Denis couldn't swing without hitting the set.

BGT had re-recorded a sort of Fat Boy Slim version of Just so Psycho, I preferred my rock version but felt I ought to comply with their wishes.

We all went home depressed, the only saving grace was we got a sneaky look as to who was on with us. The main opposition was an 11-year-old blond kid called James Hobley, he had autism and had a great story, he was a sort of albino Billy Elliot and was sure to pull the heart strings and probably win our group.

The others didn't look as though they would cause too much of a threat, Angela and Teddy the worst dog act in the world. A quick-change act, strangely called Wachrin Porn, who did get changed but certainly wasn't quick and our nemesis Gay and Allan.

Gay and fuckin Allan met at recorder class and both joined a bell ringing group, they got married and played those fuckin bells while walking down the isle.

I've always hated bells ever since stupid churches deemed it necessary to ring the damned things early on a Sunday morning waking me up after a long Saturday night before.

Gay attempted to get the sympathy vote by declaring she was never allowed a musical instrument as a child, I wonder why?

They looked like they had come from the League of Gentlemen, they had the personality of a squid and I'd seen sealions play bells better than them back in my time as a kid in the Circus.

The next couple of days I cheered up a bit and came to the conclusion that even though our aerialists couldn't swing we could get the winches going quicker and it could still look great

The 1st of June was almost upon us, I spent the eve of the show doing my VAT returns (that's showbiz) before driving to the Hilton Hotel next to Fountain Studios in Wembley where all the contestants were staying.

I got there at around 11pm and met Dave and Karen, they were on that night's show, they ended in the top three but the Judges didn't put them through. Lorna Bliss, the Brittany Spears lookalike was also in the same hotel, she had also failed in the semi finals, but the question on everyone's lips was how she even got into the semi final?

I met her briefly at The Hammersmith Apollo reveal day and she told me she had not gone through, yet the following Friday at the signing at Sony offices she was there, signing a contract with Syco and Sony, strange?

Lorna was also broadcast on Show Four, the same as us and got three 'No's from the judges. How then could it be, someone with three 'No's and was also turned down at the 'reveal show' was through to the semi final.

Apparently the judges had a re-think, twice?

Could it be the likes of Watchrin Porn, Gay and Allen, Angela and Teddy and Lorna Bliss were being lined up as cannon fodder for Simon Cowell who was returning as the 4th judge?

Another unexpected contestant was Les Gibson, he was due to appear on the Tuesday night but was moved onto the Wednesday with us.

I stayed in the hotel but I was so nervous I didn't sleep all night and I hadn't eaten for 24 hours. We arrived in the studios at 8am and the rehearsals were much better despite the restrictions on our Ariel acts by the set. Instead of Denis and Asia flying out over the crowd they could only be pulled straight up and down, it would still look OK if it were filmed correctly.

A further problem occurred as the day progressed when one of the crew over-filled our water tank and it sprung a leak, leaving Denis to emerge from a tank of smoke as opposed to a tank of water. It was a genuine accident but nonetheless spoilt part of the spectacular.

The hype was building up as the afternoon turned to night, Janey Lee Grace bigged us up on Radio 2, we were getting hundreds of good luck messages on various social network sites and Steph had travelled down to support us with her friend Doug. The flip side of the coin though saw our old friend Scott Mills championing the Bell Ringers all day on his Radio 1 show. Thanks Scott!

Show time, despite the restrictions I thought we did well, it was pretty flawless performance and received another standing ovation. The burning bible took a while to light and The Voodoo Warriors performed a little too far back but all the fireworks went off when they should have, the Ariel acts were good, Kristina's bow and arrow contortion was spot on and Sean's flaming knifes were terrifyingly close to Kristy.

Now for the judges' comments.

Surprisingly, although not bad comments, with the exception of Simon Cowell they were all downbeat, thankfully we didn't hear the dreaded buzzer but something wasn't right. I knew we had reached the end of the road.

Had David Hasselhoff said it ended fantastic but started a little slow it would have been much better than saying, you started too slow but when it got going it was fantastic.

Michael McIntire, as usual attempted a joke by criticizing the fact that there was so much going on he didn't know where to look, how can 'so much going on' be a criticism?

Both Michael and Amanda said they thought it was very entertaining and said they liked it but she too was critical, claiming we should have looked at our positioning, does she seriously think we didn't?

The Ariel acts were positioned where the winches were, this would have been fine if they could have swung but they couldn't swing because of the set, we didn't build it, but we had to live with it. I was even stood on the opposite side that I intended to stand on because the floor manger asked me to stand on the other side to get better camera angles.

It was all left to Simon Cowell, he said 'I loved it' the crowd went wild. He even corrected David Hasselhoff and went onto, rightly confront the Hoff and stated 'every show has to end big', which is exactly what we did. He did though criticize the size of Danny's fire torches this prompted me to kick Danny and say under my breath, 'cry, start to cry'. I knew if Danny had started blubbering it would have swung it for us. Forget crying kids, no one could resist a crying dwarf.

Is was now time for my reply, or was it? Any one watching may have noticed Ant and Dec didn't hand the mic to me to give me the right to reply, which they did for everyone else. Maybe they simply had to go to the commercial break and ran out of time?

Not that I was going to make excuses, I would though have been tempted to correct the Hoff, after all didn't Baywatch finish with a rescue but started in slow motion, you can't go much slower than that.

We then did another interview on the way off stage, I was trying to be upbeat but inside I couldn't really be bothered, once the Hoff made his comments I knew it was the end of the road, even though we had found a new ally in Simon, I knew it wouldn't be enough.

I was now sure we would lose and felt a huge relief surging over me, only one more possible humiliation. We were taken with the other contestants to the canteen where we had to wait until the show had ended and the votes were counted.

We then moved back in and awaited our fate, one by one, people were told either they were going home or they were in the top three.

Surpassingly Les came first, the others to reach the top three were James Hobley so no surprise there and then, the fucking Bell Ringers, Nooooooooooooooooooooooooooooooooooo. Somehow Gay and Allen had got more votes than us. This was the Benny Hill Vs T-Rex syndrome all over again.

I knew straight after the judges' comments that we weren't going to make the top three but Gay and fuckin Allen, I ask you. I got out of there as sharpish as possible, a quick interview with Stephen Mulhurn for 'More Talent', load the props and home. Oh yeah and Preston North End got relegated too. What a fuckin great night.

When I got back I watched our performance on I Player and seeing the dreadful editing by the producer and thinking about the judges comments. It was no surprise to me when we didn't make it. It may have looked fine on a cinema screen but the long shots were so wide you could see all the audience and our performers looked like ants, I would have hoped after three camera rehearsals they would have got close in on the acts at the right time. Loads of things we did were simply missed. Again, I don't think there has been anything intentional here. I believe BGT did want us to get to the final, circumstances just prevailed.

Of course with all these things there are loads of conspiracies.

The next day a blog of alleged fixing appeared on the internet, supposedly written by a Sony executive, it particularly targeted Rowan Parke. It was swiftly taken down by Syco and Sony and they vowed to find its author and take legal action against them. This all seemed to go quiet over the next few weeks though.

We did a photo shoot for that quality Sunday Paper the Sunday Sport but I also got a call from The Sun who were interested to know more about the fact that we were 'invited' to win the show and asked to see our emails. I decided not to hand them over.

The post mortem had begun though and the only conspiracies I was interested in were ours.

Would we have done better had we not gone on first?

Some people claimed they were voting tactically to get one of the 'novelty' acts such as the bell ringers to get more votes to stop some of the singers winning, if that was the case it failed, a singer did win the final.

Why was the winner of our group Les Gibson added to our night only two days previously?

Could the fact that we had already received a lot of TV exposure have backfired on us, people wanting to give someone else a chance?

Who knows the real reason, the facts are, for whatever reason we didn't get enough votes and we have to take it on the chin.

People had said to me before the show, because of the amount of performers we had and their friends and families we had a great chance, but a lot of the other acts had more performers than us and also failed.

If you look at the finalists, they were all single acts except for one.

There were no specialty acts and only one woman.

The one thing I did hope for though was a big vote from our fans, we have 16,000 subscribers to our website and a further 21,000 friends on Face Book or Myspace so you would imagine that would be significant.

Maybe it was simply that most of our fans just wouldn't watch BGT in the first place let alone spending their money voting on it.

Nevertheless I owe a huge debt of gratitude to everyone who did vote for us and who supported us.

I've always found it incredibly humbling that people use their hard earned cash to buy ticket for the show, buy my albums, vote for us on a TV show and indeed read this book.

All that is left is for me now is to leave you with the final thoughts:-

Did it serve the purpose of increasing our profile? Definitely.

Did I enjoy the experience? No.

Would I do it again? Only if Hell froze over.

Six days later I received an email from Grundy TV in Germany, asking if we would consider doing their version of the show called 'Supertalent'.

They had seen us on BGT and said there was no rules to prevent us appearing on their show.

Oh no, not again, what shall I do?

Photo credits, ITN

Oh fuck it, get the antifreeze out lets defrost Hell again,

GERMANY HERE WE COME.

Photo credits, ITN

The Moscow State Circus, photo credits, from Haze's personal collection

AND FINALLY

As the book reaches its ultimate climax The Moscow State Circus comes close to finishing its first and extremely successful tour of the UK under the directorship of myself, Paul Archer and Anthony Anderson.

The Circus of Horrors is about to trek off to foreign climes again, in this case for the first time to Finland prior to another mighty UK Theatre tour with our latest production The Ventriloquist.

2012 will see the show take on the might of the German nation when it performs on Supertalent the German version of 'Got Talent' and possibly even perform on China's Got Talent!

Preston North End are attempting another great escape this time from Division One and I still have my beautiful girlfriend Steph.

I certainly have had a charmed life and I hope you have enjoyed sharing it with me.

I would like to offer my sincere thanks to all the people (well almost all anyway) who have trod the bloody boards with Circus Beck, Fossett Bros Circus, Circus Apollo, Circus of Horrors and its predecessors, various versions of Haze or Flash Harry. Plus of course all my fellow pupils at Savick and Tulketh Schools, my fellow workers at 'my proper job' Brooks Textiles and everyone at Psycho Management.

My great friends, who have allowed me to share our combined adventures in this book, Steph, Basher Briggs, Bruce and Dawn Carter, Gerry Cottle, Psycho Skull, Paul Peculiar, Animal, Chris Cleen, Paddy Haveron, Asia and Helmut, Garry Stretch, Captain Dan, Peter Norris, Mongolian Laughing Boy, Debbie and Gina and a whole lot more.

My influences, every Preston North End squad over the last 50 years and Marc Bolan, a true rock god. Plus of course my Mum, to whom this book is dedicated.

There's also been loads of true friends who have worked tirelessly behind the screams and putting up with my madness on many projects for many years, I am of course for ever in your debt. To try and remember you all may be difficult so if I've missed you out then my memory has failed me or I don't like you, I'll leave that for you to decide which.

Until the next time.

Photo credits, Vince Ray